Dream Interpretation

Discovering the divine messages within your dreams

Guidelines,
Examples, Assignments and a
Comprehensive Dream
Dictionary

Gary Fishman

All Scripture quotations, unless otherwise indicated, are taken from taken from the New King James Version: © Copyright 1979, 1980, 1982 Thomas Nelson, Inc. Publishers. Used by permission.

Scripture indicated with KJV is from the Authorized King James Version.

Scripture indicated with Amplified Version is taken from the Amplified Bible, © Copyright The Lockman Foundation 1960, 1962, 1963, 1968, 1971, 1972, 1973, 1975, 1977. Used by permission.

Scripture indicated with NIV is taken from the Holy Bible: New International Version. © Copyright 1973, 1978, 1984 by International Bible Society. Used by permission.

Scripture indicated with NLT is taken from the Holy Bible: New Living Translation. © Copyright 1973, 1978, 1984 by International Bible Society. Used by permission.

Scriptures marked as "(CEV)" are taken from the Contemporary English Version Copyright © 1995 by American Bible Society. Used by permission.

Cover photo: Debbie Painter - debbie@photosbylastingimages.com

Cover graphic design: Jesse Painter - lovelybowtie@aol.com

ISBN-13: 978-1539990260
ISBN-10: 1539990265

Waymaker Media
Manahawkin, NJ
www.waymakermedia.com

Table of Contents

NOTE FROM THE AUTHOR'S WIFE 7

    By Norma Oquendo de Fishman 7

PREFACE 9

    By Julie Ramjit 9

FORWARD 11

    By Anna LaTona 11

INTRODUCTION TO SECOND EDITION 13

    By Russ Painter 13

INTRODUCTION 17

LESSON ONE 21

    The Purpose of Dreams 21

    What Is The Source Of Dreams? 22

    Dream Messages 24

    The Dream Subject 25

    Prophetic Character 25

    DREAM ASSIGNMENT #1 26

LESSON TWO 29

    Biblical Dream Symbols 29

    Colors and Numbers 32

    Numbers As Symbols 32

    Colors As Symbols 33

    DREAM ASSIGNMENT #2: 33

LESSON THREE 35

    Modern-Day Symbols..35

    Personal Meaning 36

    Modern-Day Transportation............................36

    Back To Details 37

    Mini–List Of Common Dream Symbols 38

LESSON FOUR 41

    People In Dreams..41

    DREAM ASSIGNMENT #3 45

LESSON FIVE 49

    Dream Settings..49

    The Symbolism Of Dream Settings.......................49

    Times and Seasons 52

    Also of Importance...53

    DREAM ASSIGNMENT #4 54

LESSON SIX 57

    Putting It All Together...57

    SAMPLE DREAM #1...57

    APPLICATION 60

    DREAM ASSIGNMENT #5 62

LESSON SEVEN 63

    In Conclusion 63

    SAMPLE DREAM #2...63

SAMPLE DREAM # 3 65

Multiple Scenes 66

Recurring Dreams.......................................67

DREAM ASSIGNMENT #6 68

SAMPLE DREAM #4...................................69

SAMPLE DREAM # 5....................................70

Comprehensive Dream Dictionary **73-317**

Dictionary Table of Contents...............................75

BIBLIOGRAPHY 319

COMPREHENSIVE INDEX...............................321

NOTE FROM THE AUTHOR'S WIFE
By Norma Oquendo de Fishman

The third edition of this book has an expanded dictionary which promises to give the reader insight into their dreams. Like the first and second editions, it is a God-inspired and biblically based book, which the author took several months to organize and complete. Of course all the glory goes to the Lord who chooses when and how to use His servants.

Norma Oquendo de Fishman

*And it shall come to pass afterward, that I will
pour out my spirit upon all flesh; and
your sons and your daughters shall prophesy,
your old men shall dream dreams,
your young men shall see visions.*

Joel 2:28

PREFACE
By Julie Ramjit

I believe we are living in one of the most exciting times from a biblical perspective where, although it appears that the world is getting increasingly darker, the body of Christ and message of the gospel is becoming brighter. As we continue to see God reveal himself in a more powerful and awesome way, I believe that God will speak even more to His people. Numbers 12:8 speaks of God's desire to speak through visions and dreams to His prophets. This book gives those who hear the voice of God through dreams and visions a powerful tool to aid in the decoding of messages coming from the throne room of God. As I have been learning, God loves to speak to His children, and the more adept we are to discerning the mediums through which He speaks, the better we can translate these messages to bring words of encouragement and exhortation not only to our own situations but also to those around us.

I have been privileged to know Pastor Gary through his dream interpretation show (dreamsnetwork.tv), and I have come to see him as another father. He truly has the heart of a servant and operates in the love of God, which I believe the Bible considers the greatest of all gifts. He is fully committed to the work of God and to using his gifts to build and mature other believers in the vineyard. This book presents dream interpretation in a completely unique and practical way and in a manner which reflects his heart. Pastor Gary has been in ministry for the past seventeen years and interpreting dreams for the past twelve years, and it is with this wealth of ministry knowledge and gifting in the prophetic that he re-releases this book as a tool to those yearning to hear and understand the voice of God.

Having recently started interpreting dreams under the guidance of Pastor Gary, I have found the book a very practical and useful guide to looking up the symbolic meanings of images in a dream and also with the application of these symbols in the message the dream is attempting to relay. As Pastor Gary would say, it has a lot to do with being sensitive to the Holy Spirit, even after we know the symbolic meaning. I believe this book provides a step by step approach to building the message of the dream, at which point the Holy Spirit links it all together for the dreamer.

I would highly recommend this book to anyone wanting to learn about the practical aspects of dream interpretation. It is relevant and easy to use and comes from the heart of someone who God Himself has entrusted to minister to others in the field of dream interpretation. I hope and pray that you will enjoy the journey of interpreting dreams as you become immersed in the Word, the symbolic meanings, and the guidance of the Holy Spirit to bring the message of the dream together from God's heart to yours.

Julie Ramjit was born to a Hindu family in the Caribbean country of Trinidad, was saved at a very young age, and started attending church. She lived for many years in Trinidad but has since moved to the UK over seven years ago where she worships at one of the UK's largest full gospel gathering. Being a dreamer herself, she was rarely able to find the people who could interpret her dreams until her brother found Pastor Gary's dreams show and submitted her dream without her knowledge. She has since connected with Pastor Gary and his dream team and has come under the pastoral and paternal guidance of Pastor Gary. Julie is now one of the dream interpreters working under the mentorship of Pastor Gary as she hopes to fulfill the purpose and calling of God upon her life.

FORWARD
By Anna LaTona

Gary Fishman is an amazing writer who is able to encourage those with the Seer anointing and dream interpreters to release what God is sharing with them in a real practical way. Gary's dream book has literally gone around the world and helped people finally interpret what God is saying accurately and simply. It allows them to apply what God is trying to share with them.

This book is clearly written and is able to bring to light what God is saying. It's a great book for those who are learning and those who are advanced in dream interpretation. As a teacher and the coordinator of prophetic teams, I use a lot of tools to help people learn how to interpret dreams symbols, numbers, and colors.

This book is such a great tool for anyone. It is laid out so easily that you can use the information in the book to really begin to interpret what God is revealing in this hour. It is so important as Believers that we hear God and interpret what He saying.

Anna LaTona
One Voice Prophetic Ministry
Author of: Prophetic Evangelism, Is the
Church Ready for a New Move of God?
Onevoiceanna@gmail.com

INTRODUCTION TO SECOND EDITION
By Russ Painter

"Every great dream begins with a dreamer. Always remember, you have within you the strength, the patience, and the passion to reach for the stars to change the world."

— Harriet Tubman

"All our dreams can come true — if we have the courage to pursue them."

— Walt Disney

"God had a dream and wrapped your body around it."

— Lou Engle

Dreams are one of the most powerful avenues through which we can receive revelation, wisdom, and direction from God. If it is true that a picture is worth 1000 words, then it's also true that God can pack a book's worth of information into a single dream!

The challenge, of course, is unpacking that information. The highly symbolic nature of dreams, where for example the kind of car you're driving can speak volumes about your purpose and destiny, requires careful interpretation in order to understand fully the message God wants to tell you.

In an age where Google searches have become second nature for many, the problem becomes one of finding reliable, trustworthy, and most importantly, Bible-based help to understand what the symbols represent. Without that, you run the very real risk of making decisions and moving in directions that ultimately prove to be unwise and possibly even harmful.

But that won't be you! No, you made the choice to acquire this excellent resource, which is all of those things — reliable, trustworthy, and Bible-based — and I congratulate you for it.

I've had the pleasure of working side by side with Gary for over 5 years in the areas of prophetic ministry, discipleship, and dream interpretation, and I can say without hesitation that he's the real deal. I've witnessed so many people get life-changing breakthroughs when they've received dream interpretations through his ministry that it's clear Father God has raised him up to equip this generation with the tools necessary to understand with great clarity all the revelation He is pouring out on us night after night.

So buckle up and get ready for a wild ride through the wonderful world of dreams and dream interpretation... where it's *always* an adventure!

Russ Painter
Executive Director
Kingdom Training Institute, Inc.
www.kingdomti.com
www.dreamsnetwork.tv
www.heavensinvasion.com

There is a God in heaven who reveals mysteries.
Your dream and the visions that passed
through your mind as you lay
on your bed are these:

Daniel 2:28

INTRODUCTION

It's impossible to read through the Bible without noticing the fact that God speaks through dreams. Throughout the Old and New Testaments, the Lord used dreams to communicate messages, both to believers and non-believers. The purpose of this manual is to equip you in the area of dream interpretation so that God's messages will not fall by the wayside. Just think for a moment about all the divine revelation that is lost because the body of Christ is so lacking in knowledge when it comes to dreams.

The 2nd chapter of Acts tells us that the last days will be marked by a great increase of prophetic revelation, including dreams and visions. We need, as the people of God, to step boldly into what the Lord desires to do on the earth in our day. When Jesus speaks to us in any manner, we cannot be content with missing even a single word. If we are to be effective and fruitful in our lives and ministries, we must become attuned to His voice. The Church has tried for too long to get by with human wisdom and the traditions of men. It's time we begin to get our strategies and blueprints directly from the One who created the heavens and the Earth. The Lord desires to speak to our hearts and minds so that we can fulfill the destinies and plans He has designed for us.

I challenge you to become fully equipped in discerning God's voice as He speaks into *your* life. In so doing, you will also place yourself into the position of learning to speak prophetically to others. These lessons will bring you one step closer to this goal.

There is one Scripture in particular that states *the* primary principal of dream interpretation. In Genesis 40:8, Joseph was asked by Pharaoh (the ruler over Egypt) to interpret a dream that none of his advisors were able to derive the meaning of. Joseph responded to him with a question: *"Do not interpretations belong to God?"* Joseph didn't mean that only God could interpret, but rather, only *with* God could he then give Pharaoh the correct interpretation. Dream interpretation is not a merely intellectual exercise of 'figuring out' a dream's meaning. If you are going to interpret a dream correctly, you have to partner together with the Holy Spirit. Just as with other forms of prophetic ministry, understanding comes from the Lord. Although there are methods and principals involved that help us unravel a dream's meaning, without the mind of the Spirit, we will be unfruitful. There are no clear-cut formulas or equations. We cannot put all the elements of a dream into a computer and come up with the interpretation the Lord intended. There is no dream book that will give us instant answers.

I have spoken to many Christians who object to dream interpretation because of its association with the occult and the New Age Movement. My answer is that the devil will always attempt to counterfeit the things of God in order to discredit them. The Bible tells us that we can expect false teachers, false prophets, false shepherds, and false doctrines. Do we then eliminate teachers, pastors, prophets, and doctrines to make sure no one falls into the traps of the enemy? Of course not. Rather, the Word tells us to use discernment and test the spirits (1 John 4:1). The existence of false, counterfeit deceptions should not dissuade us from seeking the genuine. We do not want to throw the proverbial baby out with the bathwater. The Lord has given the ministry of dream interpretation as a gift to His people (see Daniel 1:17). We must not surrender it to the enemy.

The Lord gives us scriptural safeguards when it comes to prophetic ministry, such as:

Do not put out the Spirit's fire; do not treat prophecies with contempt. Test everything. Hold on to the good. (1 Thessalonians 5:19-21)

Dream interpretation, as a form of prophetic ministry, should be embraced. The above Scripture tell us that we need to weigh out and confirm our interpretations. We need to examine them through the lens of God's written Word and to seek further confirmation from the Holy Spirit. We do not, however, want to *"put out the Spirit's fire"* by discounting a clearly biblical means of hearing the voice of Jesus, our Lord.

In Numbers 11:29, Moses reflected the heart of God when he said, *"I wish that all the LORD's people were prophets and that the LORD would put his Spirit on them!"* Today, we have the opportunity to fulfill this ancient prayer as the Spirit of Revelation is being poured out on the Church. Let it rain down on you.

This manual is divided into seven lessons that you can study alone or in a home group or Bible study, along with a dream dictionary. I do not claim that any of the topics or lists in this manual are covered exhaustively. Rather, my goal is to start you on your way and provide some firm footing.

Just as with any other ministry, the more you practice and persevere, the more adept you will become. Although some might ultimately be more gifted than others in dream interpretation, I believe that all God's children can develop basic dream interpreting skills in partnership with the Holy Spirit. Acts 2 gives us the qualifications for those people who can receive and speak out prophetic revelation:

In the last days, God says, I will pour out my Spirit on all people. Your sons and daughters will prophesy, your young men will see visions, your old men will dream dreams. Even on my servants, both men and women, I will pour out my Spirit in those days, and they will prophesy. (Acts 2:17, 18)

If you are a born again man, woman, boy, or girl, then this manual is for you. I pray that the Lord will help us as we learn to unlock the door of understanding and revelation, which is the inheritance of all God's beloved children (Ephesians 1:17, 18).

LESSON ONE
The Purpose of Dreams

I believe that the primary reason God uses dreams to speak to us is because it is the one time He knows He has our full attention. During the day, we are so often distracted by the activities, pressures, and pleasures of our lives. At other times, we may close our ears to God's voice because we do not want to hear a challenging or convicting word — perhaps because we know we're not living according to His will. Job 33:14 tells us:

For God [does reveal His will; He] speaks not only once, but more than once, even though men do not regard it. (Amplified Bible)

The Lord is always trying to get our attention. The question is, are we listening? When we dream, our conscious minds are asleep so that our defenses are down and distractions are gone. He now has a "captive audience." Job 33:15a speaks directly to this issue:

(One may hear God's voice) in a dream, in a vision of the night, when deep sleep falls on men while slumbering upon the bed. Then He opens the ears of men and seals their instruction... (Amplified Bible)

Also, a dream can leave a powerful, unforgettable image in our hearts and minds, which is not *always* the case with a spoken, prophetic word.

I often relive dreams from my past, and I can feel the emotion and the impact of the storylines as though I dreamt them last night.

What is the Source of Dreams?

Dreams can come from (1) the Lord, (2) demonic spirits or (3) our own souls or (4) bodies.

1) **The Lord**: God authors dreams to speak to us. I will discuss this at length in the next section.

2) **Demonic Spirits**: The Bible says that the enemy comes *"only to steal and kill and destroy"* (John 10:10). Demonic entities such as spirits of fear, sexual sin, rejection, anger, condemnation, etc. will at times be the origin of dreams or nightmares that release terror, depression, unbelief, or lust into our mind and emotions. (I personally suffered since childhood with 'night terrors.' I awoke many, many nights, screaming and very disoriented. It was only when I received prayer at the Toronto Revival in 1997 that they finally and forever stopped.) The Devil's purpose in these dreams is always to harm us and attempt to turn us away from God.

   Even demonically based dreams can be turned around by the Lord and be used for our good. Through these dreams, God can reveal open doors in our lives that are entry points to the enemy. These 'open doors' are often unrepentant sins. For example, if someone lusts after a member of the opposite gender, the sin can create an entry way for a demonic spirit of lust to get a foothold. It's no surprise that this spirit will have access to that individual's dream life to create lustful dreams. God allows these dreams as a means of uncovering the sin and bringing conviction so that he or she can become free.

* It is important to note that a frightening dream is not always demonically inspired (see Job 7:14). We always have to ask the Holy Spirit to help us to discern the source of a particular dream.

There can also be other open doors for the enemy to enter into our dream life. These include:

a) Movies, television shows, or music which exalt evil: Demonic spirits will often attach themselves to these forms of media. We open ourselves up to them when we watch or listen to ungodly themes and story lines. (Conversely, listening to worship music or viewing godly videos will open up the door for the Holy Spirit to touch our hearts.) As an illustration, watching today's horror films can give access to a spirit of fear to come in and give you nightmares. Watching movies or videos displaying illicit sex can open the doorway of your soul to a spirit of lust which can also manifest in your dreams.

b) Past abuse or trauma: Traumatic experiences can create an inroad through which the enemy may build a stronghold of fear, rejection, or bitterness in our lives. Awareness of this through a dream interpretation can bring inner healing and deliverance to our soul. (For me personally, I believe that a spirit of fear which gained entry through past traumas was the source of my nightmares.)

3) **The soul**: The soul is comprised of our emotions, mind, and will. Stress, inner conflicts (conscious or unconscious), emotional ups and downs, loneliness, and impeding difficult situations can influence our dreams. I recall one night when I knew that the following day would bring an extremely stressful situation. I had four different dreams that night which played out four scenarios and outcomes for what I was about to face. Just as with demonic dreams, the Lord can use these to show us ways in which our minds or feelings are influencing our behavior in a wrong manner. Ecclesiastes 5:3 tells us that *"a dream comes when there are many cares."*

4) **The body:** Bodily pain, discomfort, and unmet physical needs can affect our dreams. For instance, Isaiah 29:7-8 tells us that a person who is hungry and thirsty may dream about food and water.

Dream Messages

What are the things the Lord desires to communicate to us in dreams? I will outline several possible dream messages and note Scriptures that relate to each:

1) **Warning**: (Genesis 20:1-7, Job 33:16, Matthew 2:22) God may warn of an impending danger. He may also warn us of the consequences of our actions when we are engaged in sin or rebellion.

2) **Direction**: (Matthew 1:20, Matthew 2:13, Acts 16:9,10) The Lord, at times, gives us instructions or directions through dreams.

3) **Revelation of Destiny** (Genesis 28:11-15, Genesis 37:9) The Lord may reveal to us our ultimate calling or ministry.

4) **Strength, Encouragement, and Comfort** (1 Cor. 14:3) As with all prophetic ministry, bringing strength, encouragement, and comfort is a primary focus.

5) **Healing and Deliverance** (Isaiah 61, Luke 4:18) Jesus proclaimed: *"The Spirit of the Lord is upon me, because he hath anointed me to preach the gospel to the poor; he hath sent me to heal the brokenhearted, to preach deliverance to the captives, and recovering of sight to the blind, to set at liberty them that are bruised."*

6) **Revelation of Future Events** (Genesis 15:12-16, Daniel 2,

Daniel 7, and Amos 3:7) God reveals coming events in our lives or in the lives of others. He might even reveal a future occurrence in a church, city, or nation. At times, God may ask us to take action in light of this type of message (such as sounding a warning), but more often He wants us simply to pray for the situation in accordance with His will. Seeing into the future helps us to be watchful and discerning.

7) **Conviction of Sin** (Job 33:17) *"...to turn man from wrongdoing and keep him from pride."*

The Dream Subject

It's important to determine who the dream message is for (i.e., the dream subject). Although most of the time a dream is a message to the dreamer, it can also be for another person, a group of people, a church, a denomination, a neighborhood, a city, a state, a region, a nation, or even the world. The higher the level of prophetic calling on an individual, the more their dreams will go beyond their immediate surroundings. Still, I have seen even new believers receive dreams that give revelation on what God is doing nationally or even among the nations.

Prophetic Character

If you are going to interpret dreams or engage in any other prophetic ministry, it's vital to walk in holiness and purity and sanctify ourselves unto God. There are many reasons for this. Hearing from God requires that we keep our hearts and minds pure. Polluting our souls with music, movies, television programs, video games, etc. that give an anti-biblical, anti-God message will create confusion and cloud the channels between us and the Lord. Secondly, when we interpret dreams for others, we are speaking into a person's life, which means we are speaking to others on the Lord's behalf. We need to represent Christ not only with words, but by making our bodies a living sacrifice (see Romans 12:1). I'm not saying that you have to have your life all together for God to use you prophetically. My point is that we cannot take sin lightly. This is true for all believers but it is especially true for those who desire to be God's prophetic voice. As 2 Timothy 2:20-22 tells us:

In a wealthy home some utensils are made of gold and silver, and some are made of wood and clay. The expensive utensils are used for special occasions, and the cheap ones are for everyday use. If you keep yourself pure, you will be a utensil God can use for his purpose. Your life will be clean, and you will be ready for the Master to use you for every good work. Run from anything that stimulates youthful lust. Follow anything that makes you want to do right. Pursue faith and love and peace, and enjoy the companionship of those who call on the Lord with pure hearts. (New Living Translation)

DREAM ASSIGNMENT #1

I encourage you to keep a *dream journal*. Try to write down your dream as soon as you wake up. Note also how the dream made you feel, as emotions can reveal a lot. Occasionally, there might be significance in the time you woke up from the dream. Jot down as much detail as possible. Regardless of how insignificant a dream may seem at the time, take it seriously. The Lord often speaks powerfully in ways that we might consider foolish, and I have seen many people discard dreams or visions that come wrapped in a seemingly trivial package.

I pray in the name of Jesus that the Lord would open your spiritual eyes and ears as you endeavor to hear His voice in a new way. I also pray that the God of our Lord Jesus Christ, the glorious Father, may give you the Spirit of wisdom and revelation, so that you may know him better (Ephesians 1:17,

NLT). Amen.

LESSON TWO
Biblical Dream Symbols

Although some dreams can be taken literally, that is the exception. Most dreams are full of symbolism, which needs to be interpreted to make sense. Many people totally discount their dreams because they often seem meaningless and foolish. If you can understand the symbolic elements of a dream, you will see that what appears to be trivial and nonsensical is often deep and profound. I believe the reason the Lord wraps our dreams in symbolism is because He wants us to learn to seek Him. He wants us to become totally dependent upon Him and His wisdom. The Lord tells us in no uncertain terms:

As the heavens are higher than the earth, so are my ways higher than your ways and my thoughts than your thoughts. (Isaiah 55:9)

That leaves us with the issue of how to determine a symbol's meaning. The first thing we look at is the Bible. Scripture is full of symbolic meaning which we can often apply to our dreams. For example, let's look at some common biblical symbols for the Holy Spirit.

The Holy Spirit is often typified by:

1) **Water** (John 7:38, 39)
2) **Oil** (Matthew 25:4)
3) **Wind** (John 3:8)
4) **Fire** (Matthew 3:11)
5) **Light** (Psalm 43:3)
6) **A Dove** (Matthew 3:16)

In a dream water, oil, wind, light, or fire will often represent either the Holy Spirit Himself or the things of the Spirit.

However, we cannot say that water, for example, **always** typifies the Holy Spirit.

Water can also symbolize:

1) **The Word of God** (Ephesians 5:26)
2) **Great Obstacles** (Exodus 14, Isaiah 43:2)
3) **The Judgment of God** (Genesis 7, Job 20:28)
4) **Overwhelming Troubles** (Psalm 18:16)

Interpreting dream symbols is not as easy as looking up their meanings in a Christian dream symbol dictionary (although having one can be very helpful). There are several principles of interpretation that are vital:

1) **Ask the Holy Spirit**. Depending on the Lord is the foundation of dream interpretation in all of its aspects.

2) **Look at the Context of the Dream**. A dream basically tells a story. All the symbols have to fit together for the dream message to unfold. As an example, let's look at the dream that Joseph interpreted for the Pharaoh in Genesis 41:1-4:

When two full years had passed, Pharaoh had a dream: He was standing by the Nile, when out of the river there came up seven cows, sleek and fat, and they grazed among the reeds. After them, seven other cows, ugly and gaunt, came up out of the Nile and stood beside those on the riverbank. And the cows that were ugly and gaunt ate up the seven sleek, fat cows. Then Pharaoh woke up.

The dream symbols are seven sleek and fat cows and seven ugly and gaunt (skinny) cows. According to Joseph, the seven fat cows symbolized seven years of prosperity, and the seven skinny cows symbolized seven years of famine. The skinny cows eating the fat cows meant that after seven years of prosperity ended, there would then be seven years of famine and lack. The picture is famine swallowing up prosperity. As a result of this dream, the Egyptians were able to be prepared for the time of famine.

Can you see how the symbols relate to each other and fit into the context of the message? It's like a jigsaw puzzle in which all the pieces need to fit together and interrelate in order to get the whole picture.

3) **Look at the outstanding characteristics of the symbol**. In Pharaoh's dream, fatness equaled abundance while skinniness equaled lack. That was key. Let's go back to the symbol of water. It is important to look at details about the water in a dream which might give us more clues. Here are some helpful illustrations:

   a) Is the water **clear** or **murky**? Clear water is more likely to signify the Holy Spirit or the Word of God, while murky, dirty water is usually significant of false doctrine or something compromising or evil.

   b) Is the water **still and quiet** or **troubled and stormy**? Still water is often indicative of the peace of God, while troubled waters typify tribulation or demonic attack (Isaiah 57:20). (If it is a river being symbolized then it is the opposite. A rushing river symbolizes the moving of the Spirit (John 7:38, 39), while a stagnant river can represent complacency or dead religious activity).

   c) Is the water **suitable for drinking**, or is it **bitter**? Good drinking water can represent the Holy Spirit and the good things of God (Psalm 36: 8, 9; Isaiah 55:1), while bitter water symbolizes sin and bitterness.

Here are some other widely accepted, biblically-based symbols. You will find their Scripture references in the dictionary section of this book:

Judge, **Gardener** or **Father Figure** = *God, the Father*

Lamb, **Bridegroom**, **Teacher**, **Attorney**, **Husband**, **Doctor**, **Lion**, or **King** = *Jesus*

Dragon, **Serpent**, or **Lion** = *Satan* (Notice that a lion can signify Jesus or Satan. We should never be too quick to automatically assign meaning to a symbol.)

Sheep, **Fish**, **Child**, **Bride** or **Wheat** = *A Christian*

Milk, **Meat**, **Water**, **Hammer**, **Sword**, **Mirror** or **Honey** = *the Word of God*

Bear, **Bees**, **Wolf**, **Fox**, **Arrows**, **Rat** or a **Storm** = *Attack or deceits of the enemy.*

Colorsand Numbers

Colors and numbers have significance as dream elements. We can, for the most part, find their symbolic meanings in Scripture. (Although, as we saw in Pharaoh's dream, numbers can be taken literally.) Let's look first at numbers. I will list one meaning for each of the numbers one through ten, as well as one scriptural reference.

Numbers As Symbols

One = Unity *(Philippians 2:2)*
Two = Witness *(2 Corinthians 13:1)*
Three = God as the Trinity *(2 Corinthians 13:14)*
Four = The Earth (Four winds, four seasons, four corners of the Earth) *(Rev. 7:1)*
Five = God's enabling grace and power *(Leviticus 26:8)*

Six = The number of man (Created on the sixth day) *(Revelation 13:18)*
Seven = Completeness or perfection *(Genesis 2:2)*
Eight = A new beginning *(1 Peter 3:20)*
Nine = The Holy Spirit (Nine fruit of the Spirit, Nine charismatic Spiritual gifts) *(Galatians 5:22, 23)*
Ten = Trial and Testing *(Daniel 1:12-15)*

Colors As Symbols

As I mentioned, colors also have symbolic significance:

Red = The blood of Jesus (forgiveness, freedom), (*Ephesians 2:13*), passion or anger
Blue = Revelation or authority from Heaven (*2 Corinthians 12:1*) or sadness (the blues)
Purple = Jesus as King and Ruler (*Revelation 1:5*)
White = Purity (*Revelation 3:4*)
Scarlet, Crimson = Sin (*Isaiah 1:18*)
Green = Prosperity (*Proverbs 11:28*), life or 'Go Ahead' (given a green light)
Orange = Danger, warning
Yellow = Glory, fear or slow down and be cautious (as when a traffic light turns yellow)

DREAM ASSIGNMENT #2:

All of the above can have more than one symbolic meaning. I urge you to sit with a Bible Concordance and look up the usage of various colors and numbers in the Bible. See if you can find consistent patterns in the way each number or color is signified.

When a prophet of the LORD is among you,
I reveal myself to him in visions,
I speak to him in dreams.

Numbers 12:6

LESSON THREE
Modern-Day Symbols

Besides the symbols which can be given meaning based on their usage in the Bible, many dream symbols come from our modern-day experience. When Jesus spoke in parables two thousand years ago, He used symbols that were part of the everyday life of His listeners. Since many people in ancient Israel were familiar with farming, Jesus used activities such as *plowing, sowing, planting, reaping,* etc. as metaphors for Kingdom principles. It's the same today. The Lord speaks to us in ways we can relate to. The Lord desires to speak to all of His people, not only ministers and Bible college graduates.

Just as is the case with biblical symbols, all dream symbols can have more than one interpretation. For example, a gun can represent a demonic attack or the power of God being released. When looking at biblical symbols, I mentioned that details are very important. Say, for instance, that someone dreams they're riding in an elevator. Here are some things to look for:

1) Is the elevator going up or down? If it is going up, then it might mean that the Lord is about to elevate or promote the person. If it's going down, it could mean a fall or that the person is headed in the wrong direction in life.

2) What floor is the elevator going to? If an elevator is going up to the 8th floor, it could mean a new beginning in the dream subject's life. An elevator going down to the 6th floor may signify that the person is leaning on human advice rather than godly wisdom and counsel. (See Lesson 2 and dictionary for number meanings).

3) Who else is in the elevator? An elevator operator can

represent the Holy Spirit, a leader, a boss, or even Satan. (Remember, look at the context and ask the Lord.) Other passengers may symbolize other people in the dreamer's life.

Personal Meaning

It's important to ask the dreamer what a dream symbol means to them personally. A good example of this is a dog. To some people a dog is a symbol of love, warmth, and faithfulness. To others who have had bad experiences with dogs, it may signify anger or even an attack. When I was a teenager living in Brooklyn, I often experienced packs of wild dogs in the streets because back then many dog owners would let their dogs loose when they no longer wanted them. Because of those experiences, I don't get the same warm, cuddly feelings when I think of dogs that others might have. That is why emotions in a dream are so important. They give us clues in helping us to interpret.

Modern-Day Transportation

Typically, modes of transportation represent churches or ministries because they are symbolic of how we move together in the Lord. (Of course, they can also signify travel. An airplane, for instance, can mean a long trip or overseas missions work). Here is a list of different transport vehicles and their possible symbolic significance:

1) **Car** = An individual or small ministry

2) **Airplane** = A church or ministry that moves in the Spirit. (A large airliner usually symbolizes a large church.)

3) **Train** = A church that is steeped in tradition and ritual. A

train always takes the same route to the same place at the same time. There is no room for flexibility or being Holy Spirit led. On the other hand, a train can signify a powerful ministry or one that is continuously on the move.

4) **School Bus** = A teaching ministry or a children's ministry

5) **Ship** = Church or ministry. If the ship is on the ocean, it could signify ministry to the peoples of the nations. (Revelation 17:15)

6) **Rowboat** = Ministry that relies on human effort (also a **Bicycle**)

7) **Motorboat** = Ministry powered by the Holy Spirit

8) **Battleship** = Spiritual warfare (also a **Tank** or **Fighter Plane**)

9) **Tractor Trailer** = A ministry of bringing provision

10) **Moving Truck** = Change or relocation

Back To Details

Remember that details are significant. If the dreamer is on the *Number Three Train*, he or she is likely to be moving in the Lord. *A wrecked car* can represent a ministry being destroyed or at least headed in that direction. *A car with failing brakes* typically speaks of a ministry out of control, and *a broken down car* symbolizes a broken down ministry.

*Important note: Many negative events forecast in dreams can be averted through repentance, prayer and/or godly wisdom.

Just as is the case with the elevator operator mentioned above, the person who is driving or piloting a vehicle also has symbolic relevance. The one driving is the one in authority or in control.

Train stations, bus depots, docks and piers, airports, and parking lots usually signify a time of waiting or impending transition.

A driver looking through a rear view mirror is someone who is looking back to the past.

A vehicle stopping for gas can signify a need to stop and refuel on the Word of God and prayer.

Tires are filled with air, which is a type of the Holy Spirit. *Tires which are flat or low on air* show a church or ministry in need of the Holy Spirit's presence, guidance, and power.

Mini–List Of Common Dream Symbols

(Any symbol on this list can at times be taken literally, but I have found that to be the exception rather than the norm.)

You will find a much more complete listing in the dream dictionary:

1) **Cat** = Self-will or independence (A black cat can signify witchcraft or superstition)

2) **Vacation** = Time of Spiritual rest and refreshing

3) **Mountain** = Hindrance or obstacle – Can also be a place of encountering the Lord (Exodus 19:3, Luke 9:28)

4) **Death** = The death of a person in a dream is not typically a

bad thing. It is often symbolic of dying to the sinful flesh (Romans 8:13). It can also mean something coming to an end. You have to really hear from the Lord to take death in a dream as literal. An exception would be if a dream subject is flirting with death by engaging in potentially deadly sins such as using drugs or criminal activity. If the person is unsaved, it could also represent a warning of spiritual death (Romans 6:23) if there is no turning to Christ.

5) **Door** = An opportunity (A white door usually means that it is a door opened by the Lord.)

6) **Alligator** = Verbal attack or gossip (Alligators have very large mouths that can easily destroy.)

7) **Microwave** = Things happening quickly

8) **Earthquake** = God's power (Acts: 16:26) or judgment (Revelation 11:13)

9) **Bear** = Attack of the enemy or God's judgment

10) **Photograph** = Memory of the past

11) **Stain or Dirt** = Sin

12) **Teeth** = One's ability to comprehend the word of God (or chew on the meat of the Word) or to use wisdom. Teeth can also represent relationships.

13) **Electricity** = The power of God

14) **Spider Web** = Trap of the enemy

15) **Prison** = Spiritual bondage or addiction

16) **Tree** = A leader (Daniel 4:22), a righteous person (Psalm

92:12) or the Cross of Christ (1 Peter 2:24)

17) **Flower** = Natural beauty

18) **Sun** = Glory and light of God

19) **Moon** = The people of God (Just as the moon reflects the light of the sun, Christians have no light of their own but they reflect the Glory of the Lord.

20) **Darkness** = Lack of spiritual light or vision

21) **Map** = The Lord's direction

LESSON FOUR
People In Dreams

Just as is the case with other dream elements, most people **(though again, not all)** who appear in dreams are symbolic. At times, even the dreamer's role in a dream may be symbolic of something else. Here are some of the ways we can discover the significance of a particular person in a dream:

1) Identify something specific about that person in real life, such as an **outstanding personality, character, or temperament trait**. For example, if the person in the dream is identified as an angry person in reality, then it is possible that the Lord is revealing an anger issue in the dreamer's life. If the person is a man or woman of great faith, then it could be that the dreamer's faith is at issue. (Often, when a person dreams about someone whom he or she respects as a strong Christian, this reveals that there is indeed a message from the Lord embedded in the dream.) I usually will ask the dreamer to tell me what stands out in their mind about a particular dream character.

2) If the person in the dream is a **family member**, then look at his or her real life relationship with the dreamer. Family members can have symbolic significance, For example:

   a) **Father** = God the Father

   b) **Mother** = The Church where the dreamer is or was nurtured in the Lord

   c) **Husband** = Jesus (John 3:29)

   d) **Wife** = The Church body (Revelations 19:7) or something that metaphorically speaking the dreamer is "married "to" such as a job, a hobby, or even a car

e) **Brother** = a male Christian

f) **Sister** = a female Christian

g) **Son or Daughter** = A ministry that the dreamer birthed

3) Look at the **occupation** or **role** of the person in the dream. Here is a sample list with possible symbolic interpretations to give you a basic idea:

a) **Farmer** = A preacher, evangelist (Matthew 13:18-23), a giving person (2 Corinthians 9:10) or the Lord (Matthew 13:24-30)

b) **Soldier** = An angel or a demon, depending on whether he represents good or evil, or a Christian engaged in Spiritual warfare (Ephesians 6:10-18)

c) **Shepherd** = Jesus or a pastor

d) **District Attorney** = Satan (the accuser of the brethren) or a legalistic Christian (Galatians 3:1-3)

e) **Lawyer** = Jesus, our Advocate, or someone who defends the weak or oppressed

f) **Judge** = God, the Father, or a judgmental person

g) **Auto Mechanic** = Someone the Lord is using to help 'fix' or realign a ministry

h) **Waiter** = A teacher (one who serves 'spiritual food') or a servant (Matt. 23:11)

i) **Doctor** = Jesus or a Christian with a healing ministry

When a man in a dream is of unknown identity or is heard but remains unseen, he often represents the Holy Spirit. If such a person shows any of the functions of the Holy Spirit (protector, counselor, teacher) and/or attributes (perfectly holy, all knowing, all powerful, loving) it most likely is Him. If the person is evil, then it may mean Satan or a demon is lurking.

4) The **clothes** a person is wearing can tell you a lot. Someone dressed in white usually pictures a man or woman of God. A person wearing very dark clothes can signal evil. For example, if the dream is about a shepherd in dark clothes, he may symbolize Satan or a false teacher. A prophetic person may be dressed in blue, and a person in a dangerous situation might have on something orange. (See Lesson 2 for a list of colors and what they may represent)

*Important note: I have seen Christian books on dream interpretation that claim that a dark skinned person can symbolize an evil individual. That is untrue. The Lord never uses skin color alone to signify good or evil.

Clothes that are revealing and seductive usually speak of sexual sin or lust. When the dreamer, to his or her embarrassment, is walking in public either nude or partially nude, it often is revealing shame or a fear of being publicly exposed.

5) The **name** of a person in a dream is significant at times. I keep a book handy that gives the meaning for most names. The dream dictionary will give you the meaning of many common names.

I will now present a list of some names and their meanings so you can better understand the concept.

Alexander = Defender of mankind
Christopher = Carrier of Christ
Daniel = God is my judge
Gloria = Glory
Hillary = Happy
Jessica = He sees
John = The Lord is gracious
Jonathan = Gift of God
Joseph = God increases
Joshua = The Lord is salvation
Katherine = Pure
Kenneth = Sprung from fire
Mark = Warlike
Mary = Bitterness
Michael = Who is like the Lord?
Nicholas = People of victory
Raymond = Counselor, protector
Richard = Dominant ruler
Ruth = Friend
Tiffany = Appearance of God

From the above list, it is easy to see how a name can figure prominently in a dream. As an example, someone named Joseph in a dream may be symbolic of financial or spiritual increase. A man named John may be symbolic of the Lord's desire to show grace to the dream subject.

6) Often times, people in dreams are from the dreamer's past and may be an individual he or she hasn't seen for many years. The dreamer may appear in the dream as he or she looked as a young child, and others might look the same way they did many years before. There are several possible reasons for this:

   a) The person might be part of an **unresolved issue** from the dreamer's past. For example, an unfaithful ex–

boyfriend in a dream may point to lingering bitterness against him which needs to be forgiven and left in the Lord's hands.

b) There may be an issue of **generational sin patterns** or **curses** that the Lord wants to bring to light so that deliverance can take place.

c) On the other hand, the Lord might be pointing out **generational blessings** or **spiritual inheritances**. An example would be a dream about a grandparent or great grandparent who walked in a prophetic gifting which the Lord wants to impart to the dreamer.

d) The appearance of a person from the dreamer's past may reveal **the source of current emotional or relational problems**. For example, a person who deals with shame and rejection may dream about an abusive grandparent who helped open the door to these intense negative emotions. The root cause of the rejection and shame being uncovered can be a powerful first step toward inner healing. (If you would like to read more on this topic, I recommend the books *Healing for Damaged Emotions* by David A. Seamands, Chariot Victor Publishing and *Appointed for Significance* by Roger Lehman, Ascribe Publishing – Available from: *citystreams.org*)

DREAM ASSIGNMENT #3

Take one of your own dreams that you have recorded and list on a piece of paper:

1) Colors or **Numbers** used in the dream

2) People appearing in the dream (including name,

occupation, clothing, relationship to you, and any outstanding personal traits)

3) Any **modes of transportation** used such as a car, an airplane, etc.

4) Other **dream elements** such as animals, inanimate objects, or things in nature like the sun, rain, a river, etc.

Using the first four chapters of this manual, and in cooperation with the Holy Spirit begin to assign meaning to each element in the 4 categories listed above. You might want to use other helpful tools, such as a Bible, a Bible dictionary, and a Bible concordance. If you have questions, you can e-mail them to me at: *dreams@sanctuaryfellowship.org* I will respond as soon as possible.

Don't worry if you can't recall all the details of the dream. Just list the information you do remember.

God does speak—now one way, now another—though man may not perceive it. In a dream, in a vision of the night, when deep sleep falls on men as they slumber in their beds, he may speak in their ears...

Job 33:14-16

LESSON FIVE
Dream Settings

The issue I would like to examine in this lesson is the dream setting. In other words, where and when does the dream's storyline take place? In many dreams, the action moves from place to place. The scene may also switch from the past to the future. All of these details are significant to a dream's meaning.

The Symbolism Of Dream Settings

Here is a list of some common dream settings and their typical symbolic significance. (As I mentioned in the preface, none of the lists in this manual are exhaustive in terms of content or possible symbolic meanings.)

1) **Car, a Train or other Modes of Transportation** = (See Lesson 3)

2) **Office** = Can represent either a place of employment, financial provision, or a ministry 'office'; such as pastor, teacher, prophet, etc. (Ephesians 4:11). When someone dreams of a business owned by his or her father, in my experience that is usually speaking of the work of the Lord – *And He said to them, "Why did you seek Me? Did you not know that I must be about My Father's business?"* (Luke 2:49)

3) **Gymnasium** = Can signify competition, pride, or training for spiritual maturity (1 Timothy 4:8, 1 Corinthians 9:25-27)

4) **Hospital** = A church (place of healing) or a healing ministry

5) **Farm** = A church or ministry (1 Corinthians 3:9), sowing and reaping, provision, discipleship, or evangelism (Matthew 13:3-9)

6) **Restaurant** = Eating and drinking the Word (Hebrews 5:11-14), or drinking in the Holy Spirit (1 Corinthians 12:13)

7) **School** = A period of being tested by the Lord, a teaching ministry, discipleship, the study of the Word of God, a time of preparation

8) **Waiting Room, Parking Lot, Airport, Train Station, Bus Terminal** = Time of waiting, preparation, and/or transition

9) **Prison** = Bondage to sin, addictions

10) **Hotel** = A transitional or temporary life season, travel

11) **Swimming Pool** = Refreshing of the Holy Spirit

12) **House** = Typically a house is symbolic of the dreamer's or dream subject's life (Matthew 7:25). Various rooms and places in the house symbolize different aspects of his or her existence:

   a) **Bathroom** = Repentance, deliverance, and cleansing of sin

   b) **Attic** = Memories of the past

   c) **Basement** = Emotions that are repressed or under the surface, hidden sin

   d) **Bedroom** = Intimacy with Jesus, meditation and reflection on the Lord, rest, sexual issues, or marital intimacy

e) Front Yard or Front Door = The future

f) Backyard or Backdoor = The past

g) Living Room = The public or social part of one's life, family life, Christian fellowship

h) Kitchen = Christian service (Luke 10:38-40, MSG) eating (meditating on and studying the Bible) and drinking (receiving the ministry of the Holy Spirit)

i) Roof = The mind, God's covering and protection

j) Window = Prophetic Revelation

Note – If the dream setting is the dreamer's **childhood home**, it might mean that:

a) The dreamer perceives an issue in his or her life as if it were still the past.

b) There are issues from the dreamer's childhood that are unresolved.

c) The Lord wants to remind the dreamer of all He has set him or her free from.

d) See Lesson 4, number 6

If the dream setting is a **new house**, it could be speaking of a new chapter in the dream subject's life.

A **dirty house** speaks of sin, while a **damaged house** signifies a need for inner healing and/or restoration or physical illness (or metaphorically a "broken home"). A house in **disrepair** symbolizes the person's neglect of his or her emotional, physical, or spiritual needs.

Very often someone will dream of being at home, but it **appears different** from the way it does in real life. This could mean that the person is seeing an issue in his or her life from a wrong perspective. It can also be revealing an underlying spirit of confusion.

Times and Seasons

As I already have begun to show, noting when a dream takes place can be just as significant as where it takes place. Let's look at the four seasons. If you can tell whether a dream is set in summer, autumn, winter, or spring, it might be significant to the dream interpretation:

1) **Summer** = Rest, time of refreshing, or a season of God's favor

2) **Autumn** = Time of reaping a harvest (financial or the lost being saved), the ending of a summer season of refreshing and the transition into a season of trial, or rain in autumn speaks of the latter day outpouring of revival fire on the Earth (Joel 2:27)

3) **Winter** = A season of trial and tribulation, a lack of fruitfulness or a state of being cold in one's Christian walk, barrenness

4) **Spring** = New beginnings, the born-again experience, or the end of a season of trials (Song of Solomon 2:11, 12)

Note also the **weather conditions** and **time of day** the dream takes place:

1) **Rain** = Outpouring of the Holy Spirit, God's Word (Isaiah

55: 10,11), or God's blessing

2) **Snow** = The Word of God, or purity (Isaiah 1:18)

3) **Tornado** = The Glory of God (Ezekiel 1:4-28), a powerful attack of the enemy (Job 1:19) or God's judgment (Jeremiah 23:19)

4) **Hail** = God's judgment (Exodus 9:18)

5) **Storm** = Trials and difficulties or attack of the enemy

6) **Bright Sunshine** = The presence and favor of God (Psalm 84:11), the light of God, or healing (Malachi 4:2)

7) **Darkness** = Hidden sin, lack of direction, or the work of the enemy (Luke 22:53)

8) **Lightning** = God's judgment, the Presence of God (2 Samuel 22:13), or a sudden move of God

9) **Thunder** = The voice of God (2 Samuel 22:14), spiritual warfare, God's judgment, or a warning of an impending attack or trial.

10) **Cloudy** = *White cloud* – The presence of God (Exodus 13:21), *Dark cloud* – depression, a coming trial, a hindrance in hearing God's voice.

Also of Importance

Remember to take note of time in a dream. As I have discussed, numbers have significance. For example, if it is 5 o'clock in the dream, it could mean that a time of God's grace is at hand, or 8 o'clock might signify a new beginning. Also, write down the time you wake up from the dream, as that can also be significant.

Many dreams will change from one setting to another. There can be several possible reasons for this, which I will discuss in a later chapter.

When you dream about a future event, it does not necessarily mean that the event will take place. If you discern that it is something the Lord wants to do, then you need to partner with Him in prayer (Daniel 9:1-3, 1 Kings 18: 41-44). For example, if you dream of the salvation of a loved one, then you need to intercede for the person's salvation. As John Wesley once said, "God does nothing except in answer to prayer."

If you discern that a dream is demonically inspired and it shows a horrific event set in the future, such as the murder of a family member, then rebuke the enemy and break the spirit of fear. I have had dozens of dreams depicting terrifying events that never took place. As I said in a previous lesson, it is important when you have such dreams to ask the Lord if there is an open door to the enemy in your life or a demonic stronghold such as a spirit of fear.

DREAM ASSIGNMENT #4

In the last lesson, I asked you to take a dream and begin to look at the possible symbolic interpretations for colors, numbers, people, and other dream elements. Now begin to focus on the dream setting. Look first at where the dream took place. If it was in a house, then note the room.

Could you determine the season or the weather? Were there cars, boats, trains, or other types of transportation involved? Did the dream take place in the past, present, or future? If so, then look at the lists that I have provided to see possible meanings. Also, remember to ask the Lord to give you insight.

Without that step, the lists are meaningless.

LESSON SIX
Putting It All Together

In this lesson, I will look at an actual dream that was sent to me, and begin the process of interpretation. Now that we have examined different components of dream interpretation, let's begin to put it all together.

SAMPLE DREAM #1

The following is an actual dream from a Pastor who is in the process of starting a local church. Here it is:

I got home from a trip or something, and we were in this new apartment. I could tell that we live there now, but it was a very strange place. The weirdest thing about it was that the apartment was loaded with pets... My wife had the house full of pets... strange pets... We had a goat in the kitchen — he was tied to a large fruit basket. When I untied him to say hello and play with him, he got so excited that he peed on the bed. We had two huge beds in the room — I don't know why. We had a huge fish tank in the house with all kinds of fish. Then the strangest one — we had a skunk... But he was gorgeous... The skunk was actually bright yellow and his tail was orange. He was the coolest looking animal I've ever seen. He didn't smell, and I remember my wife telling me he was the friendliest thing around. When I sat down, he came to me and was kissing my hand... He was bright yellow and orange... There were more animals there, but I couldn't remember them when I woke up... I can't even start to imagine what all that means.

It is clearly obvious that this dream makes no sense unless it is interpreted. There is very little in it that can be taken literally. Let's first divide the dream into the categories I discussed in the previous lessons.

1) **Dream Setting:** The setting for the dream is a *new* apartment. The Pastor and has wife were in the process of planting a new church. An apartment or house is symbolic of the dream subject's life. I believe the new apartment symbolizes the new church plant which is a new and prominent aspect of their life.

2) **Dream Symbols:** There were a number of animals used symbolically in this dream. I feel that the animals are representative of the different categories of people who will be coming to this church. I will now look at them one by one and then put it all together.

   a) **Goat** = A goat can be *unruly* and *hard to manage*. At first I saw this as a negative symbol but then I realized that the goat was tied to a *bowl of fruit*. **Fruit** represents the positive consequences of the Holy Spirit working through a believer's life (John 15: 1-8). He didn't seem mean or evil, but he was messy as he "peed on the bed". I believe that the goat represented people who would come into the church needing a lot of guidance and discipleship. Although they may be hard to manage, it will be worth the work because they will bear fruit for the Kingdom of God. Perhaps the reason the goat was in the kitchen was because he was eating and drinking of the Word and the Spirit.

   b) **Fish** = Fish are typically symbolic of *souls* who have come into the Kingdom (Mark 1:17). In the dream, there were all kinds of fish. In this church, there will be people from various ethnic groups, social strata, and economic levels.

c) Skunk = A skunk is symbolic of someone who fouls up the atmosphere with sin. This skunk, however, was friendly and beautiful. I interpret this to mean that the skunk appeared to be something that he wasn't. This speaks to me of people who will come into the church and give the appearance of being holy and loving but yet they are still "skunks". Note the skunk's colors: bright yellow and orange. **Orange** often means danger or warning. **Bright yellow** can sometimes symbolically say: "Slow down and be cautious." (as when a traffic light turns yellow) These skunks may be false prophets or people living totally hypocritical lifestyles.

*Both yellow and orange can have several symbolic meanings, but in looking at the context and in seeking the Lord, I was impressed to assign the meanings I just discussed. Perhaps you will see even deeper meanings that I might have missed.

There were also **2 big beds** in the apartment. A bed speaks of God's peace and rest to those who receive salvation (Matthew 11:28-29). It is also symbolic of intimacy with the Lord (Song of Solomon 1:4). I believe that the beds are pointing to many troubled and wearied people who will come to the church and find rest in the Lord through a relationship with Jesus.

3) **Dream Subject:** I believe that the dream subject in this dream is the Pastor who dreamed it. The dream seems to contain a message for him. I see no reason to assign symbolic meaning to his presence in the dream.

4) **Dream Message:** The dream is a message of both encouragement and warning. The Lord is encouraging this pastor of a new church plant that he will bring many people into the church of all different backgrounds. Even those who are difficult to pastor at first will bear fruit. It is also a warning to use discernment, as some will come in

deceptively.

5) **Dream Source:** The source of this dream is clearly the Lord. The enemy does not bring encouragement or warning. Rather, the kingdom of darkness will release discouragement and fear. Many times when Satan is the source of a dream, you will wake up with a feeling of despair, hopelessness, or depression.

I also didn't feel that this was a soulish dream. In putting all of the pieces together, the Lord made it clear to me that this was a message from Him. A dream that originates from a dreamer's mind or emotions will typically reveal inner needs, drives, and conflicts. This dream was all about ministering to others.

This dream shows how dream interpretation can be a powerful tool in hearing and understanding what the Lord is saying. If this pastor had cast this dream aside as foolishness or the result of too many tacos for dinner, he would have missed out on a powerful message from the Lord.

APPLICATION

Once you have interpreted a dream, what should you do with the revelation? The answer to the question depends on the situation. If the subject of your dream is someone other than you, and you discern that the dream source is the Lord, then you need to ask God when and how to present it to that person.

Sometimes, when the Lord gives you prophetic revelation, He wants you just to pray for the person and not say anything. It is also important to be very careful if you feel your dream is giving direction to an individual. Many lives have been damaged by misspoken prophetic words of direction telling them to change ministries, quit their jobs, marry a certain person, etc. If you do feel that the message of a dream gives direction for someone other than yourself, really seek the Lord about whether your interpretation needs to be shared. If you are strongly impressed that you need to share your message, then go to a church leader or pastor. In that way, there is accountability and safety. If the leader tells you not to share the interpretation, then you need to submit to his or her authority (see Hebrews 13:17).

This is also true if you feel that your dream is a word of direction for a church. Share the word with the pastor. Never go around to people in a congregation and share your interpretation with them. This can cause division and rebellion, and believe me when I tell you, it happens. This is a wrong use of prophetic ministry because you are moving outside the realm of authority the Lord has given you. If the Lord directs you to share an interpretation with an individual or a group of people and you do so, then you have fulfilled your responsibility (other than keeping it in prayer). If your interpretation is ignored, then leave it at that. Don't keep badgering people if you feel they have not heeded your words. Conviction is the work of the Holy Spirit (see Ezekiel 33:7-9).

*If we stay within biblical guidelines, then dream interpretation will be safe and fruitful. If we move outside of these boundaries, we can cause great harm and even ruin lives and ministries.

If the Lord gives you a dream with a message for yourself, it is not always wise to share it. Genesis 37:1-11 tells us that Joseph had a dream that one day he would have authority over his parents and brothers. (This was actually later fulfilled.) Telling his family, however, caused anger and jealousy. Perhaps it would have been wiser to keep the dream to himself.

Also, make sure that if you do reveal your dream to others, it is never out of a wrong motive such as pride or a need for attention or recognition. Always be led by the Spirit.

DREAM ASSIGNMENT #5

Take the dream you have been working on and follow the pattern I gave you today. Begin to determine the dream's message, source, and subject.

LESSON SEVEN
In Conclusion

My goal in writing this manual is to give you some elementary skills in dream interpretation. Begin to put these basic principles into practice and allow the Lord to bring you to a higher level of prophetic maturity. In this lesson, I will look at two more actual dreams that were sent to me and give you a few more principles of dream interpretation.

SAMPLE DREAM #2

I dreamt that my mom had a new house and I visited and I counted seven toilets in her house, only on the left hand side. I counted two times. I said to her: "You have seven toilets, and that's only on this side." She said that she wanted people to be able to "go." The toilets were all beautiful, shiny and all by themselves. Some were in unusual places. I remember seeing one in a closet, with a glass door. That one had shiny wood with gold trim. They really were amazing. And my mother was soaking a lot of men's shirts, like polo shirts, she was soaking the necks of the shirts in tubs of water and the water was soapy and murky. She had the shirts laid out, one on top of the other, hanging on the floor with the neck part in the water. The shirts were different colors and patterns.

Like the first dream, this dream makes absolutely no sense when taken literally. Let's begin to see if any sense can be made out of it.

1) **Dream Setting:** The dream is set in the house of the dreamer's mother. Symbolically, a mother can represent the Church. By using the word 'Church', I am not referring to a

building. Rather, I am referring to the people of God who comprise the body of Christ.

A mother is one whose role is to love, nurture, and care for her children. This gives a picture of what the Church is called to do. So, I believe that in this case, the setting for this dream is the Church. (I will speak more on this below.)

2) **Dream Symbols:**

a) **Seven Toilets** = A toilet symbolizes cleansing and repentance. Seven is the number of perfection and completion. (Seven along with three are considered to be God's numbers.)

b) **Wood with Gold Trim** = Wood speaks of humanity, while gold symbolizes Deity. The picture is man covered by the glory of God (Exodus 37:15).

c) **Shirts** = A clean shirt symbolizes holiness, and a dirty shirt signifies a life stained with sin (Zechariah 3:1-6).

d) **Tubs of Soapy Water** = The Holy Spirit washing away sin

3) **Dream Subject:** I believe that the subject of this dream is the body of Christ. The dream might be for a specific local church, but I sense in the Spirit that it is a prophetic message for the entire body. One thing that points to this is that the shirts were different colors and patterns. This can speak of the entire Church body, which is comprised of *people from every nation, tribe, and language* (Revelation 7:9.)

4) **Dream Message:** This dream is prophetic of a move of repentance and cleansing coming to the Church. The toilet behind a glass door speaks of people repenting publicly for

all to see. As people repent and turn to the Lord, God's glory will return to His Church, and the stain of sin will be washed away. This dream is a confirmation to me, as I have seen in the Spirit that God is going to bring great conviction and cleansing to His people. Many others have prophesied this as well.

5) **Dream Source:** It is obvious to me that this dream is from the Lord.

SAMPLE DREAM # 3

I dreamt that my teenage daughter and I were preparing for a trip. We didn't have a lot of money, and it was dark and raining. We were on a college campus, and we went to the eating area where they had a small grocery store and they sold prepared food. We gathered up things to buy for our trip. I think the trip was by car, but I'm sure it was just us two.

1) **Dream Setting:** The dream took place on a college campus. A **college** can symbolize several things, but the context and the Spirit tell me that it here signifies a period of testing that the dreamer and her daughter are going through. (Again, if you feel that you have other insights, please send them to me.) Also, it was dark and raining. In this instance, I feel the darkness and rain signify a difficult period in the dreamer's life. **Darkness** also symbolizes a lack of direction. They then went to the grocery store, which speaks of a place of receiving spiritual nourishment.

*It is difficult to describe sometimes why I assign a particular meaning to a symbol, because of the element of Spiritual revelation involved. The only way to learn to interpret dreams is to start to do it and interact with the Holy Spirit. Knowledge will only take you so far.

2) **Dream Symbols:**

    a) **A Trip** = I believe that the trip refers to the next stage of the dreamer's life. While she was going through a dark and difficult time of testing, the trip signifies a new place of destiny. She was preparing for it but did not have the inner resources or the light to transition out of the place of darkness.

    b) **Food** = Food speaks of the Word of God.

    c) **"Things to buy for the trip"** = The "things" I believe are the spiritual elements (faith, God's direction, etc.) the dreamer needed for her "trip" to the next level in God's plan for her life. (Isaiah 55:1)

3) **Dream Subject:** The dream subjects are the dreamer and her daughter.

4) **Dream Message**: The dream is a call to the dreamer and her daughter to focus on their devotional lives in order to receive what they lacked from the Lord to get past the trials and testing. In the midst of the trial, they went to the grocery store (to eat of the Word and drink of the Spirit) to get what they needed for the trip.

5) **Dream Source**: If my interpretation is correct, then this dream is from the Lord.

Multiple Scenes

Many times, dreams will contain more than one scene. Even when each scene seems totally unrelated to the others, you will typically find a connection. Here are several ways in which multiple scenes might be interrelated. This is a very incomplete list. The possibilities are endless due to the Lord's boundless creativity.

1) The first scene may reveal a sin in the dreamer's life, while the next scene shows the possible consequences of that sin if there is no repentance.

2) The first scene may portray an attack of the enemy, while the next scene shows the ultimate victory.

3) The first scene might be of an event from the past, while the next scene reveals how the past issue is still affecting the dream subject.

4) The first scene may center on a problem, while the next one could reveal the solution.

5) The first scene might portray a certain behavior or attitude, while the subsequent scene shows either the Lord's pleasure or displeasure concerning it.

6) The scenes may prophetically unveil a progression of future events (Daniel 7:1-14)

*Many times, different dreams which occur on the same night are interrelated. Just as with multiples scenes, look for the ways in which these dreams may connect.

Recurring Dreams

It is important to examine the phenomena of reoccurring dreams. These are dreams you have more than once. What are some of the reasons we experience reoccurring dreams?

If you are having a *recurring nightmare,* it might signify that there is an open door in your life to the enemy that hasn't been dealt with adequately. (See Lesson One for a deeper explanation.) Let me give you an example from my own life. For years, I had a recurring nightmare that I was out of town and suddenly realized that my keys, phone, wallet, car, and money were gone. While this might not sound so terrifying, I would often wake up disoriented and trembling in fear. I believe that the reason I kept having this dream was because the enemy had a stronghold of fear and unbelief in my life. Dreams like that will expose the ongoing demonic activity so that you can be set free. This usually takes a combination of repentance and inner healing.

A recurring nightmare can also point to unconfessed ongoing sin. The Lord will continually bring warning through an individual's dream life where there is continuous sin and rebellion. Because the Lord is gracious and merciful, He will reach out to us again and again as He breaks through our often hardened hearts until His purposes are performed in our lives.

If a recurring dream is prophetic in nature, the Lord may be emphasizing the prophetic message as confirmation. For example, if someone has a recurring dream of revival coming to a city, this might be the Lord's way of affirming and highlighting the truth of the message.

In summary, recurring dreams are the Lord's way of bringing emphasis, clarity, focus, and/or confirmation to a dream message.

DREAM ASSIGNMENT #6

Using the model I gave you; begin to review your dreams on a daily basis. Remember to take your interpretations before the Lord in prayer. As you become proficient, ask others to share their dreams with you (keeping in mind the section on application in Lesson Six).

If you are going to become adept in any area of prophetic ministry, immerse yourself in the Word of God like never before. Sit quietly before the Lord and learn to discern His voice on a regular basis. Keep your life pure and separate yourself from the unholy pleasures of this World. May God bless you as you seek to know His voice in new ways. Step out of the boat, walk on the water, and let the Lord fill you with revelation.

More Sample Dreams

In this section, I am adding two more sample dreams in order to give a better understanding of how the process of dream interpretation works.

SAMPLE DREAM #4

I dreamt that I was at the zoo sitting by a large pool of water with my legs in the water. In the pool were dangerous animals swimming around and around such as snakes, alligators, and bears. I felt panic, especially when one of them would brush against my leg. The zookeeper was there, and he said, "As long as you do not respond to the animals in fear they will not hurt you." I was never hurt by any of these dangerous animals.

1) **Dream Setting:** The dream setting was a zoo. The zoo speaks of a difficult time of life for the dreamer in which there are many trials and attacks of the enemy.

2) **Dream Symbols:**

   a) **Alligator** = An alligator symbolizes verbal attack

b) Bear = A bear symbolizes an attack against one's finances

c) Snake = A snake symbolizes deception

d) Zookeeper = I believe the zookeeper in this dream represents the Lord, who is ultimately in control of all of our circumstances.

3) **Dream Subject:** The dream subject is the dreamer.

4) **Dream Message:** This dream is a message to the dreamer to put total trust in the Lord regardless of what the enemy is doing. The Lord is in total control, and even though the enemy's attacks seem constant, the dreamer will not be hurt as long as he does not become fearful and lose faith.

5) **Dream Source:** This dream is clearly from the Lord.

SAMPLE DREAM # 5

I walked over to the beach and saw a strange scene. It was daytime, and there was a group of people setting up sleeping bags, mats, and beds on the beach to sleep overnight. I walked over to a woman who had somehow brought her whole bed, frame, mattress, and headboard with her. She set the whole thing up on the beach! Around the entire bed were short shelves built into it, filled with books. I walked over to where she was because I was fascinated that she had brought everything with her. She and I started talking. I said to her, "I would love to do this!" For some reason, in the dream, I thought that I couldn't or that this wasn't really for me. She said that I could. All I needed to do was to bring my sleeping bag. Then the dream was over.

1) **Dream Setting:** The setting was the beach. The **beach** is a place of peace, rest, and joy. It can also be a place of meeting with God as it can symbolize the meeting of man (**sand**) and the Holy Spirit (Water)

2) **Dream Symbols:**

   a) **Bed, Mats, Sleeping Bag** = A bed, a mat, and a sleeping bag symbolize a place of intimacy with God

   b) **Books** = Books here speak of divine revelation

   c) **Unnamed People** = I believe that the people are Christians who are coming to seek God. The woman who brought her whole bed is someone who has truly come to a place of intimacy and rest in the Lord.

3) **Dream Subject:** The dream subject is the dreamer herself.

4) **Dream Message:** The message of this dream is a call to the dreamer to find a place in her devotional life of rest and intimacy with God. Isaiah 55:1-2 says: *"Come, all you who are thirsty, come to the waters; and you who have no money, come, buy and eat! Come; buy wine and milk without money and without cost. Why spend money on what is not bread, and your labor on what does not satisfy? Listen, listen to me, and eat what is good and your soul will delight in the richest of fare."*

God is calling her to stop her striving and spend time in His Presence where she can find peace and rest and receive revelation.

5) **Dream Source:** This is a word from the Lord.

Comprehensive Dream Dictionary

Dictionary Table of Contents

I. ANIMALS 77

II. TRANSPORTATION 91

    MODES OF TRANSPORTATION 91

    VEHICLES IN PRECARIOUS SITUATIONS.........................97

    ROAD SIGNS 100

    ROADWAYS AND PASSAGEWAYS....................................103

    DIRECTIONS 105

III. NATURE 109

    WEATHER RELATED SYMBOLS 109

    GEOGRAPHICAL SYMBOLS..114

    OUTER SPACE 119

    FLOWERS, PLANTS AND TREES.....................................121

    METALS AND PRECIOUS STONES 127

    PRECIOUS STONES 129

    OTHER SYMBOLS FROM NATURE 131

IV. FOOD AND DRINK..139

V. TIMES AND SEASONS 145

    SPECIAL DAYS AND SEASONS.......................................148

VI. COLORS AND NUMBERS 151

    COLORS...151

    NUMBERS 153

VII. NAME MEANINGS 157

VIII. PEOPLE 167

    CIRCUS PERFORMERS 188

    BIBLICAL FIGURES 189

    SERVANTS OF THE LORD 196

    IMAGINARY CREATURES OR BEINGS 208

IX. BIBLICAL PLACES, SPICES AND PERFUMES 211

    BIBLICAL PLACES 211

    BIBLICAL SPICES AND PERFUMES 217

X. MISCELLANEOUS SYMBOLS...219

    COURTROOM TERMS 219

    PARTS OF THE BODY..222

    SETTINGS AND PLACES..230

    MILITARY TERMS...239

    SPORTS TERMS 247

    FISHING TERMS...250

    MATH TERMS..251

    ACTIONS, ACTIVITIES AND STATES OF BEING...............252

    U.S. STATE MOTTOS..273

    EVERYTHING ELSE INCLUDING THE KITCHEN SINK 277

    MOTTOS OF THE NATIONS 310

COMPREHENSIVE INDEX 321

I. ANIMALS

Alligator or Crocodile = Verbal attack or gossip (Alligators have very large mouths that can easily destroy.) *alligator tail* – the backlash of the enemy or of sin (Proverbs 19:19, MSG)

Ape = The carnal nature, a mocker

Armadillo = A person who puts up a barrier between him/herself and others

Baboon = A brutish person, a coarse person, the carnal nature, ignorance

Badger = A person who constantly harasses and annoys to get his/her way (Genesis 31:36, MSG), covering or protection (Exodus 26:14)

Bear = Attack of the enemy, God's judgment of the wicked (2 Kings 2:24), financial decrease (bear market), a rude person, an emblem of Russia

Beaver = Religious spirit (stopping up the free flowing movement of the Holy Spirit), a hardworking and industrious person, constant busyness, the work of the enemy in attempting to hinder the flow of God's blessings to His people, a person who keeps down his/her emotions, an emblem of Oregon and Canada, state animal of New York

Bird(s) = A demonic spirit (Matthew 13:4, 18), a restless person (Proverbs 27:8), one who divulges things said in confidence (Proverbs 27:8), those who the enemy has set traps for (Jeremiah 5:26), the Church (Matthew 13:32) *wings* – the refuge of the Lord (Ruth 2:12), angels (2 Samuel 22:11), the Lord as our shelter and hiding place (Psalm 17:8), escape

(Psalm 55:6, Jeremiah 48:9), travel (Psalm 139:9, NKJV), soaring in the Spirit (Isaiah 40:31) *feathers* – the Lord's covering over His people (Psalm 91:3-5)

- *Albatross* = Something or someone that is a constant hindrance or burden, overwhelming feelings of great guilt and condemnation, a source of constant anxiety
- *Bat* = The occult or witchcraft, spiritual blindness
- *Chicken* = A fearful person, a young person, a person who is under the care of Jesus (Matthew 23:37)
- *Crow* = A proud person, a thief, a demonic spirit
- *Dove* = The Holy Spirit (Matthew 3:16), innocence (Matthew 10:16), a sign that a winter season of unfruitfulness and hardship is over (Song of Solomon 2:11-12), freedom (Psalm 55:6), moaning in sorrow (Nahum 2:7, NLT) **dove's eyes** – eyes that are fixed on God alone (Song of Solomon 4:1)
- *Eagle* = Prophetic ministry (Revelation 8:13), swift movement (Deuteronomy 28:49), God's care for His people (Exodus 19:4), renewed strength after a time of waiting on the Lord (Isaiah 40:31), freedom *bald eagle* – the United States
- *Hawk* = A predator, soaring in the Spirit (Job 39:26), a prophetic seer, a person who advocates war, an aggressive salesperson
- *Hen* = Nurturing and protective person, motherhood, a gossiper, Jesus (Matthew 23:37)
- *Jay* = A very gullible person
- *Loon* = Laughter, a deranged person, an emblem of Canada, state bird of Minnesota
- *Mockingbird* = A mocker, imitation, mimicking, state bird of Florida, Mississippi, Tennessee, Texas and Arkansas
- *Osprey* = A demonic attack (an osprey is a fish eating hawk, see also **Fish**)
- *Ostrich* = One who is in denial or refuses to face

difficult issues, a fearful person, carelessness and lacking wisdom (Job 39:13-18), a Christian who does not move in the Spirit (ostriches have wings but can't fly)

- **Owl** = Wisdom, evil spirit (a predator in the darkness)
- **Parrot** = Someone who repeats the words of others without understanding or thinking for him/herself, a mocker
- **Partridge** = one who is vulnerable to the enemy's attack (1 Samuel 26:20), one who gets rich through cheating, fraud or trickery and ends up with nothing (Jeremiah 17:11)
- **Peacock** = Vanity, a womanizer, national bird of India
- **Pelican** = Loneliness (Psalm 102:6, KJV)
- **Penguin** = Fasting (penguins will fast for over 100 days at a time)
- **Pigeon** = Someone who is easily fooled, a messenger, someone who betrays a confidence (1 Kings 21:10, MSG)
- **Quail** = The Lord's miraculous provision (Exodus 16:13)
- **Raven** = The Lord's miraculous provision (1 Kings 17:4), someone with an insatiable (ravenous) appetite
- **Rooster** = A proud and boastful person, a wakeup call
- **Sparrow** = God's love and provision in our lives, (Matthew 10:29-31), Living in God's presence (Psalm 84:2-4), something considered to be of little value (Luke 12:6), someone who is alone in the midst of a bad time of life (Psalm 102:7)
- **Stork** = New birth, wickedness (Zechariah 5:7-9)
- **Swallow** = An intended victim escaping an undeserved curse (Proverbs 26:2)
- **Swan** = Beauty and elegance
- **Turkey** = A foolish person, something that is a flop, giving thanks to the Lord
- **Vulture** = A devouring attack (Habakkuk 1:8), someone who preys on others, someone who is lurking and

waiting to attack

Buffalo = Intimidation, confusion, state animal of Oklahoma, something facing extinction

Bull = Economic prosperity (a "bull" stock market), an angry uncontrollable person, a stubborn person (Isaiah 1:5, MSG), a head on attack of the enemy, the occult (horoscope), national animal of Spain

Camel = Someone with great endurance through difficult circumstances, One who bears burdens, fasting (a camel can go for a month without food), an issue of great importance (Matthew 23:24), something very large (Matthew 19:24), the Arab nations

Cat = Self-will or independence, curiosity, sneaky or deceptive *black cat* – witchcraft or superstition **fat cat** – a wealthy and prideful person Psalm 73:6-8, NLT)

Cheetah = Attack of the enemy that happens with great speed

Clam or Oyster = An uncommunicative or secretive person

Cow = The Lord's great provision (Psalm 50:10), a false God (Exodus 32:8) *fat cow* – abundant resource (Genesis 41:15-35), *skinny, scrawny cow* – lack or famine (Genesis 41:15-35), *calf* – immaturity, joyful exuberance (Psalm 29:6), prayer that is answered supernaturally unexpectedly and in an unconventional manner (1 Samuel 6:7-14)

Crab = Ill-tempered person, the occult (horoscope)

Deer = Thirst for the Lord's presence (Psalm 42:1), the ability to move into higher realms of the Spirit (2 Samuel 22:34), grace of movement, state animal of New Hampshire

Dinosaur = Old patterns of thinking or dealing with matters that are no longer effective, an overwhelming issue from the past that is still affecting one's life

Donkey = An unruly hostile person, (Genesis 16:12), a stubborn person, humility, emblem of the Democratic Party

Dog = Friendship, divine judgment (1 Kings 22:38), an evil person (Psalm 22:16, Philippians 3:2), a person looked upon by others or him/herself as a "nobody" (2 Kings 8:13), loyalty, a demonic spirit **barking dog** – warning, verbal attack, *Steer clear of the* bark*ing dogs, those religious busybodies* (Philippians 3:2, MSG) **watchdog** – an intercessor, a watchman in the body of Christ who discerns the work of the enemy and warns the people (Ezekiel 33:6-8), protection

*(**A note to dog lovers***: I am applying the symbolic meanings using broad strokes and at times stereotypical images. I realize that all of these dogs can be loving and gentle pets under the right circumstances)*

- **Akita** = Emblem of Japan
- **Bloodhound, Bassett Hound, or Beagle** = Spiritual discernment, an evangelist
- **Bulldog** = A persistent or tenacious person, national symbol of Great Britain
- **Dalmatian** = Endurance
- **Doberman Pincher** = Protection, fearlessness, see also **watchdog** above
- **German Shepherd** = Loyalty, obedience, protection, pastor, alertness, see also **watchdog** above and **Sheepdog** below
- **Greyhound** = Great speed
- **Husky** = Emblem of Alaska, a servant
- **Pit Bull** = Attack of the enemy, protection, courage
- **Poodle** = Elegance

- **Rottweiler** = Attack without warning, aggression
- **Saint Bernard** = Servant, rescuer, guide
- **Sheepdog or Collie** = A pastor or anyone who provides proper guidance and oversight to Christians such as a home group leader

Dolphin = Community, love, unity

Elephant = Something of huge proportion, a prophetic person (elephants have very large ears), remembering the past (the expression "elephants never forget"), emblem of the Republican Party **ivory** – greed, luxury (Amos 3:15, NKJV)

Fish = People, both Christian and non-Christian (Matthew 13:47-48), the occult (horoscope) **big fish** – an influential person **bottom feeder** – an opportunist who takes advantage of others, a corrupt person of low morals, a scavenger

Frog =Demonic spirit, a word-curse (Revelation 16:12, 13), God's judgment (Exodus 8:4-6), rapid promotion (leapfrogging) **tree frog or coqui** – emblem of Puerto Rico

Fox = Sin (Song of Solomon 2:15), sly and crafty person (Luke 13:32), a false prophet (Ezekiel 13:4)

Gazelle or Antelope = very fast movement (2 Samuel 2:17-19), events that are unfolding very quickly, grace of movement

Giraffe = Prophetic watchman (giraffes sleep only 15 minutes per day so that they can spot predators for which they have a high perspective), teamwork (giraffes are sociable and non-territorial)

Goat = A non-Christian or a church-goer who is not right with God (Matthew 25:31-33), an unruly person, the occult (horoscope)

Groundhog = Hidden sin, a harasser, a hidden attack of the enemy a sign that a difficult season of life is nearing an end (Groundhog Day)

Hog = A selfish or gluttonous person

Horn = Strength (1 Samuel 2:1, NKJV), salvation (Psalm 18:2, NIV) authority, aggression (Exodus 21:29), a territorial spirit, anti-Christ spirit (Daniel 8:10, AMP) *ten horns* – the kingdom of anti-Christ (Revelation 17:12)

Horse = Natural human strength and power (Psalm 33:17, Proverbs 21:31) or God's strength and power (2 Kings 6:16-17), speed, warfare, the lust of the flesh (Jeremiah 5:8), *No one repents of his wickedness, saying, "What have I done?" Each pursues his own course like a horse charging into battle.*(Jeremiah 8:6, NIV), divine judgment in the end-times (Revelation 6:2-8) *high horse* – A prideful person (Jeremiah 3:18, MSG), a self righteous person (Isaiah 47:1, MSG), *Trojan horse* – The enemy coming as an angel of light or a wolf in sheep's clothing, deception

Hyena = Laughter, an attack by a group of people

Insect = A pest, a seemingly insignificant problem that can do significant damage, the enemy, sin, demonically influenced negative thoughts

- **Ant** = Hard work, wisdom (Proverbs 6:6-9), *anthill* – a community of hard workers all serving in a spirit of cooperation
- **Bees** = A swarming, stinging attack of the enemy (Deuteronomy 1:44), teamwork, evangelists, soul winners and missionaries who spread the word of God (see **Honey**)
- **Beetle or Boll Weevil** = An eating away of one's resources

- **Butterfly** = A restless and unsettled person, anxiety (Having "butterflies" in one's stomach), the beauty of the transformed Christian life, freedom
- **Caterpillar** = A person who has not yet matured
- **Chameleon** = A hypocrite, an inconsistent person
- **Cockroach** = Hidden sin in dark places, demonic spirits that "feed" on sin, an infestation of evil
- **Flea** = Something or someone seen as having insignificance (1 Samuel 26:20), a hidden attack of the enemy
- **Flies** = God's judgment (Psalm 78:45), demonic spirits
- **Gnat** = Something very small, an issue of little importance (Matthew 23:24)
- **Grasshopper** = Someone who sees him/herself as small, powerless and insignificant (Numbers 13:33), divine judgment (Psalm 78:45-47)
- **Hornet** = An angry person, torment, divine judgment (Deuteronomy 7:20-21), the Lord fighting on behalf of His people (Exodus 23:28)
- **Leech** = Someone who constantly uses others for personal gain (Proverbs 30:15)
- **Locust** = God's judgment (Joel 1:1-4), the army of God (Joel 2:1-11), a great multitude of people (Jeremiah 46:23)
- **Mite** = Hidden parasitic work of the enemy that requires divine revelation or discernment to expose, a deceptive, parasitic person
- **Moth** = God's judgment against sin (Psalm 39:11), A slow but steady erosion of one's possessions, the frailty of man (Job 4:18, 19)
- **Spider** = Trap of the enemy or of sin (Isaiah 59:5), a sense of feeling trapped, see also **Spider Web**
- **Termite** = An attack of the enemy or hidden sin that slowly erodes and corrupts

Jackal = An accomplice in an evil act, a person who performs menial tasks in the service of another

Kangaroo = Emblem of Australia, a contentious person, a rush to judgment, parental protection

Lamb = Jesus (Revelation 5:11-13), a gentle person, a new convert

Lemur = An evangelist – lemurs disperse seed (Matthew 3:18-23)

Leopard = An evil person (Jeremiah 13:23), attack of the enemy (Jeremiah 5:6), a demonic spirit (Revelation 13:2), the anti-Christ (Revelation 13:2), ambush (Hosea 13:7)

Lion = Jesus (Revelation 5:5), Satan (1 Peter 5:8), lurking attack of the enemy, royalty, a courageous person (Proverbs 30:30), a mighty warrior, the occult (horoscope), national animal of Denmark, Bulgaria, Czech Republic, England and Sri Lanka

Llama = Pastor or spiritual leader (Llamas are used to protect sheep from wolves), a mocker or one who expresses contempt (llamas are often known to spit)

Mink or **Chinchilla** = Luxury

Mole = The enemy infiltrating a Church or ministry through a false teacher, prophet, Church member, etc *mole hill* – a relatively insignificant matter

Monkey = A mocker, acting foolish, imitation

Mouse = A fearful person, hidden sin or a hidden enemy, demonic harassing attack that feeds on sin

Mule = A person who lacks understanding (Psalm 32:9), a stubborn person, the state animal of Missouri

Octopus = A false prophet or teacher (An octopus sprays toxic black ink into the water)

Ox = A servant, one who bears burdens, hard labor (Psalm 144:14)

Panda = Emblem of China

Pig or Swine = An unrighteous person who wallows in sin (Matthew 7:6)

Possum = A deceiver

Python = Spirit of divination or witchcraft (Acts 16:16, *the word for divination used in the Greek 'puthona' is the same word for Python*), a psychic or false prophet

Rabbit = Multiplication, a harasser, illicit sexuality, fertility

Raccoon = An attack of the enemy for which sin has opened the door, a thief

Ram = Head on attack of the enemy, someone applying great pressure to get their way, the occult (horoscope), sacrifice (genesis 22:13)

Rat = Judgment of God (1 Samuel 6:5), A person of evil character, A demonic attack that "feeds on" sin, disease

Scorpion = Evil person (Ezekiel 2:6), a demonic spirit (Luke 10:19), the occult (horoscope), death

Serpent or Snake = A lie or deceit (Psalm 140:3), Satan (Revelation 12:9), wisdom or shrewdness (Psalm 140:3), evil person, healing-*when on a pole* (Numbers 21:8, 2 Samuel 2:17-19), an ungodly temptation (Genesis 3:1-4) a religious hypocrite (Matthew 23:33), betrayal **snake in the grass** = a sneaky, deceptive person of evil character **venom** = bitterness, hatred, *who have sharpened their tongues like a sword. They aim venomous words as arrows* (Psalm 64:3, AMP)

Shark = Demonic attack, a con-man, a thief

Sheep = The people of God (John 10:1-6), those who blindly follow authority figures, **fleece** – putting God to the test to confirm his will (Judges 6:36) **black sheep** – a person who has been rejected or ostracized (Hosea 13:15, MSG)

Skunk = A contemptible person

Sloth = Laziness (Proverbs 18:9, NKJV), a lack of initiative or ambition

Snail = moving at a very slow pace, a curse (Psalm 58:8)

Squirrel = Someone who hordes, the storing up of provision for future use

Sting Ray = *For sin is the sting that results in death* (1 Corinthians 15:56, NLT), one who speaks curses (1 Corinthians 4:12, AMP)

Tail = The past, an ending, fleeing in fear (Isaiah 9:15, MSG), *the prophet that teacheth lies, he is the tail.* (Isaiah 9:15, KJV), one who lacks authority, finances and social standing (Deuteronomy 28:43-44)

Tiger = A major attack of the enemy, an aggressive person, a violent person, a relentless person, **Royal Bengal Tiger** – national animal of Nepal, Bangladesh and India

Turtle = A shy introverted person, someone who seems hardened on the outside but is "soft" on the inside, slow movement

Viper = a religious hypocrite (Matthew 23:33), drunkenness (Proverbs 23:31-33)

Weasel = A person of bad character, a sneaky person

Whale = Something huge in size, a vehicle used by the Lord to bring people back into His will and purpose (Jonah 1:17, *literally a "big fish"*), a wicked nation headed for ruin (Ezekiel 32:2, KJV)

Wolf = False prophet or teacher (Matthew 7:15), a predator, attack from within the church (Acts 20:29), a womanizer

Worm = Something or someone that is despised or looked down upon (Psalm: 22:6), a parasitic person or relationship, an attempt to escape (or "worm" out of) trouble by not taking responsibility, an attempt by an evil person or the enemy to "worm" his way into someone's life (2 Timothy 3:6), Jesus, who was despised and rejected (Psalm 22:6)

Zebra = A lukewarm Christian, someone who lives in moral compromise

I will pour out my Spirit on all people.
Your sons and daughters will prophesy,
your old men will dream dreams,
your young men will see visions.

Joel 2:28

II. TRANSPORTATION

MODES OF TRANSPORTATION

Abandoned Vehicle = A ministry that has been forsaken

Ambulance = A ministry to the sick or healing ministry, a ministry that helps people in emergency situations, a serious problem that requires immediate attention,

Ark = A picture of Jesus as the One who saves us and gives us refuge and protection (Hebrews 11:7), an evangelistic ministry offering the world salvation from judgment

Airplane = A church or ministry that moves in the Spirit. (A large airliner usually symbolizes a large church.), travel over a long distance, international ministry **nosedive** – total collapse or failure

Battleship = Spiritual Warfare (also a Tank or Fighter Plane)

Bicycle = An individual ministry, *stationary bike* – a ministry that doesn't seem to progress, exercising one's faith or talents

Bus (local passenger bus) = One's daily life journey

Borrowed Vehicle = Someone who attempts to duplicate the ministry of another rather than discovering his/her own unique gifting, calling, style, etc (1 Samuel 17:37-39)

Car = An individual or small ministry, a local ministry, social status, an occupation

- *Accelerator* = Increase of speed in terms of timing
- *Airbag* = The Holy Spirit cushioning the blow of a

traumatic experience

- **Antenna** = Spiritual discernment, the ability to receive revelation and prophetic words by 'tuning in' to the Lord
- **Battery** = Power of God, energy **battery charger** – the Holy Spirit
- **Brakes** = Self control, wisdom, time of waiting, decrease of speed
- **Bumper** = The Lord's protection during a clash or dispute or other difficult or traumatic situation **bumper sticker** – a statement of a ministry's mission, a message from the Lord
- **Car Seat** = Mentorship, discipleship, a call to be a spiritual parent
- **Engine** = The Holy Spirit, motivation, power
- **Fuel** = The Holy Spirit, the Word of God
- **Gas Tank** = The individual spirit of a person
- **Hazard Lights** = A ministry in trouble
- **Headlights** = The word of God (Psalm 119:105), the light of Jesus (John 8:12)
- **Horn (car)** = Lack of patience, "look out, here I come", distress
- **Horsepower** = Human strength (Psalm 33:16-17, MSG)
- **Radiator** = The ability to endure regardless of the intensity or nature of the season you are going through, **overheating** = intense anger or rage
- **Rear View Mirror** = Looking into the past
- **Seat Belt** = Wisdom, prayer, *Where there is no counsel, the people fall; But in the multitude of counselors there is safety* (Proverbs 11:14, NKJV)
- **Roll Bar** = God's protection and covering
- **Shock Absorber** = The Lord shielding you from the shock or stress resulting from difficult or bumpy situations, trust in God
- **Spark Plug** = a person who inspires others, a spiritual catalyst, a feisty or contentious person

- *Suspension* = stability through difficulty, comfort
- *Temperature Gauge* = Reveals the level of one's spiritual 'temperature' or fervency (Revelation 3:16)
- *Tires* = Tires are filled with air, which is a type of the Holy Spirit. Tires which are flat or low on air show a church or ministry in need of The Holy Spirit's presence, guidance and power, moment of truth (when the rubber meets the road)
- *Turn Signal* = Time of decision or change is at hand *see* **Right** and **Left**
- *Steering Wheel* = Change of direction
- *Transmission* = Reversal of direction, **reverse** – backsliding, backpedaling, headed the wrong way, going back to the past **neutral** – *lack of power, stuck in one place,* **drive** – *moving ahead*
- *Wheel* = Keeping grounded in the Lord, flexibility, change of direction, ability to stay on course
- *Windshield* = Prophetic revelation

Chariot = Warfare (Judges 4:3, Joshua 17:16), demonic attack (Revelation 9:8-10), human strength (2 Kings 19:22-24, Psalm 20:7), the army of God (2 Kings 6:15-17, Psalm 68:17)

Convertible = A ministry operating under an open heaven, transparency

Fishing Vessel = An evangelistic ministry

Garbage Truck = A deliverance ministry, an inner healing ministry, a need for repentance

Helicopter = A ministry capable of great flexibility, intercessory prayer

Hot Air Balloon = A peaceful rising in the Spirit

Jeep = A spiritual warfare ministry, a ministry with a great deal of flexibility, strength, maneuverability and endurance even when moving through very difficult situations

Jet = A fast moving, powerful ministry

Lifeboat = Jesus our Savior

Mobile Home = Traveling ministry

Motorboat = A powerful fast moving ministry

Motorcycle = A Spirit powered ministry, prophetic ministry, an individual ministry, independence, non-conformity, a ministry with great maneuverability, an independent spirit

Moving Truck = Change or relocation

Racecar = A ministry that moves quickly but might be motivated by competition

Raft = Moving without direction or purpose, way of escape, see also **Drifting**

Rental Car = A short term ministry assignment

Rocket Ship = See **OUTER SPACE**

Rowboat = Ministry that wrongly relies on human effort and striving, team ministry (where there is more than one oarsman)

Sailboat or Hang Glider = A ministry totally powered by the Holy Spirit

Salt Spreader = A ministry that brings the power of the Gospel into the community, see also **Salt**

School Bus = A teaching ministry, a children's ministry

Ship = Church or ministry: If the ship is on the ocean it could signify ministry to the peoples of the nations (Revelation: 17:15) *helm* – leadership or authority *rudder – It takes strong winds to move a large sailing ship, but the captain uses only a small rudder to make it go in any direction. Our tongues are small too, and yet they brag about big things* (James 3:4-5, CEV) *abandon ship* – to backslide, to walk away from a ministry assignment (Acts 13:13), to shirk responsibility *making headway* – progressing and moving ahead (Acts 27:7, NIV)

Skateboard = A ministry that has times of rapid acceleration followed by periods of slowing

Sled = A ministry that moves easily through difficult circumstances, a ministry that constantly moves on the foundation of the Word of God, see also **Snow**

Speeding Vehicle (Illegally) = A ministry that is moving ahead of the Lord's timing

Subway = The Underground Church, ministry in the city

Tow Truck = A ministry that provides help to broken people or ministries in trouble

Tractor = Evangelism, intercession, Spiritual breakthrough

Tractor Trailer or a Freight Train or a Cargo Ship = A ministry of bringing provision and supplies such as an feeding ministry, the Lord bringing great provision to the dream subject

Train or **Train Tracks** = A church that is steeped in tradition and ritual. (A train always takes the same route to the same place at the same time. There is no room for flexibility or being Holy Spirit led) a powerful ministry or one that is continuously on the move, the Lord sovereignly ordering our steps and laying out a clear path (Proverbs 3:6)

Tugboat = A ministry focused on helping other ministries move ahead or save those who are in trouble

Yacht = Wealth, luxury, ease, a ministry with great resources, a ministry to the wealthy

VEHICLES IN PRECARIOUS SITUATIONS

Alarm (Car) = A ministry crisis that requires immediate attention

Backfiring = *The trouble they make for others backfires on them. The violence they plan falls on their own heads.* (Psalm 7:16, NLT)

Broken Down = A mental or emotional collapse, fear of failure, a failure due to spiritual neglect (1 Kings 18:30) or the neglect of responsibilities such as financial accountability, a problem caused by a failure to communicate

Burning Rubber = Suddenly accelerating things too fast (in contrast to a steady pace), a need to move ahead suddenly and quickly, running away from responsibility

Collision = A clash between two or more Churches or ministries or leaders or ministry workers, a Church split, a personality clash

Crashing = Warning that there is trouble ahead, fear or a spirit of fear (Romans 8:15), falling into sin, physically or emotionally overwhelmed by the demands of ministry

Dead Battery = A lack of Spiritual power operating in a life or ministry, physical and/or emotional exhaustion

Dirty Vehicle = Sin, neglect, a pioneering or forerunner ministry going through "unpaved" territory

Drifting (Boat) = Moving without direction or purpose (Psalm 141:4, NLT), moving in spiritual darkness (John 12:35, AMP)

Engine Failure = A loss of motivation, a lack of Spiritual power due to prayerlessness or sin and disobedience, emotional burnout

Flat Tire or Low on Air = An individual or a Church or ministry in need of The Holy Spirit's presence, guidance and power.

Out of Fuel = Lacking a devotional life, a Church or ministry that has been neglecting prayer and/or the Word of God, a ministry that run's on human effort rather than God's strength and power

Overheated = A person overwhelmed by anger, an overly agitated person

Run Ashore or Aground (Boat) = Moving in the flesh rather than the Spirit

Sinking = See **Sinking or Drowning**

Speeding (Illegally) = Moving ahead of God's plan

Spinning or Out of Control = An out of control person or ministry or situation

Spinning Wheels (Without Forward Movement) = Activity that is unfruitful and nonproductive

Traffic (Stuck in) = delay, hindrance, a sign you are following the crowd rather than God

Tripping = *God's paths get you where you want to go. Right-living people walk them easily; wrong-living people are always tripping and stumbling.* (Hosea 14:9, MSG)

Turning = Change in life course direction, disobedience (Deuteronomy 5:32-33)

Unable to Get Started (Vehicle) or Take Off (Airplane) = Hindrance of the enemy, bogged down by the cares and distractions of the world, not in God's will or timing

Windshield Fogging Up = A hindrance to spiritual vision

Zig Zagging = Erratic behavior or activity

ROAD SIGNS

Bridge Ices Before Road = During your time of transition, slow down and be cautious! You can't move ahead at the pace you're going now

Bridge is Out = It is not yet time to move into your new season

Bump = There is a slight obstacle or hindrance ahead. Prepare yourself!

Caution = Be especially diligent!

Crooked Road = The path of the wicked who bring injustice and iniquity (Isaiah 59:8)

Crossroad = A major life-decision lies ahead (Jeremiah 6:16)

Curve = Prepare to expect the unexpected!

Danger = A warning of an impending dangerous situation such as an attack of the enemy or a temptation to sin

Dead End or No Outlet = The path you're on is taking you nowhere.

Detour = There are hindrances up ahead. Go around them but don't give up!

Do Not Enter = This path is closed to you. There is danger if you take it in spite of warnings

Fork In The Road = A time of decision is at hand

Hairpin Curve = A precarious situation that will require a great deal of faith and focus to make it through with little or no leeway for veering off course

Limited View or Limited Sight Distance = A lack of prophetic vision or revelation, the inability to see past an obstacle in one's life, a call to cautiously move ahead by faith in spite of the inability to see what is ahead

Low Clearance = Only the humble will make it through

Narrow Bridge = A transition which leaves no options other than total submission to the way prescribed by God, a transition that will require total trust in God to succeed

No Parking = This is not the situation or opportunity the Lord has for you right now. Keep searching in the Lord

No Passing Zone = A call for teamwork and humility

No U Turn = Continue on the path you're on and don't turn back!

One Way = *Jesus answered, "I am the way and the truth and the life. No one comes to the Father except through me.* (John 14:6, NIV)

Pothole = A destructive situation

Road Closed = This option is not available to you right now.

Road Narrows = It is time to become more focused on the Lord in your life journey. Jesus is your only option (Matthew 7:14

Rough Road Ahead or Pavement Ends = A warning that there are trials ahead

Slippery When Wet = Do not stop moving ahead but be cautious and use wisdom during this stormy period

Slow = Don't get ahead of God's leading in your life

Stop = Wait on God before moving on! (Psalm 27:14), Cease from sinning!

Tow-away Zone = See **No Parking**

Winding Road = The path you're on or are about to take is indirect with possible unexpected turns ahead.

Wrong Way = You are headed down the wrong path; turn back!

Yield = Submit to the will of God; not your own!

ROADWAYS AND PASSAGEWAYS

Alley = A sneak attack (Psalm 56:6, MSG), a dead end situation (Proverbs 4:10-12, MSG), *the lives of the wicked are dark alleys.* (Proverbs 13:9, MSG), a narrow path of transition, hidden sin

Avenue = A means of achieving a goal such as education being an avenue to getting a good job

Bridge = A transitional life season, Jesus as our passageway to the Father, a peacemaker or intermediary, a ministry that helps people to move on to new levels in their lives, a ministry that brings inner healing, a ministry that equips and trains the body of Christ *a burning bridge* – a broken relationship that will be very difficult to restore, leaving the past behind and moving on

Bypass Rte. = *The road of right living bypasses evil;* (Proverbs 16:17, MSG), ignoring God's Word (2 Kings 1:3-4, MSG), neglecting to seek wise counsel, making a decision that involves neglecting one's responsibilities, a path that avoids trouble or attack

Crossroads = A time and place of decision (Jeremiah 6:16), *I've brought you today to the crossroads of Blessing and Curse.* (Deuteronomy 11:26, MSG)

Gutter (Street) = The ultimate plight of the wicked, *Therefore this is what God, the Master, says: You've been more headstrong and willful than any of the nations around you, refusing my guidance, ignoring my directions. You've sunk to the gutter level of those around you.* (Ezekiel 5:7, MSG), sinful language or behavior

Highway = The path of holiness that leads to God (Isaiah 35:8-

9), the path of repentance and cleansing through which divine visitation comes (Isaiah 40:3) *fast lane* – a fast paced constantly driven lifestyle, a rapid rate of movement to promotion and advancement whether spiritually or naturally speaking

Road or Path = The life courses we take (Psalm 25:4, NLT), Jesus as the one narrow path that leads to the Kingdom of Heaven (Matthew 7:14, NIV, John 14:6, MSG), the path of sin that leads to death (Jeremiah 25:5, NLT, Matthew 7:13, NIV)

Tunnel = A life transition, the Lord making a way for His people to get through a major hindrance or obstacle

DIRECTIONS

Above = Heaven; the seat of God's rule (Genesis 27:39), the glory of God (Numbers 9:15, Psalm 8:1), high in authority or rulership (Numbers 16:3, Esther 5:11), God's favor (Deuteronomy 10:15), fame and honor (Deuteronomy 26:19, NIV), the Lord's greatness and superiority (Psalm 95:3, Psalm 113:4), of utmost importance (Proverbs 4:23, NIV), great in status (Isaiah 2:2)

Back = The past (Genesis 19:26), memories (Philippians 3:13)

Backwards = Backsliding (Isaiah 57:17, NKJV), retreat (Psalm 40:13-15), deterioration

Below = The earthly natural realm (Deuteronomy 4:39), death (Deuteronomy 32:22), hell (Proverbs 15:24, KJV, Isaiah 14:9), lower in authority or rank, undignified

Down = Demotion, moving away from the Lord, a fall, a season of trials and tribulations, humility, worship and honor (Nehemiah 8:6, 2 Chronicles 20:18), sad or discouraged (Luke 24:18, NIV), loss of honor or prestige (Job 14:21, NLT)

East = The glory of the Lord (Ezekiel 43:2), the light of God piercing the darkness, a beginning, the eastern nations of the world such as: India, China, Japan, Indonesia, Syria, Thailand, Korea etc, see also **Wind**

Far = In the distant future (Hebrews 11:13), separated from God (Psalm 10:1), being emotionally distant, having a great degree of disagreement, *We look for justice, but find none; for deliverance, but it is far away.* (Isaiah 59:11, NIV)

Forward = Prosperity (Genesis 26:12-14), to advance (Exodus 14:14-16), into God's presence (Numbers 12:4-5), progress

Front = The future (Philippians 3:13), the present

High = Greater level of authority (1 Samuel 18:5, NIV), Heaven as the abode of God (2 Samuel 22:17, NIV), the place of worship whether it be the worship of the One True God (1 Samuel 9:12-14) or idolatry (1 Kings 13:32), prideful and haughty (Job 10:16), promotion, the love of God (Psalm 103:11), honor (Psalm 112:9), *As the heavens are higher than the earth, so are my ways higher than your ways and my thoughts than your thoughts.* (Isaiah 55:9).

Left = Foolishness (Ecclesiastes 10:2), riches and honor as the fruit of wisdom (Proverbs 3:16), The Lord working through man's weakness, the eternal damnation of the wicked (Matthew 25:33)

Low = *Whoever exalts himself (with haughtiness and empty pride) shall be humbled (brought low)* (Matthew 23:12, AMP), those who are poor or lacking social status (Luke 1:52, KJV), lacking in authority, humility, meekness (Matthew 11:29, KJV)

Near = In the near future (Isaiah 56:1), a close relationship, *Draw near to God and He will draw near to you* (James 4:8, NKJV), having someone close by in a time of trouble

North = The throne room of God (Isaiah 14:13, Ezekiel 1:4, Job 37:22), great judgment (Jeremiah 1:14-16, Isaiah 41:25), see also **Wind**

Right = Wisdom (Ecclesiastes 10:2), authority (Genesis 48:180, 1 Kings 2:19) the power of God (Exodus 15:6, Psalm 17:7), authority, long life as the fruit of wisdom (Proverbs 3:16), the natural strength and abilities of man, the eternal life of the righteous in Christ (Matthew 25:33)

South = Freedom and restoration (Psalm 126:4, AMP), rest and refreshing (Daniel 11:40), see also **Wind**

Up = Promotion (Psalm 75:5-7, KJV), moving toward the Lord, flourishing (2 Kings 19:30, KJV), prideful (Isaiah 14:13), joyful, optimistic

West = A sign that a time of trial and difficulty is at hand, decline following success, an ending, western nations of the world such as: the United States, England, France, Ireland, Scotland, etc, see also **Wind.**

III. NATURE

WEATHER RELATED SYMBOLS

Atmosphere = The spiritual realm, the spiritual climate of a particular place or region, the emotional climate of a place or situation

Avalanche = *Wail! God's Day of Judgment is near - an avalanche crashing down from the Strong God!* (Isaiah 13:6, MSG), a sudden attack of the enemy that seems overwhelming, a situation in which someone is inundated by demands and pressures

Blizzard = a cold, difficult and overwhelming period of time where one's spiritual vision is impaired, *brutal oppressors* (Isaiah 25:4, MSG)

Cloudy = *white cloud* – The presence of God (Exodus 13:21), *dark cloud* – depression, a coming trial, a hindrance in hearing God's voice, confusion

Darkness = Hidden sin (Isaiah 29:15, NIV), lack of direction (Isaiah 50:10), the work of the enemy (Luke 22:53), misery and depression (Psalm 107:10), death (Psalm 88:11-12, NIV), wickedness (Isaiah 5:20)

Dew = The Word of God (Deuteronomy 32:2), unity among the people of God (Psalm 133:3), God's love and favor as he descends upon and covers His people (Hosea 14:4-6), something fresh and pure, human love which wavers and is temporary (Hosea 6:4) the Lord's blessings (Deuteronomy 33:13)

Drought = God's judgment (Zechariah 14:17), a dry and difficult season of life (Psalm 32:4), a season where there seems to be a lack of God's favor and His manifest presence

Earthquake = God's wrath and judgment (Revelation 11:13, Nahum 1:4-6), the Lord's power to deliver His people (Isaiah 29:5-7, Acts 16:25-26), upheaval or revolution

Eclipse = The Church lining up with God's purposes

Flood = Sudden terrors (Job 27:20), divine judgment (Job 20:28), a very difficult trial (Psalm 69:2), a great move of God (Isaiah 59:19, 20), an abundance of wealth (Isaiah 66:12), great evil (1 Peter 4:3, 4), an abundance of blessing (Malachi 3:10), A powerful and quick moving army (Daniel 11:40), **flash flood** – a sudden move of God or attack of the enemy **floodgate** – the gate of Heaven which when opened by the Lord allows His blessings to pour down upon His people (Malachi 3:10, NIV)

Fog = Obscured spiritual vision (1 Corinthians 13:12, MSG), mental confusion

Frost = a relationship that has grown cold, a person with a cold demeanor, divine judgment (Psalm 78:46-48, KJV), a frigid and dark season (Genesis 31:40, KJV)

Groundswell = A grassroots movement

Hail = God's judgment (Exodus 9:18), a plague (Revelation 16:21), God's truth (Isaiah 28:16, 17)

Haze = Confused, disoriented, unclear

Hurricane = God's judgment, great move of the Spirit

Landslide = An easy and overwhelming victory

Lightning = God's sudden judgment (Luke 10:18), the

Presence of God (2 Samuel 22:13), a sudden move of God, the voice of the Lord (Psalm 29:7) **lightning rod** – a person who often seems to attract negative attention and emotion from others, a person, church or region suddenly hit with a move of God

Mist or Vapor = Human as opposed to divine love which wavers and is temporary (Hosea 6:4), the brevity of human life (James 4:14), the Lord totally removing our sin (Isaiah 44:22), something hidden or obscured

Rain = Outpouring of the Holy Spirit (Acts 2:17), God's Word (Isaiah 55: 10, 11), God's blessing (Deuteronomy 28:12, Ezekiel 34:26), the message of the Lord (Deuteronomy 32:2), wise counsel (Job 29:23), divine judgment (Genesis 6:12-14), righteousness (Isaiah 45:8), Divine visitation (Hosea 6:3, Psalm 72:6), God's great loving kindness (Matthew 5:44-46), **spring rain**-the great end-time revival (Hosea 6:3, Acts 2:17), God's favor (Proverbs 16:15), **acid rain** – false teachings, a counterfeit spiritual movement

Rainbow = God's covenant promises (Genesis 9:13), the radiance of God's glory (Ezekiel 1:28), the mercy of God

Snow = The Word of God (Isaiah 55:9-11), purity (Psalm 51:7), a trustworthy messenger (Proverbs 25:13, NIV)

Squall = A sudden and unexpected yet brief disturbance or attack of the enemy

Storm = Trials and difficulties, attack of the enemy, God's judgment (Jeremiah 23:19), "the oppressive acts of ruthless people" (Isaiah 25:4, NLT)

Sunburst = The people who walked in darkness have seen a great light. For those who lived in a land of deep shadows — light! sunbursts of light! (Isaiah 9:2, MSG), God's revelation or wisdom suddenly dispelling confusion.

Sunshine = The presence and favor of God (Psalm 84:11), the light of God, healing (Malachi 4:2)

Temperature = The measure of spiritual fervency in a an individual life or a Church (Revelation 3:15-16), the measure of a person's emotional intensity (i.e. hot tempered or cold and aloof)

Thunder = The voice of God (2 Samuel 22:14), spiritual warfare, God's judgment (Exodus 9:23), a warning of an impending attack or trial, God's glory (Psalm 29:2-4), the sound of praise (Revelation 19:6), The Lord fighting against our enemies on our behalf (1 Samuel 7:10), a call to prepare for divine visitation

Tide = The course of events in a life, region, church, etc, *a turning tide – The hand of God has turned the tide! The hand of God is raised in victory! The hand of God has turned the tide!"* (Psalm 118:16, MSG), **low tide** – a low point in one's life, an emotional low **high tide** – a great high point in one's life

Tornado = A mighty outburst of the Glory of God (Ezekiel 1:4-28), a powerful attack of the enemy (Job 1:19) or God's judgment (Jeremiah 23:19), the dire consequences of sin (Hosea 8:7), a violent outburst of emotion

Torrent = Overwhelming anger (Proverbs 27:4, NKJV), the wrath and judgment of God (Isaiah 30:32-33, NASB), an overwhelming flow of tears (Jeremiah 9:17, The Message Bible), a massive attack of the enemy (Psalm 124:3-5, AMP)

Tsunami or Tidal Wave = An overwhelmingly difficult situation, a massive attack of the enemy, divine judgment

Volcano = An angry and volatile person, God's wrath and

jealousy (Deuteronomy 29:20, MSG), war (Hosea 10:14, MSG), the power of God (Psalm 104:32, MSG)

Waves = relentless hardships (Job 10:17, NIV), righteousness (Isaiah 48:18), restlessness of the wicked (Isaiah 57:20), false shepherds (Jude 1:12-13), one who doubts God (James 1:6), the glory of God, the turmoil of the nations (Psalm 65:7)

Wind = The Holy Spirit (Acts 2:1-4), attack of the enemy (Job 1:18-19), an elusive person (Proverbs 27:16), something that is ultimately meaningless (Ecclesiastes 1:14), troubles (Matthew 7:25), empty words (Jeremiah 5:13), *south wind* – time of refreshing, *north wind* – trial and difficulties, gossip (Proverbs 25:23), *east wind* – destruction, judgment, (Hosea 13:15) *west wind* – brings rain which can speak of blessing or hardship (Luke 12:54), the mercy of the Lord (Exodus 10:18-20)

GEOGRAPHICAL SYMBOLS

Barrens or Barren Land = Emptiness and unfruitfulness (Deuteronomy 32:10)

Beach = Rest, recreation, a boundary or limitation (Job 38:8-11), the meeting place of the flesh (sand) and the Spirit (water)

Bog or Mire or Quagmire = Deep despair (Psalm 40:2, NLT), a seemingly hopeless and desperate situation from which it seems there is no way out (Lamentations 3:55, AMP), the entanglement of sin (Ephesians 2:1-3, MSG)

Brook = The Lord's provision during a season of lack (1 Kings 17:1-5), *a bubbling brook* – wisdom (Proverbs 18:4)

Cave or Cavern = A hiding place or place of refuge (Joshua 10:17), isolation, hidden sin

Channel or **Conduit** = *Good leadership is a channel of water controlled by God; he directs it to whatever ends he chooses.* (Proverbs 21:1, MSG), communication, a passageway into a job or position such as volunteering at a hospital being a channel for getting a job there, something that serves as a transitional passageway in reaching a goal such as driving lessons being a channel to getting a driver's license, Jesus who is our conduit to the Father

Desert or Wilderness = A dry and barren season of one's life, loneliness (Jeremiah 51:43), a place of testing (Deuteronomy 8:2), a quiet place of rest (Psalm 55:6)

Field = The world (Matthew 13:38), the Church (1 Corinthians 3:9)

Forest = A dangerous situation (2 Samuel 18:7-9), God's

people gathered in worship (1 Chronicles 16:33, Psalm 96:12), something huge (James 3:5), a situation with many obstacles and restricted vision

Gold Mine = Something of great material value such as a successful business (Psalm 119:72, MSG), an abundant resource such as an encyclopedia as a gold mine of information, a source of great glory or revelation

Hill = A small hindrance or obstacle, righteousness (Psalm 72:3), the US Congress

Iceberg = A very large hindrance or obstacle, an emotionally cold person

Island = someone who is socially isolated, a Christian who is disconnected from the body of Christ, a place of rest

Jungle = A dangerous situation, a pioneering or forerunner ministry, cutthroat competition

Lake = The Holy Spirit, the peace of God

Levee (Natural) = The Lord as our place of safety from the floods of tribulation and enemy attack

Mountain = Hindrance or obstacle (Mark 11:23), a divine encounter (Exodus 19:3, Luke 9:28), the Kingdom of God (Isaiah 56:7), a place of prayer (Luke 6:12), power, a prideful person (Isaiah 40:4), peace (Psalm 72:3)

Mountain Pass = The Lord making a path for His people to walk through obstacles and hindrances

Pastureland or Meadow = Abundant provision (Psalm 23:1-3), retirement

Peak or Pinnacle = A high level of achievement, a high point of someone's life or ministry pride (Jeremiah 49:16, NLT)

Plateau = Something that has shown no sign of progress or increase over a period of time

Pool = Physical healing (John 5, John 9:7), joy and refreshing (Psalm 114:7-8)

River = The movement and workings of the Holy Spirit in and through the people of God (John 7:38), justice (Amos 5:24), the goodness of God (Psalm 36:8), great trials and difficulties (Isaiah 43:2), peace (Isaiah 48:18), many tears (Lamentations 2:18), the life-giving ministry of the Holy Spirit, the sound of angel wings (Ezekiel 1:23-25), the sound of the voice of the Lord (Ezekiel 43:2), the sound of heavenly worship (Revelation 19:6), the joy of the Lord *Jordan River* – speaks of death to the flesh (as symbolized by those going under the waters of the Jordan River in baptism) *riverbank* – a healthy Church

Sands = a worldly or fleshly foundation for one's life (Matthew 7:26), the people of Israel (Roman 9:27), a multitude of people too numerous to count (1 Kings 4:20) *sand dune* – the flesh as a hindrance to the spirit (Galatians 5:16-18), an obstacle

Sea or **Ocean** = The multitudes of people in the nations (Revelation 17:15), the people of the nations in an uproar (Psalm 65:7), the knowledge of the glory of the Lord by the people of the Earth (Habakkuk 2:14) *deep waters* - overwhelming troubles (Psalm 69:13-15), *the purposes of a man's heart* (Proverbs 20:5, NIV), *the deep things of God* (1 Corinthians 2:9-11, NIV)

Spring (of water) = The Holy Spirit's soul satisfying and life giving work in the life of the believer (John 4:14), refreshing (Exodus 15:27), love (1 Timothy 1:5, AMP) *a dried up spring* – a false prophet or false teacher (2 Peter 2:1-17) *a muddied*

spring – compromise (Proverbs 25:26) *wellspring* – a source that has an inexhaustible supply, the heart as the wellspring of life (Proverbs 4:23, NIV), understanding and wisdom (Proverbs 16:22, NKJV, Proverbs 18:4, NKJV)

Strait = A very difficult and distressful situation (2 Corinthians 6:4, AMP), Jesus as the narrow passageway leading to eternal life (Matthew 7:14, AMP), a very restrictive and confining environment

Stream = Righteousness (Amos 5:24), the presence of God (Psalm 42:1), a constant flow of tears (Psalm 119:136), the Lord's restoration (Psalm 126:4), a trend or movement

Swamp or Marsh = An overwhelming situation, something of little value, danger

Thicket = A hiding place, a place of danger (Job 38:39-40, Jeremiah 12:5), desolation (Isaiah 17:9)

Valley or Hollow = A low point in one's life, a major life decision (Joel 3:14), a humble person (Isaiah 40:4)

Wasteland = Devastation (Deuteronomy 29:23), barrenness (Psalm 107:34, NLT), gloom (Job 30:3, NLT)

Waterfall or Cascade = *Let praise cascade off my lips* (Psalm 119:171, MSG), the wicked raging of the nations (Isaiah 17:12, MSG), the rushing sound of angel's wings (Ezekiel 1:24, MSG), the refreshing of the Holy Spirit washing over the people of God, the power of the Holy Spirit rushing forth

Watershed = A dividing line or turning point in the life of a person, church, region, nation, etc – For example many consider the decision to take prayer out of American schools a watershed or turning point that moved the nation into an era of increasing sin and rebellion among the youth

Well = Salvation (Isaiah 12:3), the Holy Spirit's soul satisfying, life giving work in the life of the believer (John 4:11, 12), an abundance of knowledge or information, the deep things of the Spirit

OUTER SPACE

Alien = A Christian (1 Peter 2:11), an outsider, someone who doesn't "fit in"

Astronaut = A Christian seeking fresh encounters with the Lord, a missionary, a pastor or leader of a pioneering Church or ministry

Astronomer = A seer prophet, a visionary

Black Hole = A problem that never seems to get resolved no matter how much time and resources are thrown into it, a money and time wasting program or initiative, death (Job 3:3-4, MSG), a very difficult situation from which there is no apparent escape (Psalm 143:3, MSG)

Comet = Judgment from Heaven (Revelation 8:10), the glory of God bursting forth from His presence (2 Samuel 22:13, MSG)

Crater = A broken heart, a void in one's life

Launching Pad = Signifies that after a time of waiting a powerful ministry will be launched, a church or ministry that births other powerful churches or ministries

Meteor = Someone who rises to prominence very quickly, *falling star* – a Christian who falls into sin, a person of prominence who falls to obscurity

Moon = The Church as it reflects the glory of the Lord (2Corinthians 3:18), a mother (Genesis 37:9, 10), light shining through the darkness (Isaiah 9:2) *crescent moon (and star)* – symbol of the Muslim faith

Orbit = A sphere of influence or authority

Planet = a pioneering ministry, a missions trip to a place where others haven't ventured before

Rocket Ship = A ministry that takes off and rises very quickly, soaring in the Spirit, an angel

Satellite = A small ministry or Church under the covering of a large ministry or Church, a nation that is being dominated or unduly influenced by another nation, a sycophant

Solar Flare = The fire of God released, the wrath of God

Star(s) = Jesus (Numbers 24:17), satan (Isaiah 14:12), angels (Revelation 12:4), the multitudes of the Church and the nation of Israel (Genesis 22:17), teacher's of righteousness and soul-winners (Daniel 12:3), born again believers living in holiness (Philippians 2:15), a popular and prominent person, *morning star* – Jesus (Revelation 22:16), Satan (Isaiah 14:12) *wandering star* – a false Christian (Jude 1:13)

Sun = Jesus (Psalm 84:11, Revelation 1:16), those who love the Lord (Judges 5:31), justice (Psalm 37:6), the righteous (Matthew 13:43), a father (Genesis 37:9, 10)

Weightlessness = A state of complete abandonment in the Holy Spirit, freedom from burdens and worries that weigh one down

FLOWERS, PLANTS AND TREES

Flowers = Natural beauty which fades away (John 3:31), the fading glory of man (Isaiah 40:5-7), (Isaiah 28:1), the brevity of human life (James 1:10), a sign that a cold, barren season is over and a time of fruitfulness and renewal is at hand (Song of Solomon 2:12), romantic love **bouquet** – romance, a wedding, Jesus (Song of Solomon 1:13, MSG, Song of Solomon 1:14, NLT)),

- **Baby's Breath** = Innocence
- **Bitterroot** = Bitterness, unforgiveness (Hebrews 12:15), state flower of Montana
- **Cherry Blossom** = Emblem of Washington DC, national flower of Japan
- **Cactus Flower** = The Lord bringing beauty out of a dry and difficult situation , state flower of Arizona
- **Daisy** = a feeling of being refreshed and renewed, something fresh, innocence
- **Edelweiss** = Toughness, fortitude (this flower grows in very rugged terrain), remaining pure in a hostile environment, the national flower of Austria and Switzerland
- **Forget-Me-Not** = Loyalty, remembrance, an emotional relationship from the past, state flower of Alaska
- **Henna or Camphire** = The sweetness and beauty of Jesus (Song of Solomon 1:14)
- **Hibiscus** = Emblem of the tropics, state flower of Hawaii
- **Iris** = Emblem of France, faith, hope, state flower of Tennessee
- **Lily(ies)** = Great beauty (Luke 12:27), a Christian in the eyes of Jesus (Luke 12:27), the nation of Israel (Hosea 14:5), purity
- **Lotus** = Triumph and perseverance (even though the Lotus grows in the mud it prevails and grows into a

beautiful flower), national flower of India and Vietnam, Hinduism, Yoga

- **Magnolia Blossom** = The state flower of Louisiana and Mississippi
- **Mandrake** = Passionate love for God (Song of Solomon 7:13), magic and witchcraft, fertility (in ancient times mandrakes were believed to make a woman more fertile)
- **Narcissus** = Egotism
- **Orange Blossom** = State flower of Florida
- **Orchid** = Maturity, refinement, elegance, national flower of Venezuela
- **Pansy** = Thoughtfulness or remembrance (comes from the root word for pensive)
- **Rose** = Romantic love, a Christian (Song of Solomon 2:1) state flower of New York and national flower of the United States, passion **yellow rose** – friendship, emblem of Texas **bed of roses** – luxury and comfort
- **Sunflower** = Jesus, pride, state flower of Kansas
- **Tulip** = Emblem of the Netherlands
- **Violet** = Modesty, the state flower of Illinois, New Jersey, and Rhode Island

Plants = Those who soak in God's word (Deuteronomy 32:2), the temporary nature of human life (Psalm 37:2), young men (Psalm 144:12), one who matures quickly under the Lord's care (Ezekiel 16:7), people; both righteous and evil (Matthew 15:12-14)

- **Aloe** = Healing
- **Bamboo** = Resiliency, Emblem of Asia
- **Climbing Bittersweet** = A memory, relationship or situation that has both pleasant and painful aspects
- **Brier** = God's judgment against the wicked (Isaiah 5:6), the wickedness of the rebellious (Ezekiel 2:6)
- **Clover** = Emblem of Ireland, superstition, luxury, Used

by St Patrick in Ireland to picture the trinity

- *Flax* = human weakness and frailty (Matthew 12:20, KJV)
- *Grass* = A multitude of people too numerous to count, the godless and wicked (Job 8:11-13), the mortality of human life (Isaiah 40:6), the flourishing of God's servants,
- *Hemlock* = Judgment (Hosea 10:4) or lawsuit (NIV), murder, hatred, bitterness
- *Hyssop* = Cleansing and purification (Psalm 51:7, Leviticus 14:52)
- *Ivy* = Sin expanding if not rooted out and overtaking one's life, the upper class, college education
- *Mustard Plant* = Something very large that came from a very small beginning (Luke 13:19), the Kingdom of Heaven (Matthew 13:31-32) *mustard seed* – faith (Matthew 17:20)
- *Poison Ivy* = The danger of flirting with sin
- *Prayer Plant* = Prayer
- *Reed* = Something weak and not sturdy (2 Kings 18:21), a frail, vulnerable person (Isaiah 42:3)
- *Seaweed* = Entangling troubles (Jonah 2:5)
- *Senna* = Purging
- *Thorn* = The worries and cares of this world, or the deceptions of wealth (Matthew 13:22), a source of suffering and affliction (2 Corinthians 12:7)
- *Thistle, Bramble or Thorn bush* = Divine judgment and curse (Genesis 3:17-19), the wicked (Matthew 7:16)
- *Venus Flytrap* = The Lord's work in ensnaring the enemy, see also **Flies**
- *Weeds or Tares* = The consequences of laziness and neglect, (Proverbs 24:30-32), false Christians (Matthew 13:24-29)
- *Wheat* = True Christians (Matthew 13:24-30), the Lord's care for His people, abundance and prosperity (Joel

2:24), trial and testing (Luke 22:31), patience (James 5:7), *chaff* – useless or unsubstantial (2 Kings 19:26, MSG), the wicked and rebellious (Proverbs 20:26, AMP), false prophets (Jeremiah 23:27-28), sin (Micah 4:13, MSG) *stubble* – the wicked (Malachi 4:1), something of no eternal value (1 Corinthians 3:12, KJV) *kernel* – *The simple truth is that if you had a mere kernel of faith, a poppy seed, say, you would tell this mountain, 'Move!' and it would move.*(Matthew 17:20, MSG), see also **Grains** under **FOOD AND DRINK**

- *Wormwood* The bitter consequences of sin (Proverbs 5:4), divine end-time judgment against the wicked (Revelation 8:10)

Trees = People (Luke 3:8-9), the Cross (Acts 5:30), the Kingdom of Heaven (Matthew 13:31-33) family history (1 Chronicles 1, MSG) *tall tree* – a prideful person (Ezekiel 17:24), a leader (Daniel 4:22), *small tree* – a humble person (Ezekiel 17:24), *tree planted by the water* – a righteous man or woman of God (Psalm 1:3), *tree stump* – *A life devoted to things is a dead life, a stump* (Proverbs 11:28, MSG), *If even a tenth—a remnant—survive, it will be invaded again and burned. But as a terebinth or oak tree leaves a stump when it is cut down, so Israel's stump will be a holy seed."* (Isaiah 6:13, NLT), a remnant *also* see **Bark**, **Branches**, **Leaves**, and **Roots**

- *Acacia or Shittah tree* = *The wood from this tree was used in the tabernacle to picture the perfect life that Jesus led (Exodus 25:28)*
- *Almond tree* = The watchfulness of God (Jeremiah 1:11-12), old age (Ecclesiastes 12:5)
- *Apple tree* = Jesus our bridegroom (Song of Solomon 2:3), the Lord awakening the Church through His passionate love for them (Song of Solomon 8:5)
- *Balm of Gilead* = Healing (Jeremiah 8:22)
- *Bonsai tree* = Emblem of Japan, the dwarfing of God's

purposes in one's life

- **Cedar tree** = Powerful and mighty men (Zechariah 11:2), the prosperity of the righteous (Psalm 92:12-13), beauty, something of superior quality, those who are prideful (Isaiah 2:12-14), a great and powerful earthly kingdom (Ezekiel 31:3)

- **Cypress, Fir, Pine or Evergreen tree** = enduring or eternal, blessing and abundance in the midst of devastation (Isaiah 41:18-20), God replacing a life filled with curses and great hardships with a life of abundant blessings (Isaiah 55:13), great beauty (Isaiah 60:13), fruitfulness found in the Lord (Hosea 14:8, NIV)

- **Fig or Sycamore tree** = A sign that a season of renewal is at hand (Song of Solomon 2:12-13), a sign that Jesus' return is near **fig leaf** = shame (Genesis 3:7), self righteousness

- **Juniper or Broom tree**= Misery and defeat (1 Kings 19:3-4, Job 30:3-5, Psalm 120:3-5)

- **Magnolia tree** = A symbol of the Southern states of the US

- **Mahogany tree** = Durability and stability

- **Maple tree** = A kind sweet person, the Word of God pouring through the people of God, teachers and preachers, **maple leaf** – an emblem of Canada

- **Mulberry or Balsam tree** = Sadness (from the Hebrew word baca which mean 'weeping')

- **Myrtle tree** = A sign of God's favor and restoration (Isaiah 55:13)

- **Oak tree** = Those who are prideful and haughty (Isaiah 2:12-14), human strength (Amos 2:9), the splendor of God exhibited through the righteous (Isaiah 61:3), death (2 Samuel 18:10, Genesis 35:8) national tree of England **acorn** – speaks of small beginnings which have potential for great growth.

- **Ohio Buckeye tree** = State tree of Ohio

- **Olive tree** = Abundance (2 Kings 18:32), the prosperity of those who trust in the Lord (Psalm 52:8), Israel (Hosea 14:5-7), God's end-time witnesses (Revelation 11:3-5), the anointing, **olive branch** – a token of peace, Jews and Christians (Romans 11:17)

- **Palm tree** = the flourishing of the righteous (Psalm 92:12), praise to the King of Kings (John 12:13), the tropics
- **Willow tree** = sadness, weeping (Psalm 137:1-2)

METALS AND PRECIOUS STONES

Brass, Bronze or Copper = God's judgment in withholding His blessings from a nation because of continued wickedness (Leviticus 26:19), bondage (Judges 16:21), warfare (2 Samuel 22:35 (*Brass, bronze and copper are used interchangeably in different Bible translations. Brass and bronze are comprised primarily of copper*) 2 Samuel 21:16), to be obstinate (Isaiah 48:4), sin and corruption (Ezekiel 22:18)

Gold = Worldly riches (Acts 3:6), holiness (Job 23:10), idolatry (Psalm 115:4), royalty and authority (Daniel 2:38), the glory of God (Haggai 2:8-9), the Lord (Job 22:24-26) God's pure and holy nature, immodesty (Revelation 18:16)

Iron = God withholding His blessings because of continued wickedness (Leviticus 26:19, Deuteronomy 28:23), bondage (Deuteronomy 28:48), strength (Deuteronomy 33:25), destruction of the wicked (Psalm 2:9), stubbornness (Isaiah 48:4) people who are hard and cruel (Jeremiah 6:28, NLT), a strong mighty and dominant earthly kingdom such as the Roman Empire (Daniel 2:40)

Lead = Sin and corruption (Ezekiel 22:18), something that weighs a person down

Platinum = The wealthy upper class, durability

Silver = Worldly riches (Genesis 13:2), redemption (Numbers 3:47-49; Numbers 18:16), idolatry (Deuteronomy 7:25), the Lord as our precious treasure (Job 22:24-26), the promises of God (Psalm 12:6), godly wisdom (Proverbs 2:3-5), the words of the godly (Proverbs 10:20, NLT), God's perfect Word (Psalm 12:6)

Steel = Inflexible, strong and tough, fearless, confidence and determination (2 Chronicles 32:8, MSG)

Tin = Sin, corruption, and idolatry (Isaiah 1:25, KJV), something that looks authentic and genuine but isn't (as Tin looks like Silver), brittle or fragile

Titanium = A Christian with great unwavering faith (Titanium can withstand great extremes of temperature

Uranium = Toxic, destructive

Zinc = Healing (used in cold medicine), protection (used in sun-block and preventing diaper rash)

PRECIOUS STONES

*There is much disagreement about the exact stones found in the Bible. Diamonds, rubies, sapphires, are not considered to be the same stones that we associate these names with. That is why various Bible translations often differ in what they call a particular stone. For example what the NKJV identifies as diamond the NIV translates as emerald (Exodus 28:18.) Also many attempts to find the symbolic meanings for various stones have been based on the placement of the stones in the breastplate of the high priest (Exodus 28:17-21.) Each stone corresponded to the name of one of the sons of Jacob. The problem is that in my research I have discovered that Bible scholars disagree on which stone corresponds to which name because of the difficulty in specifically identifying ancient stones. All in all, I have sorted it out the best I can in assigning symbolic meanings to the precious stones listed below, but you might want to further research these yourself.

Agate = Joy or happiness – *Asher*

Amethyst = Royalty, the reward of the Lord – *Issachar*

Beryl or Chrysolite = dwelling place – *Zebulon*

Diamond = The stain of sin engraved on a heart that is hard toward God (Jeremiah 17:1, KJV), something of great value, flawless, wrestling or striving – *Naphtali*

Emerald = God's eternal grace and mercy (Revelation 4:3), an emblem of Ireland, joined together or united, the priesthood – *Levi*

Jacinth or Ligure = Good fortune in the Lord – *Gad*

Jasper = Purity, holiness, transparency, Jesus, the Church – *Benjamin*

Marble = Strength and endurance (Song of Solomon 5:15)

Onyx = Something of great worldly value (Job 28:16), increase from the Lord – *Joseph*

Pearl = That which is sacred and precious, wisdom, Jesus or a Christian (Matthew 13:45-46), something of great value which comes through long suffering, immodesty (Revelation 17:4)

Ruby or Sardius = The blood of Jesus, salvation, Jesus as the firstborn Son over all creation – *Reuben* (Colossians 1:15)

Sapphire = the heavens (Exodus 24:9-11), the throne of God (Ezekiel 1:26), elegance (Lamentations 4:7 NLT) or a shapely figure (AMP), the Lord's vindication in our lives, to judge – *Dan*

Topaz = The name Topaz comes from a Greek word meaning "to seek", God hearing our prayers – *Simeon*

Turquoise = Jesus; our sure foundation (Isaiah 54:11), Jesus as healer or giver of life, praise – *Judah*

OTHER SYMBOLS FROM NATURE

Acid = Harsh hurtful words, bitterness, a caustic, hurtful relationship

Air = Holy Spirit (John 20:21-23, Jeremiah 23:24)

Ashes = Great sorrow (2 Samuel 13:19), something worthless (Job 13:12), repentance (Job 42:6), a broken and sorrowful life (Proverbs 1:27, MSG), mourning (Jeremiah 6:26), divine judgment of the wicked (Jeremiah 21:10)

Bark = The outward persona, one's public image

Bedrock = The Lord as a firm foundation (Psalm 18:1, MSG)

Blossom = Joy (Psalm 65:12, NLT), righteousness (Psalm 72:7, MSG), the temporal nature of life (Psalm 103:15, MSG), Jesus (Song of Solomon 1:14, NIV), wickedness and pride (Ezekiel 7:10, NLT)

Branch(es) = Jesus (Isaiah 11:1, Jeremiah 23:5), Christians (John 15:5), worshipping Jesus as King (John 12:13), prosperity (Genesis 49:22)

Brimstone (Burning Sulfur) = Divine judgment (Genesis 19:24)

Bud = An person who has great potential but has not yet matured, a sign that a person or group of people will bear fruit in time (Isaiah 27:6), righteousness and praise (Isaiah 61:11, NIV)

Clay = Our frail humanity (2 Corinthians 4:7), something fragile and brittle (Daniel 2:42)

Coal = Cleansing from sin (Isaiah 6:6), God's wrath poured out (Psalm 11:6), the brilliance of God's presence (Psalm 18:11-13), the conviction that comes upon our enemies when we bless them (Romans 12:20), God's end time witnesses (Zechariah 4:11-13)

Crop = A sign of God's love and mercy (Acts 14:17, NIV), good works which are produced out of a godly life (Hebrews 6:5-10) or sin and evil which is the produce of a wicked heart (Proverbs 21:4, CEV, Hosea 10:13, NLT), people (Hosea 2:23, NLT, John 4:37, CEV) *failed crop* – sign of God's judgment (2 Chronicles 7:13, NLT), sign of laziness (Proverbs 20:4)

Decay = The deteriorating effects of sin (Matthew 7:17, AMP), death (Acts 13:34), *moral rottenness and corruption* (2 Peter 1:4)

Dust = The human body (Genesis 2:7), humiliation (Psalm 72:9), the feebleness of human nature (Psalm 103:13-15), too numerous to be counted (Genesis 13:16), God's judgment (Deuteronomy 28:24), a spiritual state of dryness, mourning (1 Samuel 4:11-13), total obscurity (1 Kings 16:2), total destruction (2 Kings 13:7), repentance (Nehemiah 9:1), death (Ecclesiastes 3:20), a long period of inactivity, spiritual slumber or despondency (Isaiah 52:2)

Fertilizer = Practices that enhance spiritual growth such as prayer and Scripture reading

Fire = Holy Spirit (Revelation 4:5) the Word of God (Jeremiah 20:9), destruction of the wicked (Matthew 13:42), the presence of God in the midst of the darkness (Exodus 13:21), the Lord's work in purifying His people (Malachi 3:2), God's wrath (Psalm 89:46), the glory of the Lord (Exodus 24:17), a great trial (Psalm 66:12), temptation and sin (Proverbs 6:26-28), passionate love of God (Song of Solomon 8:6), malicious or negative speech such as gossip or cursing (James 3:5-6), a devastating attack of the enemy (Nahum 3:13), the flames of hell where there is eternal suffering for those who reject salvation in Christ (Revelation 20:14-15) **firestorm** – divine judgment bursting upon the wicked (Luke 17:29, MSG, Amos 7:4, MSG), an emotional outburst, intense controversy **flint** = Unwavering boldness (Ezekiel 3:9), a heart that is hardened toward God

Fossil = An antiquated method of doing something that no longer is productive, an old memory

Fruit = See **FOOD AND DRINK**

Germ = Sin and corruption (Ezekiel 24:11, MSG), a demonic spirit

Gravity = A hindrance to moving into higher realms in the Holy Spirit

Ice = The Holy Spirit (ice is a form of water), a cold calculating person, someone who lacks compassion, a precarious situation

Infection = Sin (1 Timothy 6:4, MSG, Deuteronomy 20:8, MSG), a demonic stronghold, see also **Virus**

Leaves = An attempt to cover one's own sin before God through dead works and religion (Genesis 3:7), the flourishing of the righteous (Proverbs 11:28, NIV), a sign of life after a season of devastation (Genesis 8:11), professing Christians who have an appearance of godliness but in actuality bare no fruit (Mark 11:11-13, Matthew 3:10), shade from the sun; symbolizing God's shelter in a difficult situation

Mud = Sin and wickedness (Isaiah 57:20, MSG), slander or defamation (Ezekiel 39:7, MSG, Matthew 12:25-27), total defeat (Micah 7:10, NKJV), gossip

Oil = The anointing (Exodus 29:7), gladness and joy (Psalm 45:7), an abundant flow (Ezekiel 32:14), overflowing blessing (Joel 2:24), healing ministry (Mark 6:13), the Holy Spirit, fruitfulness that comes from brokenness

Parasite = A person who takes advantage of the generosity of others, sin (Deuteronomy 32:10, MSG), a demon

Plague = Severe divine judgment (Exodus 32:34-35), great affliction and torment (Psalm 38:11, NKJV), a widespread evil in a region or nation such as the plague of abortion

Quicksand = A worsening situation which seems inescapable (Psalm 69:2, MSG), a trap of the enemy

Rock = The Lord (2 Samuel 22:2), God as our place of refuge (Psalm 31:2), a very hard situation, an obstacle that causes one to stumble (Isaiah 8:14), desolation (Ezekiel 26:13-14), the end-time crushing of the evil governments of the world by the kingdom of God (Daniel 2:44-46), Jerusalem (Zechariah 12:3), Jesus as our firm foundation (Matthew 7:25), a hard heart toward God (Luke 8:6), *cleft of the rock* – the Lord our refuge and protector

Root = Source or origin (1 Timothy 6:10), the place where a person was born and raised, the eternal Christ (Isaiah 11:10, Revelation 5:5), the outward manifestation of the condition of the heart which begins affecting others (Hebrews 12:15), becoming settled into a new environment

Scab = An unhealed emotional wound

Seed = The Gospel message or the Word of God (Matthew 13:18-20, Luke 8:11), faith (Matthew 17:20), giving unto the Lord (2 Corinthians 9:10), a descendant; whether spiritually or naturally speaking (Galatians 3:29), sin or discord, a small beginning that has the potential to blossom into something large and powerful

Shade = Rest (Genesis 18:4, NLT), the Lord's protection over us (Psalm 121:5)

Shadow = *Our days on earth are like a passing shadow, gone so soon without a trace* (1 Chronicles 29:15, NLT), death and darkness (Job 10:20- 22), the wicked hiding in the hidden darkness to attack the righteous (Psalm 11:2), doubt cast against someone's character or integrity, the shadow of the Lord's wings which speaks of the Lord as our refuge and protection (Psalm 17:7- 9), gloom (Isaiah 59:9), healing (Acts 5:14-16), a faint picture prefiguring a future reality as for example the Sabbath day foreshadowing Jesus as our eternal rest (Colossians 2:17), something that is always shifting and changing as contrasted with God's holy character (James 1:17), a friend or companion who is constantly with you

Slate = A record of a person's past performance: *I've wiped the slate of all your wrongdoings. There's nothing left of your sins. Come back to me, come back. I've redeemed you."* (Isaiah 44:22, MSG)

Smoke = The manifest presence of God (Exodus 19:17-18) the devastation of divine judgment of the wicked (Genesis 19:27-28), the wrath of God (2 Samuel 22:8-10), false religion (Isaiah 57:13, MSG), the brevity of human life (James 4:14, AMP), something hindering one's spiritual vision, *I said to myself, "Let's go for it—experiment with pleasure, have a good time!" But there was nothing to it, nothing but smoke.* (Ecclesiastes 2:1, MSG)

Soil = The condition of man's heart toward God (Matthew 13:1-23) *hard soil* – hardness of heart, a difficult region to evangelize, a difficult ministry situation *fertile soil* – a tender heart toward God, a fruitful ministry or church, humanity

Spider's Web = A trap of the enemy or of sin (Isaiah 59:5), the fragility of the lives of the wicked (Job 27:18), the flimsy nature of the things that the godless put their trust in (Job 8:14, NLT), neglect, mental confusion

Steam = Angry words or actions (Isaiah 30:27-28, MSG), the expression of repressed emotions (letting off steam), see also **Mist or Vapor**

Sticks = People (Zechariah 3:2), the dryness that results from sin (Lamentations 4:8), a type of the cross (2 Kings 6:5- 7), discipline or abuse *firebrand (burning stick)* – *Like a madman shooting firebrands or deadly arrows is a man who deceives his neighbor and says, "I was only joking!"* (Proverbs 26:18-19, NIV), a troublemaker.

Stone = Punishment for sin (Leviticus 20:27), idolatry (Leviticus 26:1), *and You divided the sea before them, so that they went through the midst of the sea on the dry land; and their persecutors You threw into the deep, as a stone into the mighty waters* (Nehemiah 9:11, NKJV), strength (Job 6:12), a boundary (Job 24:2), Jesus: *Therefore thus saith the Lord GOD, Behold, I lay in Zion for a foundation a stone, a tried stone, a precious corner stone, a sure foundation: he that believeth shall not make haste.* (Isaiah 28:16, KJV), a hindrance (Isaiah 62:10), stubbornness (Jeremiah 5:3), a hardened heart (Ezekiel 11:19), something that blocks one's escape from a bad situation (Daniel 6:17), persecution (Matthew 23:37), rebellion (Acts 5:26), a Christian (1 Peter 2:5), hypocrisy (John 8:7) *white stone* – *To him who overcomes (conquers), I will give to eat of the manna that is hidden, and I will give him a **white stone** with a new name engraved on the stone, which no one knows or understands except he who receives it.*(Revelation 2:17, AMP), see also **PRECIOUS STONES**

Vine = Jesus (John 15:5), a fruit-bearing child of God (Genesis 49:22), Israel (Hosea 10:1)

Virus = A type of a demonic spirit as a virus requires a host to thrive (Matthew 12:43-45), sin which like a virus is infectious, a corrupting influence such as bigotry or greed

Water = The Word of God (Ephesians 5:26), the Holy Spirit (John 7:38), cleansing from sin (Hebrews 10:22), water baptism symbolizing death to the sinful nature and new life in the Spirit (Matthew 3:11), affliction (Isaiah 30:20) *lukewarm* – a compromised Christian life (Revelation 3:15- 16), something that is boring and uninteresting *boiling* – an unstable or turbulent person (Genesis 49:4, AMP), great envy, hatred and/or anger (Acts 7:9, AMP), the wrath of God (Jeremiah 44:6, NLT) *simmering* – pent-up unexpressed emotion such as anger, to calm down after an emotional outburst (simmer down) *frozen* – incapacitated by fear or shock, a detached and unfriendly person

Wood = The Cross of Jesus, human nature, an unrighteous person (2 Timothy 2:20-21), dead works (1Corinthians 3:10-13) *dead wood* – idolatry (Psalm 135:17, MSG), a person who does not fulfill his/her responsibilities or whose job is superfluous, famine (Joel 1:11-12, MSG)

IV. FOOD AND DRINK

Almond = Resurrection (Numbers 17:23)

Bitter Tasting = A time of mourning (Genesis 50:10), the bitterness of bondage and oppression (Exodus 1:14), a curse (Numbers 5:19, Judges 5:23), a distressful and unhappy season of life (Ruth 1:20), unforgiveness and hostility (2 Samuel 2:26), great suffering (2 Kings 14:26)

Bittersweet Tasting = A memory, relationship or situation that has both pleasant and painful aspects

Baloney = Foolishness, an untrue statement (Job 15:2, MSG)

Bread = Jesus (John 6:35), the presence of God (Exodus 25:30), tears (Psalm 80:5), laziness (Proverbs 31:27), adversity (Isaiah 30:20), life's basic needs (Matthew 6:11), the Word of God (Luke 4:3-4)

Butter = Kind words that are insincere (Psalm 55:21), animosity (Proverbs 30:33), walking in the favor of the Lord (Job 29:5)

Cake = A gift or offering to the Lord (Exodus 29:23) or to a false God (Jeremiah 7:18), a task that is easily accomplished, a celebration or special occasion

Carrot = Prophetic vision, patience (

Cereal = See **Grains**

Coffee = A wake-up call, addiction

Cookie = a person (a smart cookie, a tough cookie, a shrewd cookie etc)

Cream = Best or finest, decisive defeat, the elite

Egg = Potential of new things being birthed such as a ministry or a business, a new beginning

Fruit = Great Increase (Genesis 28:3), children (Deuteronomy 30:9), righteousness that comes through a relationship with Jesus (Philippians 1:11), the fruit of living in the Holy Spirit: love, joy, peace, patience, kindness, goodness, faithfulness, gentleness and self-control (Galatians 5:22-23, NIV), the consequences of our actions whether good or bad (Colossians 1:10, Ephesians 5:11), praise (Hebrews 13:15), temptation (Genesis 3:1-6), wisdom (Genesis 3:1-6), eternal life and healing (Revelation 22:1-2) *ripe fruit* – evildoers who are about to suffer divine punishment (Amos 8:1-2, NLT), spiritual maturity (Luke 8:14, AMP)

- *Apple* = The people of God, God's laws (Proverbs 7:2), speaking "the right word at the right time" (Proverbs 25:11, MSG), passion (Song of Solomon 2:5), *big apple* – Emblem of New York City
- *Date* = The good fruit of the righteous (Song of Solomon 7:7, NLT)
- *Fig* = Healing (2 Kings 20:7), abundant provision (1 Chronicles 12:39-40), Israel (Jeremiah 24:1-9)
- *Grapes* = Abundant provision (Numbers 13:24), Israel (Isaiah 65:8-9), the spilled blood of the wicked (Revelation 14:18-20)
- *Lemon* = Bitterness, something that is defective, a sour situation
- *Olives* = Jewish people (Isaiah 17:6-7)
- *Peach* = A wonderful person, a symbol of the state of Georgia, a sign that everything is going well
- *Plum* = a large financial increase, something very desirable

- ***Pomegranate*** = fruitfulness (Numbers 13:23), joy and beauty (Song of Solomon 4:3)

Garlic = The pleasures of the world (Numbers 11:5)

Grains (includes rice, corn, barley, oats, etc.) = People (Genesis 37:6-8), God's abundant provision (Genesis 27:28), an offering to the Lord (1 Kings 8:64), Israel (Hosea 14:7), the invisible work of the Lord in fulfilling His purposes (Mark 4:26-29), time and patience for the harvest (James 5:7)

Honey = The Word of God (Ezekiel 3:3), the deceptive, alluring words of an adulteress (Proverbs 5:3), pleasant words that encourage and build up (Proverbs 16:24), God's abundant provision (Jeremiah 32:22), a loved one

Juice = Vitality or strength (Psalm 32:3-5, MSG)

Junk Food = False teaching (2 Timothy 4:3-4, MSG), things of little or no value that distract us and take our attention away from what God would have us focus our hearts and minds on, ungodly entertainment, listening to gossip (Proverbs 18:8, MSG), indulgence

Liquor = Unclean or unholy (Leviticus 10:8-10), violence (Proverbs 20:1-3), drunkenness and confusion (Isaiah 28:7), spiritual stupor (Isaiah 29:9, AMP)

Marshmallow = An easy-going person, a timid person

Matzo (Unleavened Bread) = Jesus' sinless life (Matthew 26:26), sincerity and truth (1 Corinthians 5:6-8 NIV)

Meat = Gluttony (Proverbs 23:20), worldly indulgence (Isaiah 22:13), teachings from the Bible that can only be grasped by the mature believer (Hebrews 5:12)

Milk = The elementary teachings of the Christian faith (Hebrews 5:12), God's abundant blessings (Joel 3:18)

Nut = A problem that is hard to solve, an overzealous or fanatical person, a foolish person, a stubborn person *cracking open a nut* – solving a difficult problem, getting through to a "hardheaded" person

Oil = See **OTHER SYMBOLS FROM NATURE**

Onion = The process by which the Lord brings deliverance and inner healing to His people one layer at a time

Popcorn = quick, sudden and spontaneous

Pumpkin = witchcraft, the occult, harvest

Rice = A wedding, see also **Grains**

Rotten Food = False teaching, false doctrine, The wicked and rebellious (Jeremiah 29:16-18, NLT)

Salt = An eternal covenant (2 Chronicles 13:5), the Church (Matthew 5:13), God's purifying power (2 Kings 2:20, the AMP) the desolation of the wicked and rebellious (Jeremiah 48:9)

Spice = Prayer (Revelation 5:8), anointing (Exodus 35:8), abundance (1 Kings 10:10), the sweet fragrance of the Bride of Christ (Song of Solomon 4:10), zest, see also **SPICES AND PERFUMES**

Sour Tasting = The judgments, trials and persecutions written in God's Word (Revelation 10:9-10), the consequences of sin (Job 20:11-15, Jeremiah 31:29), something distasteful

Stale Food = Teaching that lacks freshness and vitality

Stew = Mental and/or emotional agitation such as worrying or simmering anger

Sweet Tasting = *Bread gained by deceit is sweet to a man, but afterward his mouth will be filled with gravel* (Proverbs 20:17, NKJV), the sweet taste of God's Word (Psalm 119:103), good fellowship (Psalm 55:14), A longing fulfilled is sweet to the soul (Proverbs 13:19, NIV), wisdom (Proverbs 24:14), sleep to the weary (Ecclesiastes 5:12), the sweetness of God's presence (Song of Solomon 2:3)

Taffy = The Lord stretching His people to new levels

Vinegar = An ill-tempered person, a bitterness of speech, a lazy person (Proverbs 10:26)

Water = The Word of God (Ephesians 5:26), the Holy Spirit (John 7:38), cleansing from sin (Hebrews 10:22), water baptism symbolizing death to the sinful nature and new life in the Spirit (Matthew 3:11), affliction (Isaiah 30:20) *cold drinking water* – refreshing of the Spirit or the Word, *Good news from far away refreshes like cold water when you are thirsty* (Proverbs 25:25, CEV)

Wine = The blood of Jesus (1 Corinthians 10:16), drunkenness (Genesis 9:21), God's wrath poured out in judgment against the unrepentant wicked (Revelation 14:10), the wickedness of the end time false religious system (Revelation 17:1-3), celebration (John 2: 1-11), **new wine** – a fresh move of the Holy Spirit (Mark 2:22), the new covenant in Christ **old wine** – tradition, old religious forms, a past move of the Holy Spirit (Luke 5:38-39), the Old Covenant based on the law of Moses

Yeast or Leaven = Boasting and pride (1 Corinthians 5:6), hypocrisy (Luke 12:1), sin and wickedness (1 Corinthians 5:8)

V. TIMES AND SEASONS

Autumn = Time of reaping a harvest (financial, the lost being saved, etc), the ending of a summer season of refreshing and the transition into a season of trial

Dawn = righteousness (Psalm 37:6), the path of the uncompromisingly just and righteous (Proverbs 4:18, AMP), the light of God flowing through the Church (Isaiah 58:8), a large and powerful army (Joel 2:2), the end of a dark season of trial and difficulty, the beginning of something new, a sudden revelation, a righteous ruler (2 Samuel 23:3-4, NLT) Japan is known as the land of the rising sun.

Daytime = Righteous behavior (Romans 13:13), see also **Sunshine**

Dusk or Twilight = A sign that a time of trial and difficulty is at hand, decline following success

Harvest-Time = The lost coming into the Kingdom of God (Matthew 9:35-38), the end of the world (Matthew 13:38-40), the end-time outpouring of God's wrath on the wicked (Revelation 14:15-20), the resurrection from the dead of all true believers in Jesus (1 Corinthians 15:20), a time of great financial gain which results from the Lord blessing the faithful giver (2 Corinthians 9:6-8), *"Those who live only to satisfy their own sinful desires will harvest the consequences of decay and death. But those who live to please the Spirit will harvest everlasting life from the Spirit."* (Galatians 6:8, NLT), a time of God's faithful promises being fulfilled in a life or ministry that continually and obediently does the good work of the Lord (Galatians 6:9), righteousness and peace that comes as a result of enduring the Lord's discipline (Hebrews 12:10-12)

Midnight = A time for giving thanks to the Lord (Psalm

119:62), death, intense darkness

Morning = A time of joy (Psalm 30:5), a time of expectant prayer (Psalm 5:3, Psalm 88:13), a time of praise and worship (Psalm 59:16), waiting and longing for the Lord (Psalm 88:13)

Nighttime = A time of sadness and weeping (Psalm 30:5), a time of desperate prayer (Psalm 77:2), terrors (Song of Solomon 3:8), drunkenness and a state of spiritual slumber (1 Thessalonians 5:7), see also **Darkness**

Noon = Justice (Proverbs 16:15, Psalm 37:6), a high point in one's life, clear direction and revelation, a mid-way point

Season = A period of time during which God deals with a person or church or ministry in a certain way. For example, a person may go through a season of refreshing (Acts 3:19), or a season of trial and testing (James 1:3, NKJV), *To every thing there is a season, and a time to every purpose under the heaven* (Ecclesiastes 3:1-8, KJV), God appointed times of dealing with a region, nation or even the world. This could be a season of judgment (Jeremiah 8:7, NKJV), prosperity (Genesis 41:29, NLT), etc

Spring = New beginnings, the born-again experience, the end of a season of trial (Song of Solomon 2:11, 12), a time for war (2 Samuel 11:1)

Summer = Rest, time of refreshing, a season of God's favor, a loss of strength (Psalm 32:4), a time to gather and store (Psalm 32:4, Proverbs 10:5), the time of Jesus' return (Luke 21:30)

Sunset = The Church shining brightly on Earth with glory at the end of the age, see also **Dusk**

Winter = A season of trial and tribulation, a lack of fruitfulness, a state of being cold in one's Christian walk, barrenness

SPECIAL DAYS AND SEASONS

*I realize that the celebrations of several of these holidays have pagan roots, but I address that under the category of IMAGINARY CREATURES OR BEINGS.

Christmas = The birthing of God's purposes on Earth, family, celebration

Day of Atonement = Jesus as the atonement for our sin (Romans 5:11), the future judgment (Revelation 20:11-12), repentance

Day of Pentecost, Feast of Weeks, or Shavuot = Outpouring of the Holy Spirit (Acts 2), the beginning of harvest-time (Exodus 34:21-22)

Easter = God's resurrection power, a new beginning in the Lord

Feast of Tabernacles or Succoth = God dwelling in the midst of His people (Leviticus 23: 39-43), thanking God for His abundant blessings, celebration of the harvest

Feast of Trumpets or Rosh Hashanah = The return of Jesus for His Church (1 Thessalonians 4:16), a call to repentance

Freeze Free Season = A time of favor and refreshing

Fourth of July = Freedom and liberty (Galatians 5:1, NKJV)

Halloween = Witchcraft, paganism, satanic worship

Hanukkah = The rededication of a life to the Lord (John 10:22), the Lord's miraculous provision, the Lord driving out our enemies *menorah* – Jesus as the Light of the world giving light to His people

Jubilee = Freedom from debt and bondage (Leviticus 25), redemption, restoration

New Year's Eve = A sign that a new beginning is at hand, worldly revelry

Passover = Freedom and deliverance (Deuteronomy 16:1), Jesus' death on the cross bringing us salvation (1 Corinthians 5:7)

Purim or the Feast of Esther = The Lord's often unseen hand giving us victory over every plot of the enemy (Esther 9:24)

Sabbath = Jesus as our eternal rest from dead works (Hebrews 4: 6-11), a time of rest

St. Valentine's Day = Love, romance

Thanksgiving = Thanking God for His provision and blessings (1 Chronicles 16:8)

VI. COLORS AND NUMBERS

COLORS

*Note: None of the colors listed below refer to skin color as indicative of a particular race. All people are equally precious in the sight of God.

Amber = The fullness of God's glory (Ezekiel 1:4)

Black = Famine and death (Revelation 6:5), darkness (Proverbs 7:9), mourning (Jeremiah 4:27-29) the occult (black magic), a financial profit

Blue = Revelation (*2 Corinthians 12:1*) sadness (the blues), heavenly or earthly authority (Ezekiel 23:6), intercession, baby boy, color of the Democratic Party

Bronze = See **METALS**

Brown = Earth, humanity, the withering of what was once alive and vibrant, wood hay and stubble or dead works (Corinthians 3:12-13)

Emerald = See **GEMSTONES**

Gold = See **METALS**

Gray = Compromise, *gray hair* – old age (1 Samuel 12:2), maturity, wisdom and experience (Proverbs 20:29, the Amplified Bible)

Green = Prosperity (*Proverbs 11:28*), life (Job 39:8), 'Go Ahead' (given a green light), healing, jealousy or envy, new beginnings (the color of spring), fertility, immature, the national color of Ireland

Multi-Colored = Favor (Genesis 37:3, KJV)

Orange = Danger, warning, fire of God, passion

Purple = Jesus as King and Ruler (*Revelation 1:5*), royalty (Judges 8:26), prosperity (Proverbs 31:22)

Red = The blood of Jesus: forgiveness, freedom, sacrifice (*Ephesians 2:13*), war and bloodshed (Revelation 6:4), passion, anger, Stop! (red light), financial loss, color of the Republican Party

Scarlet, Crimson = Sin (*Isaiah 1:18*)

Silver = See **METALS**

Turquoise = See **GEMSTONES**

White = Purity and righteousness (*Revelation 3:4*), innocence, angels (Acts 1:10)

Yellow = Glory, fear, hope, Slow down and be cautious (as when a traffic light turns yellow.)

NUMBERS

*Through the use of the principles of biblical numerology it is possible to ascribe symbolic meaning to many more numbers than I have listed here. I do not however feel comfortable enough with that process to use it. I prefer to stick to meanings that are evident either in Scripture or everyday life.

One = Oneness, unity (Philippians 2:2), the beginning

Two = Witness (2 Corinthians 13:1), division or difference, duality

Three = The Triune God (2 Corinthians 13:14), the Third Heaven (2 Corinthians 12:2)

Four = The Earth; e.g. there are four winds, four seasons, four corners of the Earth (Revelation 7:1), worldwide

Five = God's enabling grace and power (Leviticus 26:8), the five–fold ministry (Ephesians 4:10-12)

Six = The number of man (Created on the sixth day)

Seven = Completeness or Perfection (Genesis 2:2), rest (Sabbath)

Eight = New beginning (1 Peter 3:20)

Nine = The Holy Spirit: Nine fruit of the Spirit (Galatians 5:22, 23), nine charismatic Spiritual gifts (1 Corinthians 12:4-11), on the Day of Pentecost the Holy Spirit fell at nine in the morning (Acts 2:14-19), new birth

Ten = Trial and Testing (Daniel 1:12-15, Genesis 31:7), God's divine law and order (Exodus 34:28), tithing

Eleven = Incomplete, short of God's perfect plan (Luke 24:9, 1 Chronicles 11:1), transition, at the last possible moment (11th hour)

Twelve = Government and leadership (Numbers 17:2, Acts 6:2), Israel (1 Kings 18:31)

Thirteen = Rebellion (Genesis 14:4, *also* Israel rebelled 13 times in the wilderness), superstition, number of original American colonies

Fourteen = The death of Jesus our Redeemer on the cross; the Lamb of God sacrificed for sin (Exodus 12:1-6, Numbers 29:12-14)

Fifteen = Rest (Leviticus 23:39, Esther 9:18, Leviticus 23:33-35), celebration, harvest (Leviticus 23:39), The Lord extending ones years (2 Kings 20:6)

Sixteen = Love (There are 16 characteristics of love mentioned in 1 Corinthians 13:4-8)

Eighteen = Suffering and bondage (Judges 10:8, Luke 13:11, Jeremiah 52:27, 29, Judges 3:14), life (In Hebrew, the figures for the number 18 also spell out the word *chai* which means 'life')

Twenty = A trial of great length coming to an end by the hand of the Lord (Genesis 31:38, Judges 4:1-3, 1 Samuel 7:1-3)

Twenty-Four = Perfection in government (Revelation 4:40)

Twenty-Six = Number of nations who are members of NATO

Thirty = Maturity for ministry (Numbers 4:47, 2 Samuel 5:4,

Luke 3:23), mourning and sorrow (Numbers 20:29, Deuteronomy 34:8)

Forty = Judgment (Genesis 7:4, Numbers 14:34, Judges 13:1), testing (Deuteronomy 8:2, Matthew 4:1-2)

Fifty = Freedom, liberty, debt cancellation, restoration, inheritance, jubilee (Leviticus 25), Outpouring of the Holy Spirit (Pentecost means 50 – see Acts 2)

Fifty-Two = Number of nations that have a primarily Muslim population

Sixty-Six = the Bible (which contains 66 books)

Seventy = Captivity or the time of the end of captivity (Jeremiah 29:10), body of elders (Ezekiel 8:11, Numbers 11:16)

Hundred = Full reward from the Lord (Mark10:30, Genesis 26:12)

Three Hundred = God's faithful remnant (Judges 7:8)

One Hundred Ninety-Two = Number of member states in the United Nations

One Hundred Ninety-Three = Number of recognized independent nations in the world

Six Hundred Sixty-Six = Antichrist (Revelation 13:18)

One Thousand = Warriors in battle (1 Samuel 29:2, Joshua 23:10, Numbers 31:5)

One Hundred Thousand = mighty men of valor (2 Chronicles 25:6)

VII. NAME MEANINGS

*Many times a person's name is significant in understanding a dream. I have included some of the more common names (common at least in NYC) whose meanings have possible prophetic significance.

Aaron = Exalted, shining light

Abraham = Father of a multitude

Abigail or Gail = My father rejoiced

Adelaide, Ada = noble, nobility

Aida = Help

Aidan = Fiery

Aisha = Life or lively

Albert or Alberto or Alberta = Noble and bright

Alexander or Alexandra = Defender of mankind

Alexis = Helper

Alice or Alicia = Noble

Alyssa = Rational

Amy = Beloved

Angel or Angela or Angelina = An angel or messenger

Anthony = Priceless

Ariel = Lion of God, used as a name for Jerusalem (Isaiah 29:1)

Aurora = Dawn

Ava = Like a bird

Barbara = Foreign

Beatrice = Voyager

Belinda = Beautiful Snake

Bernice = One that brings victory

Brian or Brianna = Strength

Bridget = Resolute strength

Brittany = From England

Buffy = God's promise

Caleb = Brave or bold

Carrie = free man, strong

Cassandra = Shining upon man

Charles or Carla or Carlene or Karl or Charlotte = Strong one or free man

Catherine or Katrina or Kayla or Karen = Pure

Christian or Christine or Kirsten = Anointed or Christian

Christopher = Carrier of Christ

Claude or Claudia = Lame or crippled

Connor = Strong willed

Constance or Connie = Steadfastness

Daniel or Danielle = God is my judge

David = Well beloved

Donald = From Celtic words meaning world and power

Dora = Gift

Edward or Eduardo = Blessed guard

Edwin = Blessed or rich friend

Elizabeth or Isabella or Betty or Beth = My God is abundance or pledged to God

Elliot or Elijah or Elias = Jehovah is God

Emily or Amelia = Industrious

Emma = Universal

Ephraim = Very fruitful

Esther = Star

Ethan = Steadfast or firm

Eva, Evelyn, Evita = Life

Faith = Faith

Felix or Felicia = Happiness

Gabriel or Gabrielle = Champion of God

Giselle = pledge

Gloria = Glory

Haley = Hero

Hanna or Hannah or Anna = Favor or grace

Heidi = Noble

Henry or Henrietta or Enrique = Ruler of the home

Hilda = Woman warrior

Hillary = Happy

Inez = Pure

Irene or Irena = Peace

Iris = Rainbow

Isaiah = Salvation of Jehovah

Isabella = Consecrated to God

Isla = Island

Jacob or James or Diego or Jacqueline or Jackie = Supplanter or deceiver

Jaden = He will judge

Jaleel = Great, exalted, expectant of God

Jason = Healer

Jeremy or Jeremiah = Appointed by God

Jesse = God exists

Jessica = He sees

Jocelyn, Joy, Joyce = Happy

John or Juan or Juana or Jane or Giovanni or Joanna or Joanne = The Lord is gracious

Jonathan = Gift of God

Jordan = Descend or descendant

Joseph or Jose = God increases

Joshua = The Lord is salvation

Judith or Judah = Praise or Jew

Juliet = Youthful

Justin or **Justine** = Fair minded

Kelly = Warrior

Kenneth = Sprung from fire

Kylie = boomerang or graceful

Lakeisha = Favorite one

Laticia = Joyful

Laura = Laurel; which speaks of victory

Laverne = Born in the spring

Leah = Weary

Leonard or Leonardo = Strong or brave as a lion.

Liam = Unwavering protector

Linda = Beautiful

Louis or Luis or Louisa = Renowned warrior

Lynn = Waterfall or Cascade

Madeline or Magdalene or Migdalia = Tower

Manuel = God is with us

Margaret or Margarita or Margot or Peggy = Pearl

Mark or Martin or Martina = Warlike

Mary or Maria or Molly or Marian = Bitterness

Matthew = Gift of God

Megan = Great

Michael or Miguel or Michelle or Mitchell = Who is like the Lord?

Molly = star of the sea

Monica = Advisor

Nancy = Full of grace

Naomi = Lovable or my delight

Natalie or Natasha = The Lord's birthday

Nathaniel = Given by God

Neil = Champion

Nicholas or Nicole = People of victory or victory of the people

Noah = Comfort or rest

Oliver or Olivia = Olive tree

Paige = Assistant

Patrick or Patricia = Noble one

Paul or Pablo or Paula = Small

Raphael = God has healed

Raymond = Counselor, protector

Rebecca or Becky = Captivating, a noose

Richard or Ricardo = Dominant ruler

Robert or Roberto or Roberta = Shining with fame

Rocco = Rest

Rosalie or Rosa or Rose = Rose

Ruth = Friend

Ryan = Royalty

Samuel or Samantha = Heard of God

Salvador = Savior

Sarah or Sally = Princess

Saul = Asked for

Sean or Shawn or Shauna = God is gracious

Serena = Tranquil or Serene

Seth = Appointed one

Shaquille = Handsome

Sofia = Wisdom

Stacie = Resurrection or fruitful

Steven or Stephen or Stephanie = Crown

Susan or Suzanne = Lilly

Tammy or Tamara = Palm tree

Theodore or Dorothy = Gift of God

Theresa or Tracy or Teri = To reap or harvest

Tiffany = Appearance of God

Timothy = Honoring God

Todd = Fox

Veronica = True image

Victor or Victoria = Conqueror

William or Guillermo = Determined guardian

Zachary = The Lord has remembered

VIII. PEOPLE

*Of course any of the people I list below can be taken literally in a dream. For example, if you dream about your mother, the dream might be speaking literally about your mother. A terrorist could signify an actual terrorist attack. My purpose in writing this dictionary is to show symbolic meanings only.

Accountant = Financial responsibility and stewardship

Accuser = satan: *And I heard a loud voice saying in heaven, Now is come salvation, and strength, and the kingdom of our God, and the power of his Christ: for the accuser of our brethren is cast down, which accused them before our God day and night.* satan in his work of attacking the hearts and minds of God's people with condemnation and shame

Acrobat = A person who quickly changes his/her opinion on an issue to suit the circumstances

Actor = A hypocrite or pretender (Luke 6:42, AMP), a drama ministry

Adulterer = See **Adultery**

Adventurer = God, who got you started in this spiritual adventure, shares with us the life of his Son and our Master Jesus. He will never give up on you. Never forget that. (1 Corinthians 7:9, MSG), One who seeks out new challenges and is willing to take risks to succeed when directed by God, a person who takes unnecessary chances with negative consequences, one who diligently seeks after wisdom (Proverbs 2:3-5, MSG)

Advocate = *May the Lord therefore judge which of us is right*

and punish the guilty one. He is my advocate, and he will rescue me from your power!" (1 Samuel 24:15, NLT), the Holy Spirit (John 14:16, AMP), *And if any man sin, we have an advocate with the Father, Jesus Christ the righteous:* (1 John 2:1, KJV)

Air Traffic Controller = The Holy Spirit, who directs, leads and guides according to the timing of the Lord

Ambassador = A Christian as Christ's representative on Earth (2 Corinthians 5:19-21)

Ancestor = A family curse or blessing (Exodus 20:5-6), generational sin patterns (2 Chronicles 30:7), spiritual heritage and inheritance (Psalm 45:16-17)

Archaeologist = Having an unhealthy focus on digging up the past, Uncovering information to be used as gossip (Job 10:6, MSG, Proverbs 3:29, AMP), seeking out treasures hidden in God's word, *I will give you **hidden** treasures, riches stored in secret places, so that you may know that I am the Lord, the God of Israel, who summons you by name. (Isaiah 45:3 NIV)*

Archer (Bow and Arrow) = The devil or a demon launching an attack (Ephesians 6:16), the Lord pouring out judgment on the wicked (2 Samuel 22:14-16), the Lord fighting on behalf of His people (2 Samuel 22:7-16), victory and deliverance (2 Kings 13:16-17), the wicked attacking the righteous (Psalm 11:1-3), the Lord's rebuke (Psalm 38:1-2, MSG), gossip and slander (Psalm 64:2-4, Proverbs 25:18, NLT), the occult (as an astrological sign)

Architect = God as designer and creator (Hebrews 11:9-10, NIV), wisdom (Proverbs 8:29-31, NLT)

Athlete = Competition, a Christian who denies him/herself sinful pleasures in order to fully live out his/her God given destiny (1 Corinthians 9:24-26) **athletes in a team sport or sports team** – team ministry, a family working together in the Lord, cooperation

Audience = The great cloud of witnesses; who are the souls of the saints (sanctified ones) who have gone before us, cheering us on from Heaven (Hebrews 12:1), a congregation that is experiencing worship or other ministry as a performance rather than entering in themselves, a sign that a preacher, teacher, worship leader, etc is more concerned with pleasing man than pleasing God (Galatians 1:10)

Aunt = A different church or ministry than the one the dreamer or dream subject is a member of, a false Church, actual positive or negative qualities of one's aunt

Author = Jesus as: *the author of life* (Acts 3:15, NIV), *the author of eternal salvation* (Acts 16:1, AMP), *the author and promoter of peace* (2 Corinthians 13:11, AMP), *the author and perfecter of our faith* (Hebrews 12:2, NIV) and the *author of God's creation* (Revelation 3:14, AMP)

Auto Mechanic = Someone the Lord is using to help 'fix' or realign a ministry

Baby = A new ministry that has been birthed (or will be) that is still in its beginning stages, a new believer (1 Peter 2:2), an immature believer (1 Corinthians 3:1-3, Hebrews 5:12-14), dependence

Blacksmith = The work of the enemy in creating weapons to use against God's people (Isaiah 54:16-17)

Bodyguard = The Lord (Psalm 34:20, MSG), an angel (Psalm 91:11)

Boyfriend = Something that takes the place of Jesus in one's life, actual positive or negative qualities of one's boyfriend

Boy Scout or Girl Scout = A moral and virtuous person, a helpful person, a good citizen

Brother = A male Christian (Philemon 1:16), actual positive or negative qualities of one's brother, **older brother** – a judgmental, self righteous Christian (Luke 15:28-32)

Brother or Sister-in-Law = A false Christian, a legalistic Christian, a Christian who belongs to another Church or denomination, actual positive or negative qualities of one's brother or sister-in-law

Builder = God (Hebrews 3:3-4), an apostle (1 Corinthians 3:9-11), a Christian (1 Corinthians 3:13, NLT)

Bully = A person who uses words to intimidate and get their way (Matthew 10:29-31), the enemy, *"I brought Israel up out of Egypt. I delivered you from Egyptian oppression—yes, from all the bullying governments that made your life miserable.'* (1 Samuel 10:18-19, MSG)

Busboy = Humble servant, minister or ministry worker in training

Cannibal = But if you bite and devour one another, beware lest you be consumed by one another! – Galatians 5:15 (NKJV)

Carjacker = Someone out to take down a ministry or Church leader in order to hijack control

Carpenter = Jesus (Mark 6:3), a kingdom builder; whether God's or man's

Celebrity = Someone who ministers or does religious acts in order to get the praise and attention of man (Matthew 6:16-18,

MSG), a sign that there will be an opportunity to minister to people of influence, a sign that the ministry of the dream subject will be brought to the forefront, idolatry

Champion = The Lord who is the victor over all (Genesis 49:24, MSG), an angel (Job 33:23, MSG, Daniel 12:1, M S G), a victorious child of God

Cheerleader = An enthusiastic and vocal supporter, a great encourager

Child = Immaturity in thought, speech and actions (1 Corinthians 13:11), a Christian (Galatians 4:7), a non-Christian (1 John 3:9-11), Jesus (Revelation 12:5), a Christian with simple child-like faith and trust (Matthew 18:3, Matthew 11:25), innocence, the dreamer as a child, the inner child of the dreamer, ***adopted child*** – a born-again Christian (Romans 8:14-16), a ministry that the dreamer or dream subject didn't birth but has taken leadership of, a spiritual son or daughter

Coach = The Holy Spirit, a pastor, a Church leader, a ministry leader, a mentor

Commander in Chief = Jesus as Lord of hosts (angelic army) (1 Samuel 15:2)

Conductor (Musical) = The Holy Spirit, a worship leader, a pastor or leader

Counselor = The Holy Spirit (John 14:26), God's laws and principles (Psalm 119:23-24)

Cook = A pastor or teacher's work in preparing lessons, sermons, written works that break down the Scriptures in ways that people can digest, see also **Meat**

Cowboy = A reckless person who takes unacceptable risks, an independent spirit, an adventurer, an emblem of the western U.S.

Co-Worker = A fellow Christian in the Lord's service (Philippians 2:25, NLT), actual positive or negative qualities of one's co-worker, Jesus as our co-laborer in the harvest (2 Corinthians 6:1)

Craftsman = *The heavens proclaim the glory of God. The skies display his craftsmanship.* (Psalm 19:1, NLT)

Critic = *"Do you still want to argue with the Almighty? You are God's critic, but do you have the answers?"* (Job 40:2), *"Don't pick on people, jump on their failures, criticize their faults— unless, of course, you want the same treatment. That critical spirit has a way of boomeranging. It's easy to see a smudge on your neighbor's face and be oblivious to the ugly sneer on your own.* (Matthew 7:1-2m MSG), one who appoints him/herself to publically judge and criticize ministries and/or ministers on social media

Delivery-Person (Food) = An evangelist who brings the gospel to homes, A home group teacher

Deep Sea Diver = A Christian who is seeking the deep things of God (1 Corinthians 2:9-11, NIV), one who ministers to people going through great difficulties

Dispatcher = God; as He sends angels out on assignment (Psalm 78:49, NLT, Matthew 24:30-31, MSG), God; as He sends His people out on assignment (Exodus 4:19-21)

District Attorney = Satan; the accuser of the brethren (Zechariah 3:1-3), a legalistic Christian (Galatians 3:1-3)

Doctor = Jesus as healer (Luke 5:30-32), a Christian with a healing ministry

Drug Dealer = satan as the tempter (1 Thessalonians 3:4-5), the sinful nature (Ephesians 2:3), witchcraft, see also **Drugs (Illegal)**

Enemy = satan and his demons (1 Peter 5:8)**,** death (1 Corinthians 15:26), *You adulterous people, don't you know that friendship with the world is hatred toward God? Anyone who chooses to be a friend of the world becomes an enemy of God. (James 4:4),* the sinful nature as an enemy of the Spirit (Galatians 5:16-18), sin

Ex-Husband or Ex-Boyfriend = One's life before knowing Jesus, the world, a prior sin or addiction, satan

Explorer = *I devoted myself to search for understanding and to explore by wisdom everything being done under heaven.* (Ecclesiastes 1:13, NLT), a non-believer who is seeking truth, a Christian who moves into new realms of the Holy Spirit

Exterminator = The Holy Spirit as He uncovers and destroys the hidden work of the enemy, the Holy Spirit as He uncovers and eradicates hidden sin in the life of a submitted believer

Family = The Church as the household of faith (Galatians 6:9-10)

Farmer = See **Planter** and **Harvester**

Father = God the Father, a true spiritual mentor (1 Corinthians 4:15), the Devil – if evil (John 8:44), actual positive or negative qualities of one's earthly father

Father-in-Law = A false god, a spiritual leader from another Church or ministry, a legalistic Church leader, actual positive or negative qualities of one's father in-law

Firefighters = Leaders who quench the fire of the Holy Spirit by disallowing prophetic utterances (1 Thessalonians 5:1), Christians whose faith in the midst of the battle acts as a shield to quench the fiery darts of the enemy (Ephesians 6:16)

First Born = Special blessing received from the father (Genesis 27:4, AMP), double portion inheritance (Deuteronomy 21:17), birthright (Genesis 25:31-33) Jesus: *He is the image of the invisible God, the firstborn over all creation.* (Colossians 1:15, NIV)

Fisherman = Evangelist, soul winner, outreach worker (Matthew 4:18-19), You have made men like fish in the sea, like sea creatures that have no ruler. The wicked foe pulls all of them up with hooks, he catches them in his net, he gathers them up in his dragnet; and so he rejoices and is glad (Habakkuk 1:14-16, NIV) a scam artist or con-man

Forest Ranger = The lord protecting and guiding us through difficult life situations, a person with a ministry that helps people navigate through situations and seasons they can't see their way out of, a counselor

Fortuneteller, Medium, Psychic, Soothsayer, or Spiritist = A false prophet (Isaiah 44:25, AMP), witchcraft and the occult (Deuteronomy 18:9-11)

Friend = An obedient Christian as a friend of Jesus (John 15: 14-15), a carnal person as a friend of the world (James 4:4), Jesus, actual positive or negative qualities of the particular friend

Gardener = God the Father (John 15:1), a ministry that helps people to grow in the Lord

Giant = A large intimidating obstacle (Numbers 13:33, AMP)

Glutton = A person who has a great appetite for sin, a person given to great excess, a Christian with a ravenous appetite for the Word of God, a person with a remarkably great desire or capacity for something (for example: a glutton for punishment)

Graduate = One who has been tested by the Lord and has been found faithful (Exodus 15:25, NLT, Revelation 2:10), a sign of promotion (Psalm 75:6-7, AMP), one who reaches a new level of spiritual maturity (1 Corinthians 2:6, AMP)

Grandparent = Generational blessing (Psalm 112:1-2), generational curse (Exodus 34:7), past family issues, spiritual inheritance (2 Timothy 1:5), actual positive or negative qualities of one's grandparent

Guide = The Holy Spirit (John 16:12-14), Jesus (Matthew 4:19, AMP), the Word of God (Psalm 119:98, NLT), the light and truth of the Lord (Psalm 43:3, NLT), a godly leader (Psalm 78:72), the wise teachings of a parent (Proverbs 6:20- 22), wisdom (Ecclesiastes 7:23, NLT), Galatians 5:18, AMP), a pastor (Titus 2:1-3, MSG), a teacher, a counselor *blind guide* – an ungodly leader or teacher who lacks spiritual vision (Matthew 15:12-14)

Harvesters or Reapers = Angels (Matthew 13:38-40, NIV), Evangelists and those who reach out to the lost (Matthew 9:35- 38), *"Those who live only to satisfy their own sinful desires will harvest the consequences of decay and death. But those who live to please the Spirit will harvest everlasting life from the Spirit."* (Galatians 6:8, NLT), see also **Harvest-Time**

Heir = Jesus (Mark 12:6-8), a born-again Christian (Romans 8:16-18), Israel (Acts 3:25)

Homeless Person = A refugee, *For this world is not our permanent home; we are looking forward to a home yet to come.*

(Hebrews 13:14, NLT), poverty, a spiritually lost person, A Christian without a Church home or place of fellowship

Husband = Jesus as our heavenly bridegroom (John 3:29), something that metaphorically speaking the dreamer is "married to" or extremely devoted to such as a job or a hobby, actual positive or negative qualities of one's husband

Imposter = A false Christian (2 Timothy 3:12-13), the devil masquerading as an angel of light (2 Corinthians 11:14), a womanizer presenting himself as a gentleman or vice-versa

Interloper = Someone who interferes and meddles in the lives of others

Intruder = Someone or something that is intrusive such as someone who interrupts one's private times with the Lord, a sickness or disease, sinful or tempting thoughts that intrude into one's mind

Investor = *Be generous: Invest in acts of charity. Charity yields high returns.* (Ecclesiastes 11:1, MSG), *God has been too long involved with Israel, has too much invested, to simply wash his hands of them.* (Romans 11:2, MSG) see **Sower**

Jockey or Horseback Rider = Someone who relies solely on human rather than divine strength, see also **Horse**

Judge = God the Father (John 8:50), a judgmental person (Romans 2:1), an intermediary (1 Corinthians 6:1-4)

King = Jesus (Revelation 19:16), anti-Christ or satan (Revelation 17:10-12), *To Him who loved us and washed us from our sins in His own blood and has made us kings and priests to His God and Father* (Revelation 1:5-6)

Knight = The Lord who rescues His people (2 Samuel 22:2,

MSG), an angel – (Luke 2:13, AMP) **evil knight** – satan or a demon

Landlord = God the Father (Matthew 21:33-42)

Lawyer = Jesus our Advocate (1 John 2:1-2), a legalistic Christian (Acts 21:19-21), an advocate

Life Guard = The Lord, an angel (Psalm 91:10-12)

Magician = A sorcerer or enchanter operating through demonic powers (Deuteronomy 18:9-11), a false prophet (Genesis 41:23-25, Isaiah 44:25, AMP), the anti-Christ spirit (2 Thessalonians 2:8-10), a deceiver delivering illusions (Isaiah 30:9-11, AMP), see also **Magic**

Master = Money (Matthew 6:24), Jesus (Matthew 9:10-12 KJV), sin and addiction (1 Corinthians 6:12), satan for those who do not serve the Lord (Colossians 1:13)

Matchmaker = The Holy Spirit in His role of bringing people to Jesus the Heavenly Bridegroom, a soul winner

Merchant = Jesus: *Again, the kingdom of heaven is like a merchant looking for fine pearls. When he found one of great value, he went away and sold everything he had and bought it* (Matthew 13:45-48, NIV)

Messenger = An angel (Daniel 4:13), a prophet (Haggai 1:13, 2 Chronicles 36:16), a priest (Malachi 2:7), Jesus (Malachi 3:1), an afflicting demon as sent by Satan (2 Corinthians 12:7), an apostle (Matthew 10:2, AMP), Christians as God's messengers bringing the Gospel to the World (Romans 11:31, AMP)

Midwife = A person the Lord has placed in the life of a dreamer or dream subject in order to facilitate the birthing of a ministry or other life purpose, a ministry designed to help people in birthing God's purposes in the lives of His people

Milkman = One who teaches or disciples new converts in Christ (Hebrews 5:13)

Model = A Christian whose life is a godly example for others to follow, an unrealistic and unattainable standard of worldly beauty, the fashion and design industry

Mother = The Church where the dreamer or dream subject is or was nurtured in the Lord, source or origin, a spiritual mother (Titus 2:3-5), actual positive or negative qualities of one's mother

Mother-in-Law = An apostate Church, a legalistic Church, a Church other than the one you attend, actual positive or negative qualities of one's mother in-law

Mountain Climber = A prideful person (2 Kings 19:23, NIV), *Who may **climb the mountain** of the LORD? Who may stand in his holy place? Only those whose hands and hearts are pure, who do not worship idols and never tell lies. They will receive the LORD's blessing and have a right relationship with God their savior. Such people may seek you and worship in your presence, O God of Jacob.* (Psalm 24:3-5, NLT), a person who is attempting to overcome an obstacle

Murderer = satan (John 8:44), a demon, one who carries hatred toward his brother
(1 John 3:15)

Musician = Worshipper – whether worshipping the One True God (1 Chronicles 15:27) or false gods or worldly idols such as self, sinful pleasure, money, etc (Exodus 32:18), rejoicing (1 Samuel 18:6), the Lord's delight and love for His people (Zephaniah 3:17), celebration (1 Kings 1:40-42) deliverance (1 Samuel 16:23), prophecy (2 Kings 3:14-16), worldly pleasure

(Amos 6:4-6), Spiritual warrior (2 Chronicles 20:20- 22), see also **Singing** and **Music**

Nanny = A discipler of new Converts, a children's ministry worker, an angel (Matthew 18:10)

Nomad = A Church hopper, a person without roots, a travelling ministry

Nurse = Healing, sacrificial service, nurturing

Niece or Nephew = A ministry that has been birthed by someone other than the dreamer, actual positive or negative qualities of one's niece or nephew

Orchestra = symbolic of working together in unity and harmony with others, Worshippers in unity (Psalm 98:5)

Orphan = A person without God in his/her life (John 14:18), a Christian who lacks a true spiritual father or mother

Paparazzi = Promotion, favor, fame, elitism, idolatry, a superstar mentality in the Church

Paramedic = Healing or inner healing ministry to those in a crisis, healing evangelism, a sign that a situation is at a crisis point and cannot be overlooked

Partner = *He who robs his father or mother and says, "It's not wrong"— he is partner to him who destroys. (Proverbs 28:24, NIV), God will do this, for he is faithful to do what he says, and he has invited you into partnership with his Son, Jesus Christ our Lord. (1 Corinthians 1:9, NLT)*

Passenger = A member of a Church or ministry who is not the pastor or leader, one who is not in control of a situation

Pastor = Jesus as the shepherd of the His people (Acts 20:28)

Photographer = See **Photograph**

Pioneer = A missionary to an unreached people group (Romans 15:17-21, MSG), a forerunner ministry, the trailblazing fathers and mothers of our Christian faith who have gone before us (Hebrews 12: 1-3, MSG)

Pilot or Captain = The Lord, a pastor, a Church or ministry leader

Pirate or Marauder = The devil or a demon (John 8:44), wicked leaders in the House of the Lord (Hosea 6:8-10, NIV), a predator (Isaiah 33:21)

Planter or Sower = An evangelist or a Christian who shares his/her faith (Matthew 13:18-19), a troublemaker who "sows mistrust and suspicion in the minds of the people" (Acts 14:2, MSG), one who gives financially to the work of the Lord (2 Corinthians 9:6), the enemy as he places false Christians in the Church (Matthew 13:38-40), one who ministers to the people of God such as a teacher (1 Corinthians 9:11), one who performs good works in the Lord (Galatians 6:7-9), a doer of evil and corruption (Galatians 6:7-9), a peacemaker who spreads seeds of peace (James 3:18)

Plumber = The Holy Spirit as He unclogs the stopped up drains through which repentance and cleansing from sin flow, see also **Water** and **Shower**

Police = Authority, the Lord, protection against the enemy, an angel, *traffic cop* – direction for life or ministry

Politician = Governmental authority (Romans 13:1-4), a church leader who attempts to move ahead through maneuvering and manipulation

Postman = A prophet, a preacher, someone who delivers a prophetic message, the Holy Spirit

Potter = The Lord as He creates, shapes and molds us (Jeremiah 18:1-10, Romans 9:20-21)

Pregnant Woman (or in some dreams, a man) = A sign that a ministry or the purposes of God are about to be birthed, "He who is pregnant with evil and conceives trouble gives birth to disillusionment" (Psalm 7:14, NIV), "Lust gets pregnant, and has a baby: sin! Sin grows up to adulthood, and becomes a real killer." (James 1:13-15), Israel (Revelation 12:1-2), *fetus* – a ministry, business, career, etc that is still in the formative process, a pre-Christian, see also **Birth**

Prince = Jesus as the Prince of Peace (Isaiah 9:6), Satan as *the Prince of this world* (John 12:30-32), a male Christian as a child of the King

Princess = A female Christian as a child of the King, an entitlement mentality

Principal = The Lord, a pastor or leader, director of a teaching ministry

Prisoner = An unforgiving person (Matthew 18:21-35), one who is bound by sin (Romans 7:23, NIV), a non Christian (Galatians 3:22), a Christian as a willing servant of Jesus Christ (2 Timothy 1:8), *But the Scripture declares that the whole world is a prisoner of sin, so that what was promised, being given through faith in Jesus Christ, might be given to those who believe. Before this faith came, we were held prisoners by the law, locked up until faith should be revealed* (Galatians 3:22-23, NIV)

Prison Guard = satan and his demons keeping people in

bondage, a legalistic or false Church leader (Galatians 2:4), sin and addiction (Galatians 3:22)

Prostitute = Idolaters (Exodus 34:152, Chronicles 21:11,), someone who turns to the occult or a medium instead of God (Leviticus 20:6), a person controlled by their lusts (Numbers 15:38-40), the false, apostate Church (Revelation 17)

Psychologist = The Lord working inner healing in our hearts and minds

Puppeteer = Satan as he controls the lives of the wicked, a very controlling or manipulative person, a nation that totally dominates a less powerful nation under its control (Isaiah 7:4-6)

Quarterback = The Holy Spirit, a team leader

Queen = Israel (Lamentations 1:1), The Church as the Bride of Christ the King (Psalm 45:9) *queen of heaven* – idolatry and paganism (Jeremiah 44:25)

Rebel = *The careless, the rebellious, and the unbelieving, who go against the purposes of God* (Ephesians 2:2, AMP)

Record Keeper or Registrar = An unforgiving person who keeps a record of wrongs done to him/her (1 Corinthians 13:5), a person who keeps a journal of prayer, dreams, testimonies etc, the devil who keeps an account of our sins and uses that to bring condemnation (Zechariah 3:1-3)

Referee or Umpire = The Holy Spirit as the one who lets us know (convicts us) when we break the rules (are disobedient), the Holy Spirit as the final authority, the Lord as the one who punishes sin

Refiner of Metals = The Lord as he purifies and purges our lives from sin (Malachi 3:2-4, 1 Peter 1:7)

Rescuer = The Lord who rescues us from our enemies (Luke 1:74, 2 Timothy 4:18), Jesus our Savior (Colossians 1:13), God who rescues us from our troubles (2 Timothy 3:10-11, 2 Peter 2:9), a Christian who partners with the Lord to bring the lost into the Kingdom of Heaven (Jude 1:22-24, NLT)

Savior = Jesus (2 Peter 1:10-11)

School Bus Driver = A teacher, a children's ministry leader

Security Guard = An angel (Psalm 91:11), *We are guides into God's most sublime secrets, not security guards posted to protect them.* (1 Corinthians 4:1-2, MSG), the Holy Spirit

Servant = **Jesus** (Matthew 12:18), a humble and obedient Christian (Matthew 20:20-26), an angel (Revelation 19:9-10), someone in financial debt (Proverbs 22:7)

Shepherd = **Jesus** (John 10:11) a pastor or overseer of a Church or ministry (Acts 20:28)

Shoemaker = The Lord as the giver of peace (Ephesians 6:15), the Lord as our provider (1 Timothy 6:6)

Sister = A female Christian (1 Corinthians 9:5), wisdom (Proverbs 7:4), actual positive or negative qualities of one's sister

Slave = A Christian who lives in total obedience to God (Romans 6:22, Ephesians 6:6), a sinner as a slave to fear (Romans 8:15-16) sin and corruption (2 Peter 2:19 NLT) or money (Matthew 6:24), a legalistic Christian (Galatians 2:4)

Soldier = An angel or a demon; depending on whether he represents good or evil, a Christian engaged in Spiritual warfare (Ephesians 6:10-18), one who willingly endures suffering and hardship for the Lord (2 Timothy 2:3)

Son or Daughter = A ministry that the dreamer birthed or will birth, a child of God (Romans 8:21), actual positive or negative qualities of one's son or daughter, a spiritual son or daughter (1 Timothy 1:2, 2 Timothy 1:2, Titus 1:4)

Spy = A false Christian (Galatians 2:4), one who can prophetically discern the plans of the enemy (2 Kings 6:8-12) *double agent* – a church-goer who is living in compromise

Squatter = The enemy taking ground in the lives and possessions of God's people (Matthew 8:16)

Stalker = Sinful temptation (Proverbs 6:26, AMP), poverty (Isaiah 17:4, NLT), disease and war (Ezekiel 5:17, NLT), the devil (1 Peter 5:8), a demon

Student = A Christian (Matthew 10:23-25), someone going through a season of the Lord's testing (James 1:2-4)

Surgeon = The Holy Spirit as he performs healing in our physical body or in our emotions, The Holy Spirit's work of removing sin from our lives, *scalpel* – the Word of God (Hebrews 4:12, MSG), delicate precision in cutting through hard issues *operating table* – a spiritual posture of submission to the work of the Lord as he cuts away harmful sin, wrong attitudes and emotional baggage, place of healing

Swimmer = See **Swimming**

Teacher = **Jesus** (John 13:13, Matthew 19:16), the Holy Spirit (John 14:26)

Terrorist = Distress and anguish (Job 15:24, NIV), a demonic spirit of fear (2 Timothy 1:7), a fearful heart (Deuteronomy

28:67), sickness and disease (Deuteronomy 28:60, MSG), distress and anguish (Job 15:24), One who the "voice of the enemy" speaks through such as a gossiper or slanderer (Psalm 55:3-4) the devil (Psalm 55:3-4), a demon, the wicked and unjust (Proverbs 22:8, NLT)

Thief = The enemy (John 10:10), a sudden unexpected event (1 Thessalonians 5:4), an activity that robs our time with God

Tutor = A discipler in the faith, *Therefore the law was our tutor to bring us to Christ, that we might be justified by faith.* (Galatians 3:24, NKJV), a mentor in sin and rebellion

Twins = Fruitfulness, double anointing, multiplication anointing

Tyrant or Dictator = A wicked leader or ruler (Isaiah 14:5, AMP), the demonic powers (Colossians 2:15, MSG), a very controlling person, one who leads through intimidation and control

Uncle = A mentor outside of your own Church or ministry, a false god, a false shepherd or teacher, actual positive or negative qualities of one's uncle

Unseen or Unknown Man = The Holy Spirit, an angel, satan, a demon, the new move of the Spirit where the average "no-name" believer is being raised up to walk in supernatural power and glory

Unseen or Unknown Woman = Wisdom (Proverbs 1:20, Proverbs 4:6), an angel, a demon (Acts 19:27), temptation (Proverbs 7:6-27), justice, the Church

Vagabond = An irresponsible person with no sense of purpose or direction, a church-hopper

Ventriloquist = A demonic spirit who speaks evil words such as slander or gossip through human vessels who submit to his control – *And the tongue is a flame of fire. It is a whole world of wickedness, corrupting your entire body. It can set your whole life on fire, for it is set on fire by hell itself.* (James 3:6, MSG), a lying spirit speaking lies through the mouth of a false prophet (2 Chronicles 18:21)

Virgin = A born-again Christian (Matthew 25:1-13), Israel (Amos 5:2, Jeremiah 31:21)

Visionary = A prophet with a seer anointing (Deuteronomy 13:1, MSG)

Waiter = A teacher (one who serves 'Spiritual food'), a servant (Matt.23:11)

Watchman = One who discerns the work of the enemy and warns the people of God (Ezekiel 33:6), a prophet who warns the people of God of their sin with the goal of bringing them to repentance (Ezekiel 33:7-9), a pastor or leader responsible for watching over God's people (Isaiah 56:10-11, NLT)

Weather Forecaster = A prophet who discerns God's times and seasons (Luke 12:55-57)

Weightlifter = One who is bearing heavy burdens (Matthew 11:28, NLT), the Lord building up our faith, patience and endurance through allowing trials and difficulties in our lives (James 1:3-4)

Whistle Blower = A person who uncovers and reports dishonesty and corruption within an organization, a prophetic watchman who sees and signals danger ahead (Ezekiel 33:6) *Don't blow the whistle on your fellow workers behind their backs; They'll accuse you of being underhanded, and then you'll be the guilty one!* (Proverbs 30:10, MSG), *When I whistle to* *them, they will come running, for I have redeemed them.* (Zechariah 10:8, NLT)

Wife = The Church body (Revelations 19:7), something that metaphorically speaking the dreamer is "married to" such as a job or a hobby, actual positive or negative qualities of one's wife

Witch = A rebellious person (1 Samuel 15:23), a false prophet (Isaiah 44:25, AMP, Jeremiah 14:14, AMP), a worker of counterfeit miracles which are performed using satanic powers (2 Thessalonians 2:8-10), a seductress (Proverbs 7:21), a legalistic teacher or leader who leads God's people into a gospel of works rather than grace (Galatians 3:1-3), one who is controlling and manipulative

X-Ray Technician = The Holy Spirit as he looks into the innermost condition of our hearts in order to expose sin, fear and wrong motives (Psalm 44:20-21, Psalm 139:23-24)

CIRCUS PERFORMERS

Clown = A foolish person, someone who keeps his/her true feelings hidden, joy

Contortionist = A deceitful person who twists words

Juggler = Someone who has a very hectic schedule, a manipulative person

Knife Thrower = A gossiper or slanderer

Lion Tamer = The Lord; who thwarts the devouring attack of the enemy (Daniel 6:1-23)

Strongman = The devil or a demonic power (Matthew 12:28-29)

Sword Swallower = A Christian who devours the Word of God

Tightrope Walker = Someone in a very precarious situation

BIBLICAL FIGURES

*Under each Bible character I will list just a few characteristics or functions for each as described in Scripture. This is not meant to give a comprehensive picture by any means.

Aaron = High Priest who interceded with the Lord on behalf of the people, yielded to the will of the people instead of standing firm in the Lord, received supernatural confirmation of his ministry before the people

Abraham = Man of radical faith and obedience, willing to sacrifice everything for the Lord, God called him His friend

Angel = Spiritual being, protector of God's people (Psalm 34:7), the Lord's messenger (Judges 2:4), carries out the Lord's judgments (2 Samuel 24:15-17), a heavenly worshipper of the Most High God (Psalm 148:2), wars against demonic powers of darkness (Daniel 10:12-13, NLT)

Anna = Prophetess, she patiently waited many for God's promise to be fulfilled and she was rewarded for her faithfulness

Balaam = Prophet who lived in compromise and greed

Barnabas = Encourager, spiritual father, helped launch others into their callings in spite of their past failures (Acts 9:26-28, Acts 15:36-40)

Cain = Wanted to serve God on his own terms which was unacceptable to the Lord, murdered his brother in a jealous rage

David = Passionate worshipper who loved God's word and His

Presence, was shown mercy by God in spite of his great sin, a man after God's own heart (Acts 13:22)

Daniel = Man of prayer, received many heavenly visitations, a prophet of great character, found victory in an impossible situation, stood in the gap in prayer for the sins of his generation and past generations, interpreted dreams

Deborah = Female leader, prophetess and liberator of God's people

Demon = Evil spiritual beings who serve the devil in his work of attempting to hinder God's people in every way (Ephesians 6:11-13), demons can possess a non believer's body, soul and spirit (Matthew 8:28-29), demons can cause affliction and sickness (Matthew 17:14-20, Luke 13:11), demons are the source of witchcraft, fortunetelling and other occult practices (Acts 16:16-18)

Elijah = Miracle working prophet, man of great faith, confronted the false prophets of his day

Elisha = A prophet with a double portion anointing, received his anointing and mantle after a season of humble and faithful servitude to Elijah, did great miracles but remained humble and compassionate

Enoch = Walked with God in great faith and intimacy

Esther = Interceded with the king on behalf of the people, willing to face death in order to accomplish the Lord's assignment, *Esther obtained favor in the sight of all them that looked upon her"* (Esther 2:15, KJV)

Ezekiel = Name means: God will strengthen, had visions of the glory of God and the River of God, uncovered corruption and idolatry going on behind the scenes in the Holy Temple, was transported in the Spirit

Gideon = An ordinary person (who saw himself as a nobody) raised up by God as a mighty leader who brought deliverance to God's people, after a season of great victory he slipped into idolatry

Goliath = An enemy that appeared undefeatable who taunted the people of God, was eventually defeated by David who totally trusted in God for the victory, symbolizes major obstacles and hindrances

Good Samaritan = Helped a badly beaten robbery victim whom everyone else passed right by, sacrificed time and money to help the man

Haman = Plotted to destroy the Jewish people and in the end he himself was destroyed

Hannah = Persisted in prayer until the Lord answered her request, dedicated her son to the service of the Lord

Hosea = Displayed great forgiveness and mercy to his spouse as a picture of God's great love and mercy toward His people

Isaiah = Had a great vision of the throne room of God

Jacob = Got his way through crafty and deceptive means, he tenaciously wrestled with God for His blessing,

Jeremiah = A prophet who was broken for God's people and wept over them, his prophetic ministry was virtually totally rejected, walked at times through emotional darkness

Jezebel = Extremely controlling and seductive queen, used intimidation and violence to get her way, brought witchcraft and idolatry to God's people

Job = Worshipped God in the midst of great loss and suffering, man of great favor, suffered rejection and criticism but overcame

John = Beloved of Jesus, visited Heaven and received great revelations, preacher of love

John Mark = Failed miserably on a missions trip as he abandoned his traveling companions because of fear one of whom was Paul, John Mark was restored through the ministry of Barnabas and Paul later said of him *"Get Mark and bring him with you, for he is useful to me for ministry"* (2 Timothy 4:11, NKJV)

John the Baptist = Forerunner ministry, preacher of repentance

Jonah = Rebelled against the Lord's calling in his life, saw a nation transformed through his ministry, received a second chance after failure

Joseph (OT) = Great patience in suffering, refused to compromise at any cost, interpreted dreams, had great favor with his father and the king

Joshua = Led the people into the land of promise, loved to sit in the presence of God, challenged God's people to walk in greater levels of holiness and faithfulness, God promised to give him victory everyplace he *"set his foot"* (Joshua 1:2-4, NIV)

Judas Iscariot = Traitor, thief

Lazarus = Resurrected from the dead, was Jesus' friend

Lot = *Lot lived right and was greatly troubled by the terrible way those wicked people were living. He was a good man, and day after day he suffered because of the evil things he saw and*

heard. So the Lord rescued him. (2 Peter 2:7-8, CEV)

Martha = Busyness, servanthood, distraction

Mary (Mother of Jesus) = An ordinary girl used mightily by God

Mary (of Bethany) = Deep worship and adoration

Michal (David's Wife) = Mocked David as he freely worshipped and danced before the Lord for which God cursed her with barrenness

Mordechai = Uncovered the plot of the enemy, spiritual father and mentor

Moses = *"When a prophet of the LORD is among you, I reveal myself to him in visions; I speak to him in dreams. But this is not true of my servant Moses; he is faithful in all my house. With him I speak face to face, clearly and not in riddles; he sees the form of the Lord.* (Numbers 12:6-8, NIV), leader with great humility, had tremendous hunger for the presence of God, *He regarded disgrace for the sake of Christ as of greater value than the treasures of Egypt, because he was looking ahead to his reward* (Hebrews 11:26)

Noah = Lived righteously before God in the midst of great evil, showed great faith in the midst of rejection and persecution, a preacher of righteousness

Paul = True apostolic father, suffered greatly for Jesus but never complained or gave up, missionary, Church planter, moved in great miraculous power and authority, fought against and exposed legalism

Pharaoh = Had a hardened heart toward God, symbolic of satan, was an evil and wicked ruler oppressing God's people

Peter = Tremendously effective soul winner, apostle to the Jewish people, radically transformed when he was filled with the Holy Spirit

Rich Young Ruler = Claimed to be righteous based on keeping the law but his money was an idol in his life, he walked away when Jesus told him to give his money to the poor

Samson = A man of great anointing whose ministry was overcome by fleshly desires, repented and was greatly used by God at the end of his life, man of great strength and power but displayed little character

Samuel = Remained a righteous and faithful priest and prophet in the midst of a corrupt religious and governmental system, prophesied God's judgment against the corrupt priesthood of Eli, *and the boy Samuel continued to grow in stature and in favor with the Lord and with men* (1 Samuel 2:26, NIV)

Sarah = Miraculously had a child when she was well past child bearing age

satan or the devil = Tempts people to sin (Genesis 3:1, AMP), the spiritual adversary and enemy of God's people (Job 1:12, AMP, 1 Peter 5:8), source of sickness and suffering (Job 2:7), the father of lies (John 8:44), *You used to live in sin, just like the rest of the world, obeying the devil— the commander of the powers in the unseen world. He is the spirit at work in the hearts of those who refuse to obey God.* (Ephesians 2:2, NLT), accuser and slanderer of God's people (Revelation 12:10)

Saul = A leader whose desire to be praised by man was greater than his desire to please God, success by those under him was met with jealousy, envy and murderous hatred, was physically impressive but lacked inner character

Shadrach, Meshach, and Abednego = Refused to bow down to idols even at the cost of their lives, were thrown into the fire but the Lord miraculously spared their lives

Solomon = Had great wisdom, in spite of his wisdom and zeal for the Lord he was overcome by greed and compromise, had great wealth which he realized in the end was meaningless in light of eternity, a picture of Jesus Our Bridegroom in the Song of Solomon

Stephen = Martyr, bold and fearless speaker of truth

Thomas = Told by Jesus to: *Stop doubting and have faith!"* (John 20:27, CEV)

SERVANTS OF THE LORD

*Often in dreams a prominent minister of the Gospel will appear as a dream character. As with most dreams elements these appearances are typically symbolic. I have listed here a number of prominent men and women of God of the past and present and describe a few elements of their ministries. I also included websites for further research. (A great website for reading about many other past giants of the faith is *godsgenerals.com;* It also contains videos of actual miracles done through men of the 50s healing revival.)

Doug Addison = Prophetic evangelist, author, Life Coach and stand-up comedian, he is known for his Daily Prophetic Words – *dougaddison.com*

Che Ahn = He is the founder of Harvest International Ministry which is an international apostolic fellowship, the International Chancellor of Wagner Leadership Institute which is designed to equip and prepare believers for ministry, ministers under a powerful healing anointing, formerly the founding pastor of a very large Church – *harvestim.org*

Carlos Anacondia = Argentinean evangelist with a tremendous deliverance ministry, the Lord uses Carlos to perform many miraculous healings – *reachingsouls.com*

John and Carol Arnott = Pastored the Toronto Blessing which had as its centerpiece the impartation of the Father's love, they equip the body of Christ in achieving great intimacy with the Lord through soaking prayer – *tacf.org*

Heidi Baker = Missionary to Mozambique who has planted thousands of churches and built many orphanages, Heidi and her husband Rolland have seen tremendous miracles and

God's mighty provision in the mission field all birthed out of Intimacy with the Lord – *irismin.org*

Jim Baker = Popular Christian TV host, he was a pioneer of Christian Television; Fell into disgrace after establishing an enormous international ministry but he has since been restored, often teaches on the end times- *jimbakkershow.com*

Todd Bentley = Todd holds worldwide evangelistic crusades, his teams win many souls through signs, wonders and miracles, he spend hours soaking in the presence of God which he considers one of the major keys to the anointing. His ministry has been the object scores of social media critics. – *freshfireusa.com*

Mike Bickle = Founder of the International House of Prayer in Kansas City which ministers to the Lord in prayer and worship 24 hours per day 7 days per week, he teaches with great passion on the unconditional love of God for His people – *ihop.org*

Shawn Bolz = An international prophet who flows in very accurate words of knowledge, Shawn planted a church in Hollywood, CA with a strong emphasis on reaching the entertainment industry and the poor for Jesus, his main emphasis is on touching the nations by displaying the grace and love of God. – *bolzministries.com*

Reinhard Bonnke = Ministering primarily in Africa he has won millions of souls to the Lord through evangelistic crusades (48 million from 1995-2005), Many miracles occur in his meetings including the dead being raised – *cfan.org*

William Branham = Powerful leader of the 1950s healing revival, he had many angelic visitations, Brother Branham moved in a highly accurate prophetic gift with incredibly on target words of knowledge – *godsgenerals.com*

Dr. Michael L. Brown = Founder and president of FIRE School of Ministry, popular TV and radio host, a key part of the Brownsville Revival in the late 90s., engages often in Jewish outreach and debates rabbis, heavily involved in the culture wars, often participates in theological debates – *askdoctorbrown.org.*

Juanita Bynum = A prophetess and prophetic songstress who challenges the Church to walk in increasingly greater levels of holiness and purity – *juanitabynum.com*

Jonathan Cahn = Messianic rabbi, Jewish believer in Jesus, teaches extensively on the Jewish roots of the Christian faith, author of the Harbinger and The Mystery of the Shemitah: both of which give warning of God's coming judgment poured out on America – *bethisraelworshipcenter.org*

Mahesh Chavda = A pastor who was a former Hindu, the glory of God is wonderfully manifested in his meetings and tremendous miracles take place – *maheshchavda.com*

David Yonggi Cho = Pastor of the world's largest church located in Seoul, South Korea, he built up the local church by organizing cell groups which began to multiply in a very short amount of time – *davidcho.com*

Randy Clark = Revivalist who ignited the Toronto Blessing in 1994, he has a powerful healing gift, he was totally burned out in his pastoral ministry before being radically impacted by the Lord through Rodney Howard-Browne – *globalawakening.com*

Kim Clement = Prophet to the nations, he ministers through powerful prophetic music – *kimclement.com*

Jack Coe = Evangelist of the 1950s who held massive healing crusades, many times in his meeting or through his radio ministry people would grow back body parts that had been lost – *jackcoe.org*

Bobby Conners = "For almost five decades, Bobby Conner has been ministering around the world as a seasoned prophet of God. Bobby is uniquely anointed with a profound, passionate love for the Lord Jesus Christ and a fervent desire to discern and herald God's voice to prepare the Lamb's Bride to establish the Kingdom of God. Specifically, Bobby is called to sound the alarm and awaken the warriors to arise and contend for the true faith." – From *Bobby Conners.org*

James Dobson = Teacher, author and radio personality who defends and promotes Christian values in our nation and teaches families to live victoriously in Christ – *focusonthefamily.com*

John Eckhardt = He is an apostolic reformer called to perfecting the saints by imparting biblical truths, including deliverance and spiritual warfare, and activating the gifts of the Spirit in order to raise up strong ministries in the body of Christ. (Quoted from his website) – *johneckhardtministries.com*

Jonathan Edwards = Led the Great Awakening which was a great revival in 18th century colonial America, became a missionary to the Native Americans, was a prolific theological author – *.jonathan-edwards.org*

Lou Engle = Founder of the Call which is a movement focused on challenging the young people in the body of Christ to a radical lifestyle of prayer, fasting, holiness and obedience, also the founder of the Cause which their website describes as: *a grassroots movement of prayer and fasting to contend for the return of righteousness and justice to America.* – *thecauseusa.com*

Maria Woodworth-Etter = *Within a short time after Maria*

Woodworth-Etter responded to God's call to "go out in the highways and hedges and gather in the lost sheep," people were thronging to hear her speak with signs and wonders following. By 1885, without a public address system, crowds of over twenty-five thousand pressed in to hear her minister while hundreds fell to the ground under the power of God. Woodworth-Etter not only shook up denominational religion, she rocked the secular world with life-altering displays of God's power. (Quoted from godsgenerals.com)

Charles Finney = Played a prominent role in the Second Great Awakening in the 19th century, he fought for social justice and preached against slavery, led over 100,000 souls to the Lord of which 85% never strayed (as cited on *gospeltruth.net/lawsonbio.htm*), at times people would fall under the conviction of sin even as he passed them on the street – *charles-finney.com*

Jentzen Franklin = Pastors a "multi-campus church with a global reach", a New York Times best-selling author, teaches extensively on the benefits of fasting, worldwide conference speaker – *jentezenfranklin.org*

James Goll = A prophet, teacher and author with a worldwide ministry, teaches and imparts the *"power of intercession, prophetic ministry, and life in the Spirit"*, promotes unity in the Body of Christ – *encountersnetwork.com*

Billy Graham = An evangelist who has brought many thousands into the Kingdom through mass evangelism crusades, television and radio – *billygraham.org*

Franklin Graham = Evangelist who heads up Samaritan's Purse which is an evangelistic relief organization with an annual budget of 264 million dollars, they minister to the needy in more than 100 nations – *samaritanspurse.org*

John Hagee = Founding and Senior Pastor of a 20,000+ member Church, strong supporter of the Nation of Israel, has a popular TV ministry – *sacornerstone.org*

Kenneth Hagen = Preached and demonstrated the power of faith, he taught that God wants His people to be prosperous and free of sickness – *rhema.org*

Jack Hayford = The founding pastor of Church on the Way which is a very large church in Van Nuys California and also the founder of The King's College and Seminary, Dr Hayford has written almost 50 books many of which teach on living a victorious spirit- filled and empowered life and he has also written many worship songs, has a prolific television and radio teaching ministry, he often serves as a bridge in the body of Christ by bringing together different cultural groups and divergent streams – *jackhayford.com*

Ruth Ward Heflin = Her revival meetings were often marked by the appearance of gold dust as well as jewels signifying the glory ream of Heaven poured out on Earth, she had a powerful ministry in Israel – *calvarycampground.org/rheflin.htm*

Steve Hill = The evangelist of the Brownsville Revival who preached a message of holiness and repentance while seeing tens of thousands run to the altars over 5 years. He also served as a pastor/evangelist as he saw souls saved worldwide – *heartlandfamily.com*

Benny Hinn = Pastor, worldwide evangelist, televangelist, teacher and bestselling author with a powerful healing anointing. As Benny Hinn worships, the presence of God floods the atmosphere and powerful miracles regularly break out among the attendees. His ministry has often been embroiled in controversy and he is the regular target of social media critics – *bennyhinn.org*

Rodney Howard-Browne = Brings joy to the Church through holy laughter as the River of God is released through his ministry, he has been a catalyst for many moves of God worldwide despite being blasted by self styled 'critics'. – *revival.com*

John Paul Jackson = Equipped the body of Christ in dream interpretation and prophetic ministry –*streamsministries.com*

Cindy Jacobs = A powerful prophetess and intercessor, she mobilizes strategic worldwide intercession – *generals.org*

TD Jakes = Pastors a multi-racial, multi-ethnic, debt-free church of 30,000 in Dallas, Texas, he is also a successful entrepreneur and prolific writer, Pastor Jakes produced several God glorifying movies – *tdjakes.org*

Bill Johnson = Pastor who equips and releases the body of Christ to walk in supernatural revelation and power as part of everyday life – *ibethel.org*

Bob Jones = A prophet who received clear visions of what is to come on the Earth, he received many angelic and divine visitations as well as heavenly encounters – *bobjones.org*

Rick Joyner = An apostolic leader who has had a great hand in launching the prophetic movement in the U.S., he has written extensively about his many visions and divine encounters – *morningstarministries.org*

John Kilpatrick = Pastored the Brownsville Revival which followed two and a half years of intense prayer, he teaches on the power of the spoken blessing, he ministers often on the blessings of living a holy life – *partnersinrevival.org*

Patricia King = Trains believers to enter into the throne room of God and experience the supernatural realm, she equips and mobilizes prophetic evangelism teams to reach the lost – *extremeprophetic.com*

Kathryn Kuhlman = Held evangelistic meetings in which the power of God was greatly manifested and many miraculous healings took place -*kathrynkuhlman.com*

John G. Lake = Brought revival to Africa as a missionary through signs and wonders, according to healingrooms.com. John G. Lake: *was responsible for raising over 1,000,000 converts, 625 churches and 1,250 preachers in five years of ministry,* after returning to the U.S. he saw over 100,000 healings through his ministry in Spokane, Washington – *healingrooms.com*

C.S. Lewis = Author of Christian fiction as well as non-Christian books, his fiction works were popular even among secular readers, held academic positions at both Oxford and Cambridge Universities, decades after his death his works of Christian-based fantasy (Narnia series) have been made into hit Hollywood movies – *cslewis.com*

Jerame Nelson = is a prophetic revivalist, author, international conference speaker and a crusade revivalist to the nations, Jerame has a powerful word of knowledge and healing gift, along with a strong anointing for miracles and the supernatural – *livingathisfeet.org*

Joel Osteen = Since becoming pastor of Lakewood Church (after the death of his father and former pastor John Osteen) in Houston, Texas, in 1999, it has grown into a mega-Church, he is seen extensively on television preaching a message of God's love and grace – *joelosteen.com*

Cal Pierce = Redug the wells of John G. Lake's healing revival in Spokane, Washington and has reestablished the ministry of healing rooms resulting in hundreds of healings, his ministry is to equip the average believer to heal the sick – *healingrooms.com*

Chuck Pierce = *He is known for his accurate prophetic gifting which helps direct nations, cities, churches and individuals in understanding the times and seasons we live in.* (quoted from *glory-of-zion.org*), he helps to oversee intercessory teams who are sent out on assignment throughout the Earth, teaches the Church an understanding of the Jewish roots of the faith – *glory-of- zion.org*

Derek Prince = Derek was a renowned teacher with a daily radio show and over 40 books to his credit, he had a tremendous anointing for deliverance – *derekprince.org*

Oral Roberts = His pioneering healing ministry has touched many, many lives through his television broadcasts, over 120 books and worldwide crusades, he founded ORU which has become a top university in the nation – *orm.cc*

Sid Roth = Jewish believer in Jesus, evangelist to the Jewish communities of the nations, Christian TV and radio talk show host with an emphasis on the supernatural, – *sidroth.org*

John and Paula Sanford = They minister inner healing and inner freedom from sin and unforgiveness – *elijahhouse.org*

R.W. Schambach = Evangelist who known for powerful healings and miracles, mostly held his outdoor evangelistic meetings in tents, , he ministered often among the poor, he ministered regularly through TV and radio broadcasts – *schambachfoundation.org*

Aimee Semple McPherson = She innovated using the arts as a means of spreading the Gospel over 70 years ago, as one of the first female revivalists she ministered in the power of the

Holy Spirit, she founded the Foursquare Gospel denomination
– *www.foursquare.org*

William Seymour = The major leader of the Azusa Street
Revival in the early 1900s which started in Los Angeles and
touched the world, asked the Lord to fill him with *"the real
Holy Ghost and fire with tongues and love and power of God
like the apostles had." – williamjseymour.com*

Dutch Sheets = A pastor/teacher who also ministers to the
body of Christ worldwide, He is particularly known for his
teachings on prayer and intercession – *dutchsheets.org*

Kim Walker Smith = "She is a passionate worship leader with
an anointing to bring an entire generation into an encounter
with God." – *jesusculture.com*

Charles Stanley = A pastor of a very large Baptist Church in
Atlanta, Georgia and a renowned teacher and author, through
his TV and radio ministries Dr. Stanley's teachings are heard
worldwide – *intouch.org*

Perry Stone = Teaches often on the Jewish roots of the
Christian faith, international evangelist, teacher of end-times
Bible prophecy – voe.org

Tommy Tenney = Ministers to the hearts of believers to
passionately pursue the presence and glory of the Lord –
godchasers.net

Jason Upton = A passionate worship leader who believes that
intimacy with the Lord is the centerpiece of worship and a
victorious life – *jasonupton.net/com*

Kris Valloton = Senior Associate Leader of Bethel Church in
Redding, California and co-founder of Bethel School of

Supernatural Ministry. Kris travels internationally training and equipping people to successfully fulfill their divine purpose, Kris has a powerful prophetic gift and he is the author of many books. – *krisvallotton.com*

C. Peter Wagner = International apostolic leader, teacher, theologian, author and founder of Wagner Leadership Institute which is designed to equip and prepare believers for ministry – *wagnerleadership.org*

Lance Wallnau = An international speaker, teacher and business consultant, has influenced thousands of leaders around the world. he often teaches on the subject of cultural transformation – *lancewallnau.com*

Rick Warren = Wrote the book the Purpose Driven Life which is the best selling hardcover book in American history, he pastors Saddleback Church in California which averages 22,000 attendees per Sunday and 300 community ministries, he is deeply involved in helping the poor both locally and worldwide – *purposedrivenlife.com*

John Wesley = Preaching in 18th century England, he held mass evangelistic crusades in open fields, as most churches closed the door to his biblical message. Wesley and his followers were often persecuted and attacked by mobs. He was the founder of the Methodist Church. He spoke out about many social issues of his day, including prison reform and the abolition of slavery. He raised up many itinerant evangelists who travelled and preached the gospel. – *godrules.net*

Todd White = Former drug addict and atheist who became a powerful street evangelist, operates in powerful healing and prophetic gift, desires to equip the Body of Christ in living a supernatural lifestyle – *lifestylechristianity.com*

John Wimber = Held powerful healing meetings, trained the body of Christ to heal the sick and encouraged the Church to take the miracle working power of God into the streets, founded the Vineyard Fellowship of churches, spoke against hype and materialism in regards to ministry = *johnwimber.net*

IMAGINARY CREATURES OR BEINGS

Alien = See **OUTER SPACE**

Boogeyman = Satan who lurks in the darkness waiting to attack or frighten the innocent

Bugs Bunny = A Christian who is one step ahead of the enemy

Cupid = Human rather than divine love

Cyclops = A false prophet

Dragon = The devil (Revelation 12:7-9)

Dr Jekyll and Mr. Hyde = A religious hypocrite, a double minded person (James 4:8)

Easter Bunny = Paganism and idolatry, the religious spirit, counterfeit

Energizer Bunny = A person of great persistence and endurance

Frankenstein Monster = The wages of sin are death – creator killed by his creation (Romans 6:23), the dangers of scientists and doctors "playing God" (genetic engineering, abortion, euthanasia, etc)

Genie = A false image of God as having to meet our demands

Goblin = A demon working his evil through a person

Gremlin = A demonic root of a problem or disturbance

Grim Reaper = The spirit of death (Jeremiah 9:21)

Grinch = A bitter and spiteful person

Harry Potter = Witchcraft, satan appearing as an angel of light

Legion of Superheroes = The people of God moving in the power of God

Mermaid, Sea Nymph or Siren = A seductress or a seductive spirit that will lead to ruin

Mickey Mouse = Something trivial or unimportant, an organization that keeps a low standard of quality, childishness, innocence

Monster = A dangerous wicked person (Psalm 31:11 MSG, Ezekiel 29:2-4), a powerful enemy (Isaiah 27:1), the kingdom of anti-Christ (Daniel 7:18-20, MSG), a demonic spirit, a huge problem or trial

Mummy = A past sin that had been repented of and forgiven but now has again become a temptation, a past hurtful memory was healed but now seems to coming again to the surface, the spirit of death (Jeremiah 9:21)

Ogre = An exceptionally cruel, wicked and destructive person

Peter Pan = Immaturity

Phantom = An illusion or delusion, believing a lie

Pinocchio = A liar

Road Runner (Cartoon) = Outwitting the enemy

Sandman = The religious spirit which lulls God's people to sleep

Santa Claus = Worldliness, idolatry, the religious spirit, counterfeit religion

Scrooge = A miserly and uncompassionate person

Superhero = Jesus, a believer in Jesus doing might works to help others, a supernatural fight against spiritual forces of darkness (2 Corinthians 10:4-5)

Super Villain = The devil, a false image of the enemy as being a foe equal to God.

Troll or Gnome = A hidden attack of the enemy, witchcraft, a hindering spirit

Vampire = A demonic spirit of death (Jeremiah 9:21), an evil person that preys on and exploits people

Werewolf = The sinful nature manifesting itself above the spirit (Galatians 5:16-22), a person given to sudden fits of rage

Wiley Coyote = A thwarted attack of the enemy

Zombie = Voodoo or the occult, spirit of death (Jeremiah 9:21), an apathetic or lifeless person, an unsaved person who lacks the life of God

IX. BIBLICAL PLACES, SPICES AND PERFUMES

BIBLICAL PLACES

*At times a dream will take place in the setting of an ancient biblical town, city or country. I am listing the name meaning for each of the location listed below. All meanings in this section are taken from Hitchcock's Bible Names Dictionary, The International Standard Bible Encyclopedia or Smith's Bible Dictionary. I am also detailing one biblical association for each.

Baca = Weeping – The Israelites had to pass through this "valley of weeping" on their pilgrimage to visit the sanctuary of the Lord in Jerusalem. David prophesied however that: *When they walk through the Valley of Weeping, it will become a place of refreshing springs. The autumn rains will clothe it with blessings. They will continue to grow stronger, and each of them will appear before God in Jerusalem.* (Psalm 84:6-7, NLT)

Bethany = House of affliction or misery – Town where Jesus raised Lazarus from the dead (John 11)

Bethel = House of God – The place where Jacob dreamt: *that there was a ladder set up on the earth, and the top of it reached to heaven; and the angels of God were ascending and descending on it! And behold, the Lord stood over and beside him and said, I am the Lord, the God of Abraham your father [forefather] and the God of Isaac; I will give to you and to your descendants the land on which you are lying.* (Genesis 28:11-13, AMP)

Bethlehem = House of Bread – Birthplace of both David and Jesus (1 Samuel 17:12, Matthew 2:1)

Bethsaida = House of fishing – The city where Jesus fed a multitude with five loaves of bread and two fish (Mark 6:32–41)

Calvary or Golgotha = Place where Jesus was crucified (Luke 23:33)

Cana = Zeal; jealousy; possession – The village where Jesus performed His first miracle by turning water into wine at a wedding celebration (John 2:1 -10)

Canaan = Merchant; trader; or that humbles and subdues – God spoke to Abraham and said: *"The whole land of Canaan, where you are now an alien, I will give as an everlasting possession to you and your descendants after you; and I will be their God."* (Genesis 17:8, NIV)

Capernaum = The field of repentance;.city of comfort – A city that saw so many miracles and yet the people refused to turn to the Lord (Matthew 11:23)

Corinth = Ornament = Although the Church in Corinth operated in spiritual gifts their moral standards were often not much different than those of the world (1 Corinthians 5)

Damascus = A sack full of blood – It was on the road to Damascus that Paul had a divine encounter with the Lord (Acts 9:3-4)

Dead Sea = Nothing living can exist in the Dead Sea, the minerals found in the Dead Sea have healing and therapeutic qualities

Egypt = That troubles or oppresses; anguish – Country where God's people Israel were afflicted with bondage and oppression (Exodus 2:23)

Elim = Strong trees – An oasis of rest, refreshing, and nourishment in the midst of the desert (Exodus 15:27)

Emmaus = People despised or a hot spring – It was on the road to this city that Jesus after His resurrection rebuked two disciples because of their unbelief and disappointment with the Lord: *Then Jesus said to them, "You foolish people! You find it so hard to believe all that the prophets wrote in the Scriptures. Wasn't it clearly predicted that the Messiah would have to suffer all these things before entering his glory?"* (Luke 24:25, NLT)

Ephesus = Desirable – Jesus had this to say to the Church of this city: *Yet I hold this against you: You have forsaken your first love. Remember the height from which you have fallen! Repent and do the things you did at first. If you do not repent, I will come to you and remove your lampstand from its place.* (Revelation 2:4-6, NIV)

Galatia = White – It was the Galatian Church in which Paul found that legalism and a works gospel had replaced a gospel of grace through faith (Galatians 3:1-14).

Gethsemane = Oil press – Garden where Jesus struggled in deep intercession the night before His death. After a time of intense agonizing prayer He proclaimed to the Father: *Abba, Father, all things are possible unto thee; take away this cup from me: nevertheless not what I will, but what thou wilt.* (Mark 14:36).

Gibeon = Hill city – The Gibeonites deceived the Israelites (who did not seek the Lord on the matter) into signing a treaty with them (Joshua 9)

Gilgal = Circle or rolling – *Then the LORD said to Joshua, "Today I have rolled away the reproach of Egypt from you." So the place has been called Gilgal to this day.* (Joshua 5:9, NIV)

Goshen = Drawing near – When the Lord brought plagues to punish Egypt none of them fell on Goshen which was the region in Egypt where God's people dwelt (Exodus 8:22)

Hebron = Friendship or society – The region where Abraham encountered the Lord and entertained angels (Genesis 18)

Jericho = Place of fragrance – The walls of the city fell after God's people marched, shouted and sounded the trumpet, opening the way for victory (Joshua 6)

Jerusalem = Vision of peace – The place where God's glory dwelt in the Old Testament temple (Psalm 26:8)

Joppa = Beauty – Place where Peter raised Dorca from the dead (Acts 9:36 – 40)

Jordan River = Descender – Place where John the Baptist baptized repentant sinners, river that miraculously parted to allow the Israelites passage into the Promised Land (Joshua 3:15-17)

Laodicea = Justice of the people – The Church of this city was found by the Lord to be lukewarm (Revelation 3:13-16)

Mt Mariah = Mountain on which the Holy Temple stood (2 Chronicles 3:1), Place where Abraham was willing to sacrifice his son as an act of obedient worship unto the Lord (Genesis 22:1-3)

Mt. Sinai = Mountain where Moses received the revelation of God's laws during a forty day period of divine and angelic visitation (Exodus 34:27-29)

Nazareth = Separated or sanctified – *Jesus said to them, "Only in his hometown, among his relatives and in his own house is a prophet without honor." He could not do any miracles there, except lay his hands on a few sick people and heal them. And he was amazed at their lack of faith.* (Mark 6:4-6, NIV)

Pergamum = Height; elevation – This city was so wicked that it was labeled by Jesus as the city "where Satan has his throne" (Revelation 2:13)

Philadelphia = Brotherly love – *"And to the angel of the church in Philadelphia write, 'These things says He who is holy, He who is true, "He who has the key of David, He who opens and no one shuts, and shuts and no one opens" "I know your works. See, I have set before you an open door, and no one can shut it; for you have a little strength, have kept My word, and have not denied My name."* (Revelation 3:7-8, NIV)

Philippi = Named after Philip of Macedonia – The people of the Philippian Church were very generous in giving of their finances to the cause of the gospel (Philippians 4:14-16)

Philistia = Land of sojourners – The Philistines constantly fought and harassed the people of God. (Ezekiel 25:15) For this reason the Philistines are often seen as a type of the flesh or sinful nature which is at odds with the Spirit: *For the desires of the flesh are opposed to the (Holy) Spirit, and the (desires of the) Spirit are opposed to the flesh (godless human nature); for these are antagonistic to each other (continually withstanding and in conflict with each other), so that you are not free but are prevented from doing what you desire to do.* (Galatians 5:16-18, AMP)

Samaria = Watch mountain or watchtower – The people of Samaria practiced a religion that was a mixture between the biblical faith and paganism (2 Kings 17:25-29)

Sardis = Prince of Joy – *"And to the angel of the church in Sardis write, 'these things says He who has the seven Spirits of God and the seven stars: "I know your works, that you have a name that you are alive, but you are dead. 2 Be watchful, and strengthen the things which remain, that are ready to die, for I* *have not found your works perfect before God"* (Revelation 3:1-2, NKJV)

Smyrna = Myrrh (symbolic of death) – The Christians of this city were slandered, persecuted and imprisoned (Revelation 2:8-11)

Sodom = Burning – A city destroyed by God because of its great sin (Genesis 19: 23-25)

Thessalonica = Victory over the Thessalians – In spite of great suffering and persecution in that city the Church shined in the darkness. As Paul wrote them in his letter: *We continually remember before our God and Father your work produced by faith, your labor prompted by love, and your endurance inspired by hope in our Lord Jesus Christ.* (1 Thessalonians 1:3, NIV)

Thyatira = A perfume; sacrifice of labor – In the words of Jesus to the Church of this city: *"Nevertheless, I have this against you: You tolerate that woman Jezebel, who calls herself a prophetess. By her teaching she misleads my servants into sexual immorality and the eating of food sacrificed to idols".* (Revelation 2:20, NIV)

Ziklag = Measure pressed down – David's camp in Ziklag was raided and the enemy carried off the possessions and families of David and his men. David however: *found strength in the Lord his God* and took back all that was stolen by the enemy (1 Samuel 30:3-6, NIV)

BIBLICAL SPICES AND PERFUMES

Aloe = Healing

Balm of Gilead = Healing (Jeremiah 8:22)

Calamus = Sacrificial Worship (Isaiah 43:24)

Cassia = The word cassia in Hebrew means 'stripped'. It signifies being stripped of pride and set apart, the worship of the saints (Psalm 45:7-8)

Cinnamon = The enticement of sin (Proverbs 7:12-17), the sweet smelling fragrance before the Lord of a child of God who is consecrated unto Him – cinnamon was a key ingredient of the anointing oil used in the Temple (Exodus 30:23)

Coriander = Manna from Heaven (Exodus 16:31, Numbers 11:7)

Frankincense = Prayer (Revelation 5:8, Psalm 141:2)

Galbanum = Sacrifice (Galbanum smells sweet when burned)

Myrrh = Death (John 19:38-40)

Spikenard = Precious and costly (Mark 14:3 AMP), the pouring out of oneself in worship and devotion to Jesus (John 12:3)

X. MISCELLANEOUS SYMBOLS

COURTROOM TERMS

*Again please keep in mind that I am listing symbolic meanings of these terms. I am not stating the obvious meanings.

Accuse = satan bringing accusation and slander against God's people (Revelation 12:10), Christians speaking evil about each other (James 4:11, AMP)

Adversary = satan as an adversary of the righteous (Job 2:2, AMP), the Lord and the angelic hosts as adversaries of the wicked (Numbers 22:21-23, NKJV)

Advocate = See **PEOPLE**

Acquit = To offer forgiveness to someone who hurt you (Luke 6:37, AMP) ... we are justified (acquitted, declared righteous, and given a right standing with God) through faith (Romans 5:1a)

Capital Offense = *The wages of sin is death* (Romans 6:23, KJV)

Condemned = Sentenced to eternal hell for rejecting Jesus as Savior (John 3:18), having overwhelming feelings of guilt even though the sin has been forgiven (Romans 8:1)

Convicted = The work of the Holy Spirit in revealing areas of sin and unrighteousness in our lives (John 16:7-9)

Dismissal = The Lord dismissing the slanderous accusations that satan makes against the children of God (Zechariah 3:1-5)

District Attorney = See **PEOPLE**

Evidence = The testimony of Jesus Christ (Revelation 1:9, AMP), miracles (John 14:11)

Guilty = *For the person who keeps all of the laws except one is as guilty as a person who has broken all of God's laws.* (James 2:10, NLT)

Judge = See **PEOPLE**

Judgment = *For we must all appear before the judgment seat of Christ, that each one may receive what is due him for the things done while in the body, whether good or bad.* (2 Corinthians 5:10, NIV), the final Great White Throne judgment of the dead at the end of the age (Revelation 20:11- 14), God's wrath poured out on the unrepentant wicked (2 Peter 2:5), The Lords discipline and chastening of his people for the purpose of bringing restoration and repentance (1 Peter 4:17), *then let us no more criticize and blame and pass judgment on one another, but rather decide and endeavor never to put a stumbling block or an obstacle or a hindrance in the way of a brother.* (Romans 14:13, AMP)

Law = The commandments and requirements of the Lord (Luke 1:6, Amplified Bible)

Lawyer = See **PEOPLE**

Mercy = The Lord's willingness to show grace and forgiveness (Psalm 78:38)

Murder = A heart full of anger, hatred or malice toward another (Matthew 5:22, 1 John 3:15), speaking curses over someone's life (Proverbs 18:21)

Offense = Sin and disobedience to the Lord (Leviticus 5:19)

Pardon = *I am writing to you, little children, because for His name's sake your sins are forgiven (pardoned through His Name and on account of confessing His Name)* (1 John 2:12, AMP)

Testimony = The truth of God's Word (Isaiah 8:20), a miraculous work of healing or deliverance as a testimony of God's love and mercy (Matthew 8:3-5), *and this good news of the kingdom (the Gospel) will be preached throughout the whole world as a testimony to all the nations* (Matthew 24:14, AMP), *worship God: for the testimony of Jesus is the spirit of prophecy.* (Revelation 19:10b, KJV), The testimony of one who has witnessed God's power, love, provision, etc working in or through his/her life (John 4:39)

PARTS OF THE BODY

Arms = God's Power and strength (Deuteronomy 4:34), mans power and strength (2 Chronicles 32:8) **broken arm** – lacking strength or power

Back = The past, the part of a person that is most vulnerable to attack

Belly or Stomach = Human appetite for worldly pleasures (Philippians 3:19, Romans 16:18, NKJV), lust of the flesh (1 Corinthians 6:13), emotions, our innermost spiritual being (John 7:38, KJV)

Blood = Our natural, earthy lives (1 Corinthians 15:50, MSG), justice and retribution (2 Samuel 1:16), anguish (Luke 22:44) **blood of Jesus** – purification from sin (1 John 1:7), forgiveness of sin (Matthew 26:28), the new covenant (Mark 14:24), the cost of Jesus' sacrifice (Acts 20:28), salvation and justification (Romans 5:9), guilt (Isaiah 59:3)

Body = The Church – *so in Christ we who are many form one body, and each member belongs to all the others.* (Romans 12:5, NIV)

Bones = The human body (Job 2:5), Israel (Ezekiel 37:11), the essence of a person (Genesis 2:23)

Brain = The mind

Breast = The Church giving spiritual milk and care to the new believer, idolatry as spiritual prostitution (Ezekiel 23:1- 7), love and nurture from a wife (Proverbs 5:18-20), sexual temptation (Proverbs 5:20), overflowing abundance (Isaiah 66:10-11, NIV), motherhood, **beating one's breast** – repentance for sin (Luke 18:13) or great sorrow (Nahum 2:7)

Cheeks = Trial and persecution (Job 16:10, Isaiah 50:6), love and patience (Matthew 5:38-40), countenance (Song of Solomon 5:13), expressions of emotions

Ears = Listening attentively with understanding (Proverbs 2:2, Isaiah 48:8), hearing and obeying God's voice (Revelation 2:7), a counselor, prophecy *deafness* – refusing to listen to God's voice (Psalm 106:25), refusing to hear the cries of the needy (Isaiah 47:15, NLT), unwilling to hear the truth (Acts 7:51, NLT), those who turn a deaf ear to wisdom and wise counsel (Proverbs 5:1), *earwax* – blockage in hearing God's voice, inability or unwillingness to accept spoken truth

Elbow = *Appoint Aaron and his sons to minister as priests; anyone else who tries to elbow his way in will be put to death.* (Numbers 3:10, MSG)

Eyes = The ability to see into the supernatural spiritual realm (Numbers 24:15, Numbers 22:31), jealousy (1 Samuel 18:9), the lust of the eyes (Matthew 5:29, Numbers 15:39), favor (Genesis 30:27), a prophetic seer (Numbers 24:4), a person's mindset or way of perceiving something (Numbers 27:14, Deuteronomy 25:3), tears and sadness, discernment (Proverbs 20:8), the watchman (Ezekiel 33:6), visual prophetic revelatory experiences such as visions (Ezekiel 1:1), seduction (2 Kings 9:30), just retribution; eye for an eye (Exodus 21:24) *blindness* – unable to recognize one's own sin (Psalm 36:2, NLT), *blinded by tears of pain and frustration.* (Psalm 88:9, MSG), those with no true spiritual vision or direction (Matthew 15:14), *The god of this age has blinded the minds of unbelievers, so that they cannot see the light of the gospel of the glory of Christ, who is the image of God.* (2 Corinthians 4:4, NIV), one who sees others through eyes of hatred (1 John 2:10-11) *cataract* – a hindrance to prophetic vision *black eye* – a ruined reputation (Proverbs 6:24, MSG)

Face = Expression of emotion (Genesis 4:6), the radiance of the glory of God (Exodus 34:30), a good reputation, a surface appearance of something, dignity, God's favor (Numbers 6:25) *hidden face* – shame or fear (Genesis 4:6), the withdrawal of the favor of the Lord (Deuteronomy 31:18), great sorrow (2 Samuel 19:4) *facedown* – humility, reverence and honor before God (Joshua 5:14) *face to face* – a direct confrontation, deep intimate friendship (Exodus 33:11)

Fat = One who gives him/herself over to worldly sinful pleasures (Job 15:27, AMP), the proud who are wealthy by the world's standards but lacking in the eyes of God (Psalm 119:69-71, NKJV), gluttony (Proverbs 23:19-20), a low self image, financial waste

Feet = Evangelism (Isaiah 52:6-8), taking territory from the wicked as an inheritance for the godly (Joshua 14:9), one's walk with the Lord (Psalm 17:5), the ability to stand in higher realms of the Spirit (2 Samuel 22:34), victory (2 Samuel 22:40, Romans 16:20) *bare feet* – weeping and mourning (2 Samuel 15:30, Micah 1:8), standing in the presence of the Lord (Exodus 3:5), poverty, humiliation (2 Chronicles 28:15) *lame foot* – putting confidence in an unreliable person in times of trouble is like ... walking on a lame foot. (Proverbs 25:19, NLT) *footsteps or footprints* – *He followed in the footsteps of his father, serving and worshiping the same foul gods his father had served.* (2 Kings 21:21, MSG), *He behaved well in the eyes of God, following in the footsteps of his father Amaziah. He was a loyal seeker of God* (2 Chronicles 26:4, MSG), the path one walks in life (Psalm 119:133

Forehead = One's thoughts (Exodus 13:9), one's willfulness or determination (Isaiah 48:4, Ezekiel 3:9)

Gall Bladder = Bitterness

Hair = Dedication or consecration to the Lord (Numbers 6:19), seduction (2 Kings 9:30), the Lord's great love and care for His people (Luke 12:7), a covering (1 Corinthians 11:15) *beard* – dignity, maturity and manhood **pulling out own hair** – repentance, grief, mourning (Ezra 9:3), overwhelming stress

Hands or Fingers = Human work and labor (Deuteronomy 2:7), human power and strength (Deuteronomy 8:17), warfare (Job 15:25), **the hand of God** – God's creative power (Isaiah 48:13), God's power to deliver His people (Exodus 32:11), signs wonders and miracles (Deuteronomy 7:19), God's mighty deeds (Deuteronomy 3:24), divine judgment (1 Samuel 5:11) **outstretched or uplifted hands** – prayer (1 Kings 8:22), worship (Nehemiah 8:6), the Lord's grace and love in calling people to come to Him (Proverbs 1:23-25), one who is reaching out to God (Job 11:13), pronouncing a blessing (Luke 24:50) giving, **one hand raised** – a vow or oath (Ezekiel 20:15) **folded hands** – prayer, laziness, inaction **pointing finger** – self righteous accusation or gossip (Isaiah 59:3), **Finger of God** – the Holy Spirit or the manifestation of the power of God (Luke 11:20), **right hand** – human strength **left hand** – God's strength made perfect in our weakness **dirty hands** – sin and evil (Psalm 26:10,NLT), hard work (Nehemiah 3:5, MSG), **laying on of hands** – commissioning into the Lord's service (Numbers 27:22-23), impartation (Deuteronomy 34:9), healing prayer (Matthew 8:3), **fingerprint** – individuality, leaving a mark or imprint in a person's life or a situation **all thumbs** – ineptitude

Head = Jesus as the Head of the body of Christ (Ephesians 4:15), authority (1 Corinthians 11:3), the Greek word for head which is *kephale* can also be translated "source" or "beginning", place of honor (1 Samuel 9:22), the mind (thoughts, reason, intellect, etc), one who is blessed with authority, finances and social standing (Deuteronomy 28:12-14) **big head** – pride (Job 20:6), **head down** – shame, sorrow or grief (Job 10:15, Psalm 35:14), **uplifted head** – dignity (Psalm 3:3) hope, pride **head shaking** – scorn or derision

(Psalm 64:8), disbelief

Heart = The inner man (Ephesians 3:16, NKJ), feelings and emotions (Genesis 6:6, Genesis 34:3), one's thought life (Genesis 6:5, Ecclesiastes 3:17), courage (Deuteronomy 1:28, Joshua 5:1), deep desires (2 Samuel 3:21, Job 19:27), one's affections and devotion (2 Samuel 15:61, Kings 11:2), one's moral character (1 Kings 9:4), the core of an issue, one's motives (Proverbs 12:20)

Jaw = A dangerous and distressful situation (Job 36:16), the ultimate inability of the wicked to escape judgment (Isaiah 30:28)

Knees = Prayer and supplication (1 Kings 8:54), honor and reverence (1 Kings 1:31, Esther 3:2), worship (Psalm 95:6), submission (Psalm 22:28-30)

Legs = Human strength (Psalm 147:10, Daniel 5:6), grace in movement (Song of Solomon 7:1)

Lips = The words we speak whether good (Exodus 13:9, Job 33:3) or evil (Exodus 23:13, Psalm 12:3), shouts of joy (Job 8:21), seductive words (Proverbs 5:3), see also **Mouth**

Liver or Kidney = The cleansing power of the Holy Spirit (1 John 1:9), the blood of Jesus (Hebrews 9:13-14)

Loins = Strength and endurance (1 Kings 18:46, NKJV), righteousness (Isaiah 11:5, NKJV), a clear and sober mind (1 Peter 1:13), the potential for new birth (Jeremiah 30:6, NKJV)

Mouth = Words we speak, intimacy with Jesus (Song of Solomon 1:2) a spoken curse or lie (Job 31:30, Psalm 59:12), a spoken blessing (Proverbs 11:11) laughter (Job 8:21), encouragement (Job 16:5), mocking and jeering (Job 16:10), the sweet taste of evil to the wicked (Job 20:12), wise instruction (Job 22:22), singing praises to the Lord (Psalm 40:3), prayer (Psalm 54:2), spoken vows to the Lord (Psalm 66:14), carnal appetites (Ecclesiastes 6:7), the confession that Jesus is Lord (Romans 10:9) *the mouth of the Lord* – God's promises (2 Chronicles 6:15), God's provision of our needs such as food and water (Nehemiah 9:20), the Word of God (Job 23:12),

Neck = The human will, authority (Daniel 5:16), strength (Song of Solomon 4:4), elegance or stateliness (Song of Solomon 7:4) *stiff-necked* – stubborn or proud (Psalm 73:6), a rebellious attitude toward God (Deuteronomy 31:27) *bowed neck* – bondage and defeat (Psalm 105:18, Jeremiah 27:11), prayer

Nose = Spiritual discernment (1 Corinthians 12:10), defeat and domination (2 Chronicles 33:11), see also **Odor** and **Fragrance**

Palm = God's strength and power (1 Chronicles 29:12, MSG), the great love and care that Jesus has for us evidenced by His death on the Cross (Isaiah 49:15-16), abuse (Matthew 26:67)

Scar = An emotional wound or trauma that hasn't healed, *for I bear on my body the (brand) marks of the Lord Jesus (the wounds, scars, and other outward evidence of persecutions-- these testify to His ownership of me)!* (Galatians 6:17, AMP),

Shoulder = Burden bearing or carrying a heavy load (Genesis 49:15, Isaiah 9:4), rest and security for God's beloved children (Deuteronomy 33:12), governmental authority (Isaiah 9:6, Isaiah 22:21-23)

Skeleton = Occult, rebellion, death, a secret that if uncovered would bring disgrace or scandal (Job 10:5-7, MSG, Daniel 6:4, MSG), a basic framework

Skin = Personal boundaries, outward appearance *thin skinned* – easily offended *thick skinned* – not easily offended *rash* – an issue of setting proper boundaries with others, shame, making a *'rash'* decision as a play on words

Spine or Backbone = Courage and determination (2 Chronicles 32:8, MSG), flexibility

Teeth = Wisdom (Psalm 37:30, MSG), understanding of the Word of God, God's wrath (Job 16:9), oppression of the poor by the wicked (Proverbs 30:13-14), viscous attacks against the people of God (Psalm 124:6), a personal relationship (Song of Solomon 4:2), the ability to think a matter through, children suffering for the sins of past generations (Jeremiah 31:29), a ferocious tearing attack of the enemy (Joel 1:6), just retribution (Exodus 21:24, Leviticus 24:20), *false teeth* – Worldly wisdom or philosophy, an ungodly personal relationship, a wrong understanding of a situation *gnashing or grinding teeth* – great sorrow of the unsaved whose final plight is outer darkness (Matthew 13:42), mocking disdain displayed by the ungodly (Psalm 35:16, NIV) *teeth falling out* – a lack of wisdom or proper understanding, a broken relationship, a reflection of inner shame and rejection, reflects undue concern or anxiety over one's outward appearance *rotting teeth* – neglect of God's word, neglect of a relationship that is going bad *broken tooth* – *Putting confidence in an unreliable person in times of trouble is like chewing with a broken tooth* (Proverbs 25:19, NLT)

Thigh = Strength and power (Revelation 19:16, Psalm 45:3)

Tongue = eloquence or slowness of speech (Exodus 4:10), slander and false accusations (Job 5:21, NLT, Psalm 31:20), curses, lies and threats (Psalm 10:7, NIV), verbal expressions of joy (Psalm 16:9, Psalm 126:2), great thirst (Psalm 22:15), praise unto the Lord; whether spoken or sung (Psalm 35:28, Psalm 51:14), harmful and deceitful words (Psalm 52:4), God' people sharing testimonies of His righteous deeds (Psalm 71:24, NLT), the verbal threats of the wicked (Psalm 73:8-10), lying (Psalm 78:36), words of wisdom bringing healing (Proverbs 12:18), cursing and blessing imparting death or life (Proverbs 18:21), false flattery (Proverbs 28:23), false prophets (Jeremiah 23:31), speaking in unknown tongues as a part of one' prayer language or as a corporate expression that needs to be interpreted (1Corinthians 14:2, 1 Corinthians 14:27)

Umbilical Cord = An unhealthy co-dependent relationship, a soul tie

Womb = The potential for the birthing of a ministry, business, etc, the origin of something (Job 38:29, NIV)

SETTINGS AND PLACES

Animal Shelter = A ministry to those who feel neglected, abandoned, unwanted and/or alone, homeless ministry

Aquarium = A church (fish in this case symbolizing Christians)

Ballroom = Fun, worldliness, intimacy with Jesus our Bridegroom, a call to dance ministry

Bandage = A healing ministry, emotional wounds being healed by God (Psalm 147:2-6, MSG)

Band-Aid = A temporary solution to a problem, a quick fix, healing

Bank = The sure promises of God, money as an idol (Job 31:24, MSG), the need to save up, worldly wealth as opposed to true riches (Proverbs 3:13, MSG), greed, our heavenly rewards (Matthew 6:19-21)

Barn = Kingdom of God (Luke 3:17), the Lord's great provision (Psalm 144:13, NIV), hoarding and greed (Luke 12:15-22)

Beauty Parlor = Vanity (Proverbs 31:30, KJV), a ministry that brings restoration and wholeness into the lives of broken women

Building = The Body of Christ (Ephesians 2:21)

Cabin = A place of peace, rest and refuge (Psalm 55:6-8, MSG, Jeremiah 9:1, MSG)

City = The Church (Hebrews 12:22, Matthew 5:14), a place of refuge (Numbers 35:25)

Courthouse = The judgment seat of Christ (2 Corinthians 5:10), the great white throne judgment of the dead (Revelation 20:11-12), the heavenly court (Daniel 7:9-10), conviction of sin by the Holy Spirit (John 16:8), the condemnation and accusation of God's people by the enemy (Revelation 12:10)

Doctor's Office = A ministry of physical healing, Jesus as healer, see also **Doctor**

Factory = A Church or ministry with a lack of creativity, diversity or spontaneity, a productive Church or ministry

Farm = A church or ministry (1 Corinthians 3:9), giving and receiving (2 Corinthians 9:6) outreach ministry (Matthew 13:3-9), see also **Farmer, Harvest-Time,** and **Planting**

Fortress = The Lord as our protector and defender (Psalm 18:1-3), the Lord as our Savior (Psalm 28:8, NIV), the Lord as our place of refuge in times of trouble (Psalm 59:16, NIV)

Gas Station = A Church or ministry that provides an atmosphere for God's people to receive ministry from the Lord, an individual's devotional life

Gym = Competition, pride, training for Spiritual maturation (1 Timothy 4:8, 1 Corinthians 9:25-27)

Hangar = A time of waiting for something to "take off" such as a ministry or a business

Hospital = A Church (place of healing), or a healing ministry
ICU – an acute or dire situation requiring immediate attention
emergency room – an emergency situation showing that ignoring it or neglecting to address it is no longer an option

Hotel = A transitional or temporary life season, travel

House = Typically a house is symbolic of the dreamer's or dream subject's life (Matthew 7:25.) Various rooms and places in the house symbolize different aspects of his or her existence. *house in disrepair* – spiritual, physical or emotional neglect *damaged house* – a need for inner healing and restoration, sickness, a broken home

- **Attic** = Memories of the past
- **Backyard** = The past
- **Basement** = Emotions that are repressed or under the surface, hidden sin, hidden agendas, hidden motives
- **Bathroom** = Repentance, deliverance and cleansing of sin **dirty bathroom** = a person, church, etc that neglects repentance or inner healing
- **Bedroom** = Intimacy with Jesus, meditation and reflection on the Lord, rest, sexual issues or marital intimacy
- **Ceiling** = A spiritual covering, a hindrance in the life of someone who desires to go to a higher spiritual realm in the Lord, a hindrance or limitation to one's promotion or prosperity
- **Cesspool** = A nation, city region, organization, etc totally overrun by sin and or/ idolatry (Jeremiah 23:10-12, MSG), moral filth
- **Childhood Home** = The dreamer perceives an issue in his or her life as if it were still the past, issues from the dreamer's childhood that are unresolved, the Lord wants to remind the dreamer of all He has set him or her free from, generational blessings, curses and or inheritance
- **Closet** = Place of secret prayer and intimacy (Matthew 6:6, KJV), A Christian who is not willing to openly declare his/her faith (Acts 19:8, MSG), stored up past memories, hidden sin (NLT)
- **Corridor** = A passage from one phase or season in your life to another, transition
- **Cornerstone** = Jesus: *Therefore thus saith the Lord God,*

Behold, I lay in Zion for a foundation a stone, a tried stone, a precious corner stone, a sure foundation: he that believeth shall not make haste. (Isaiah 28:16, KJV)

- **Door** = Jesus as the only way to salvation (John 10:9), the entryway to the heart (Revelation 3:20, Genesis 4:6-7), *A person without self-control is like a house with its doors and windows knocked out.* (Proverbs 25:28, MSG), ***door mat*** – one who suffers abuse and indignation (Proverbs 29:21, MSG), ***open door*** – opportunity for ministry (Colossians 4:3, 1 Corinthians 16:9, NLT), an open entryway into a desirable situation such as a job opportunity, an open portal for the enemy to enter into a situation ***closed door*** – hidden sin (Job 31:33, MSG, Psalm 58:1, MSG), Secret plans of the enemy (Isaiah 8:12, NLT), protection from enemy attack (Nehemiah 6:9-10, NIV), secret prayer (Matthew 6:6), the eternal damnation of the wicked (Luke 13:24-25), a seeming opportunity that doesn't materialize, a secret meeting ***narrow door*** = Jesus as the only entryway into the Kingdom of Heaven (Luke 13:23-25) ***back door*** – the past, a means of escape, an entryway to the intrusion of the enemy coming in an unexpected way

- **Doorstep** = Transition, something too close at hand to be overlooked (Isaiah 9:8, MSG), "When you enter a town and are received, eat what they set before you, heal anyone who is sick, and tell them, 'God's kingdom is right on your doorstep!' (Luke 10:8-9. MSG)

- **Driveway** = The beginning or the end of a journey

- **Facade** = An illusory or deceptive appearance

- **Fire Escape** = *If any person's work which he has built [on this foundation, that is, any outcome of his effort] remains [and survives this test], he will receive a reward. But if any person's work is burned up [by the test], he will suffer the loss [of his reward]; yet he himself will be saved, but only as [one who has barely escaped] through fire.* (1 Corinthians 3:14-16AMP), a way of escape from a dangerous situation, a way of escape when a Christian is tempted to sin (1 Corinthians 10:13)

- **Fireplace** = The heart, family, the comfort of the Holy Spirit, romance
- **Foundation** = Whatever the dream subject has built his or her life on; whether God, money, power, career, etc. Jesus is the only firm foundation on which to build a life (Luke 6:47-49, NLT), God's truth (2 Timothy 2:19, NLT), faith (Hebrews 11:1, MSG), a victorious, overcoming Christian (Revelation 3:12)
- **Front Yard or Porch** = The present or future, outreach and evangelism
- **Furnace** = God's future burning judgment against the wicked resulting in total destruction (Malachi 4:1, NIV, Genesis 19:27-29), an extremely painful and oppressive situation (Deuteronomy 4:19-21), affliction and suffering in our lives which the Lord uses to test and refine us (Isaiah 48:9-11), the eternal fires of hell (Matthew 13:41-42)
- **Kitchen** = Christian service (Luke 10:38-40, MSG) eating (meditating on and studying the Bible) and drinking (receiving the ministry of the Holy Spirit), see also **Eating** and **FOOD AND DRINK**
- **Living Room** = The social part of one's life, family life, Christian fellowship
- **New Home** = A new season of life, one's life since becoming born again
- **Pillar** = Jesus as our strength and support (Song of Solomon 5:1), the Church (1 Timothy 3:15), strong leaders in the Church (Galatians 2:9)
- **Roof** = The Mind, God's covering and protection
- **Stairs or Elevator** = See **Up** and **Down**
- **Wall** = Emotional Boundaries, sin boundaries, social boundaries, lack of transparency, protection (1 Samuel 25:16, NLT), an obstacle or hindrance (2 Samuel 22:30, NLT) *gap in the wall* – a way left open for enemy attack (Ezekiel 13:4-6), intercession and spiritual warfare =

Ezekiel 22:29-30, someone with poor social and/or emotional boundaries, a breakthrough in a difficult situation

- **Window** = Prophetic Revelation (Matthew 6:22), way of escape (1 Samuel 19:11-12) *locked window* – protection from the enemy (Jeremiah 9:21), *open window* – blessings from Heaven (Jeremiah 47:1-4),way of escape (1 Samuel 19:11- 12), open portal for the enemy, *back window* – the past, *front window* – the present or future

Laundromat = The Lord's work in removing our sin and clothing us in righteousness (Zechariah 3:2-4, MSG)

Lawyer's Office = Entering into the presence of Jesus who is our advocate with the Father, a legalistic Church or ministry, see also **Lawyer**

Library = Bible study, keeping a journal, authoring or writing, divine revelation, heaven where the books are kept such as the Book of Life (Revelation 3:5) and books which keep an account of each person's life (Revelation 20:12, Daniel 7:10)

Lighthouse = Jesus as the light of the world (Isaiah 42:5, MSG, John 8:12), the Church reflecting the light of Jesus (Matthew 5:14)

Locker Room = Preparation and readiness, a sign that a big opportunity is near

Mansion = God the Father's house in Heaven (John 14:1-3, KJV), the wealth of the wicked (Amos 5:11, NIV, Amos 3:14-15, NLT), a Church as a place of great spiritual riches, a Churches that is materialistic and worldly minded, great prosperity

Museum = A church, ministry or denomination that display their past victories while having little interest in what God would have them do today

Oasis = rest, peace and provision in the midst of a difficult season (Exodus 15:27)

Office = A place of employment, financial provision, a ministry 'office' such as pastor, teacher, prophet, etc. (Ephesians 4:1)

Orphanage = A Church that lacks leaders who serve as true spiritual fathers and mothers

Palace = The Lord's throne room in Heaven (Psalm 18:6, MSG, Amos 9:6, NIV), a ruler or authority (John 18:28), the wealth of the wicked (Amos 3:14-15, NLT)

Pharmacy = Physical healing, addiction, dependence on man rather than God

Power Plant = The Kingdom of Heaven as the source of divine power or the kingdom of hell as the source of demonic power

Prison = Bondage to sin, (Romans 7:23, NIV), addictions, the unsaved who have not tasted the freedom that is found only in Christ, (Galatians 3:22), the bondage of unforgiveness (Matthew 18:21-35)

Psychologist's Office = A ministry of inner healing, Jesus as the one who heals our minds and emotions, see also **Psychologist**

Restaurant = A Church or ministry as a place of eating the word (Hebrews 5: 11-14) and drinking in the Holy Spirit (1 Corinthians 12:13), A ministry of feeding the poor (Matthew 25: 34-36), blessing your enemy (Romans 12:20)

Saloon = A place of sin (Psalm 1:1, MSG), drunkenness,

addiction, worldly pleasures, see also **Liquor and Wine**

School = a period of being tested by the Lord, a teaching ministry, discipleship, the study of the Word of God, a time of preparation, a Church, a situation or problem in the present that is similar to a circumstance during the time the dreamer or dream subject was in school **university** – a high level of testing, see also **Teacher**

Shrine = Idolatry (1 Kings 12:31, NKJV)

Skyscraper = The prideful and arrogant (Isaiah 2:11-17, MSG), the Kingdom of God, man's kingdom (Ezekiel 31:3, MSG), a large multi-faceted ministry, ministry in a big city

Slaughterhouse = God's wrath poured out in judgment on the wicked (Isaiah 34:5-7, MSG), great wickedness and violence, murderous rage

Spa = Rest, refreshing, vanity

Sports Arena or Stadium = Competition, teamwork, see also **Athlete**

Supermarket = A Church offering a great variety of ministries related to feeding the Body of Christ

Tent = A place of 24 hour/ 7 days per week prayer and worship as established by King David (Acts 15:16, 1 Chronicles 9:32-34), a place of encountering God (Exodus 33:7), the heavens (Psalm 104:2), the human body as a temple of the Holy Spirit (2 Corinthians 5:1)

Theater = Hypocrisy, emotional drama, a drama ministry, see also **Actor**

Tower = The Lord as our shelter and strength (Psalm 61:3), rebellion against God (Genesis 11:3-5), God our Savior (2 Samuel 22:51, KJV), the place of the watchman who discerns the work of the enemy and warns the people (2 Kings 9:16-17, KJV), the Lord as higher than our enemies (Psalm 144:2), the name of the Lord (Proverbs 18:10), the arrogant and prideful (Isaiah 2:14-15, NLT), see also **Watchman**

Waiting Room, Parking Lot, Airport Terminal, Train Station, Bus Terminal = Time of waiting or transition, travel is in store, see also **MODES OF TRANSPORTATION**

Warehouse or Storehouse = Greed and hoarding of wealth (Luke 12:17-19, AMP), the heart (Luke 6:45, AMP, Matthew 12:35 AMP), a sign to beginning saving one's resources (Genesis 41:35), the Church (Malachi 3:10), memories of the past

MILITARY TERMS

About Face = A total change in one's life direction, total change in one's way of thinking, *Life ascends to the heights for the thoughtful— it's a clean about-face from descent into hell.* (Proverbs 15:24, MSG)

Absent without Leave or a Deserter = A backsliding Christian who is no longer in fellowship (Daniel 11:35, AMP), a Christian who walks away from the ministry God called him/her to, a parent who walks away from his/her children

Air Raid Siren = The cry of the prophetic watchman that an attack of the enemy is at hand (Ezekiel 33:1-4)

Ambush = *The words of the wicked are like a murderous ambush, but the words of the godly save lives* (Proverbs 12:6), an unexpected and sudden surprise attack of the enemy (Hosea 6:9), sin and temptation that lurks in the darkness to entrap those who do not guard their hearts in the Lord (Proverbs 7:12, AMP)

Ammunition = *I'd rather die than give anyone ammunition to discredit me or impugn my motives* (1 Corinthians 9:15, MSG)

Anti-Aircraft Artillery = Spiritual warfare prayer

Armor = *Therefore, put on every piece of God's armor so you will be able to resist the enemy in the time of evil. Then after the battle you will still be standing firm. Stand your ground, putting on the belt of truth and the body armor of God's righteousness. For shoes, put on the peace that comes from the Good News so that you will be fully prepared. In addition to all of these, hold up the shield of faith to stop the fiery arrows of the devil. Put on salvation as your helmet, and take the sword of the Spirit, which is the word of God.*

Army = *Then suddenly there appeared with the angel an army of the troops of heaven (a heavenly knighthood), praising God* (Luke 2:13, AMP), The Church as the army of God (Song of Solomon 6:4, Philippians 2:25, NIV), *spiritual forces of evil in the heavenly realms* (Ephesians 6:12, NIV)

Assassination = An attempt to destroy someone's reputation through slander or gossip

Barricade = divine protection, angelic protection, limitation, hindrance

Battle = A confrontation between one's flesh and spirit (James 4:1), a clash between the Kingdom of Heaven and demonic powers (Revelation 16:14), a fight between angelic and demonic beings (Daniel 10:13), conflicts in relationships, anger or rage

Battle Fatigue = One who has become worn down and wearied by life's struggles

Battleground = A place where there is great spiritual warfare, emotional conflicts or constant arguments

Bayonet = A verbal assault, an up-close personal attack, the Word of God

Bomb = A volatile situation that will explode if not dealt with, underlying anger that is about to erupt, an idea that is not going to succeed

Bombardment = A relentless attack of the enemy, a strategy of sustained Spiritual warfare prayer against the strongholds of satan

Booby Traps or Land Mines = The hidden traps set by the wicked or the enemy: *They booby-trapped my path; I thought I*

was dead and done for. They dug a mantrap to catch me (Psalm 57:6, MSG)

Breastplate = *But since we belong to the day, let us be self-controlled, putting on faith and love as a breastplate* (1 Thessalonians 5:8a, NIV), righteousness (Ephesians 6:14, NKJV)

Bulletproof Vest = God's protection, forgiveness, faith, righteousness

Camouflage = *For such men are false apostles, deceitful workmen, masquerading as apostles of Christ* (2 Corinthians 11:13, NIV), the devil disguising himself as an angel of light (2 Corinthians 11:14)

Cease Fire = An end or temporary end to hostilities and division

Civil War = A Church split, great division within a Church, organization, family, etc.

Counterattack = Hitting back at the enemy through prayer, outreach, etc after receiving a demonic attack, the enemy attacking the church after a time of victory or great soul-winning

Defense = *...for God is my Defense, my Fortress, and High Tower* (Psalm 59:17, AMP), wisdom (Ecclesiastes 7:12, AMP), faith, Ephesians 6:16), God's truth and faithfulness, (Psalm 91:4, AMP)

Divide and Conquer = The enemy's work of bringing division among God's people thereby destroying unity (1 Corinthians 11:17-18)

Encroachment = The enemy making gradual inroads into

one's heart or mind, sin gradually advancing and taking ground in one's life (Song of Solomon 2:15)

Enemy = satan and his demons (1 Peter 5:8), death (1 Corinthians 15:26), *You adulterous people, don't you know that friendship with the world is hatred toward God? Anyone who chooses to be a friend of the world becomes an enemy of God. (James 4:4),* the sinful nature as an enemy of the Spirit (Galatians 5:16-18), sin

Frontal Assault = A head-on attack of the enemy

Gas Mask = Shows the need to discern and protect oneself in a toxic spiritual environment

Grenade = A volatile issue or situation, gossip or malicious words, the power of God destroying the works of the enemy

Gun = The power of God, murderous rage, demonic attack, slanderous words, *Don't shoot off your mouth, or speak before you think* (Ecclesiastes 5:2, MSG)

Helmet = The confidence of our salvation (1 Thessalonians 5:8, NLT), protecting one's mind against enemy attack

High Ground = Holiness and integrity (1 Corinthians 7:24, MSG), pride (Romans 2:1, MSG), a place of safety in the Lord (Romans 2:1, MSG)

Infiltration = *What has happened is that some people have infiltrated our ranks (our Scriptures warned us this would happen), who beneath their pious skin are shameless scoundrels.* (Jude 1:4, MSG), the demonic work of placing unholy thoughts in the minds of believers (2 Corinthians 10:5)

Invasion = *My repose is shattered, my peace destroyed. No rest for me, ever—death has invaded life."* (Job 3:26, MSG), the intrusion of sickness or disease, an onslaught of sin or wickedness in a community, city, nation, etc (Psalm 55:10, NLT), the Church invading the kingdom of darkness through prayer, evangelism, etc

Military Strategy = The plotting and planning of the enemy against God's people (Isaiah 8:10, MSG), God's strategy for His children in prayer, worship, evangelism, etc to tear down the devil's strongholds and advance the Kingdom of Heaven (Joshua 6:1-7)

Minefield = A potentially dangerous situation, a situation that is laden with traps

Mine Sweeper = The Lord's work of uncovering and destroying the hidden traps of the enemy

Peace = ...*freedom from all the distresses that are experienced as the result of sin* (Luke 7:50b, AMP), *freedom from fears, agitating passions, and moral conflicts* (1 Peter 5:14, AMP), a heart at rest in the Lord's love and protection (Psalm 4:8), peace between God and man because of the sacrifice of Jesus (Isaiah 53:5), forgiveness and reconciliation (Matthew 5:23-25, CEV), harmony among brothers and sisters in Christ (Mark 9:49), a church that lacks disorder and confusion (1 Corinthians 14:33)

Radar = Spiritual discernment, prophetic revelation of an approaching enemy attack

Raid = A sudden surprise attack of the enemy (Job 1:15, NLT), an intensive outreach campaign designed to take souls away from the hands of satan and bring them into the Kingdom of Heaven

Reconnaissance = Spiritual mapping: *"Superimposing our understanding of forces and events in the spiritual domain onto*

places and circumstances in the material world." – from <u>The Last of the Giants</u> by George Otis Jr., 1991 Chosen Books

Retreat = *The Devil retreated temporarily, lying in wait for another opportunity.* (Luke 4:13, MSG), *When I pray, LORD God, my enemies will* **retreat***, because I know for certain that you are with me.* (Psalm 56:9, CEV), backsliding into sin (Hosea 11:7, AMP), shrinking back because of shame or fear (Hebrews 10:38-39, AMP)

Rubble = A life that has been battered and broken by abuse and great hardship, a life that has crumpled because of sin and rebellion, God's judgment (Micah 1:6)

Shell Shocked = A person who is stunned and emotionally broken by a constant barrage of traumatic situations

Shield = Faith: *Above all, taking the shield of faith, wherewith ye shall be able to quench all the fiery darts of the wicked.* (Ephesians 6:16, KJV), the Lord as our Protector (Psalm 3:3), the favor of the Lord (Psalm 5:12)

Siege = An attack of the enemy with the intent of cutting off the victim from others including the Lord, a relentless enemy attack (Psalm 27:2-3), continual and specifically targeted Spiritual warfare prayer that attacks the strongholds of the kingdom of darkness

Smoke Screen = Deceit (Proverbs 12:17, MSG), hypocrisy (Matthew 5:33-34, MSG), insincere flattery (1 Thessalonians 2:5, MSG), the glory of God blocking the vision of the enemy

Soldier = See **PEOPLE**

Sword = The Word of God (Hebrews 4:12, Ephesians 6:17), division (Matthew 10:34), violence (Matthew 26:52), divine judgment (Job 19:29), slanderous evil words (Psalm 55:21), an adulteress (Psalm 55:21), lying or giving false testimony (Proverbs 25:18), a calling to preach or teach the Word of God **double edge sword** – *For the word of God is living and active. Sharper than any double-edged sword, it penetrates even to dividing soul and spirit, joints and marrow; it judges the thoughts and attitudes of the heart.* (Hebrews 4:12, NIV), something than can do good but also cause harm, an adulteress (Proverbs 5:3-5, NIV)

Stronghold or Beachhead = The Lord as our fortress of protection (Psalm 18:2, NIV, Joel 3:16, NIV), anyplace in our hearts or minds where satan has gained a foothold (Ephesians 4:26-27), *We are human, but we don't wage war as humans do. We use God's mighty weapons, not worldly weapons, to knock down the strongholds of human reasoning and to destroy false arguments. We destroy every proud obstacle that keeps people from knowing God. We capture their rebellious thoughts and teach them to obey Christ.* (2 Corinthians 10:3-5, NLT), a pioneering forerunner church that opens the door for Kingdom advancement in a region

Surrender = Giving in to sin and allowing it to control one's life (Romans 6:16, AMP), Giving ourselves over to the Lord thereby submitting to His will rather than our own (Romans 6:16, AMP), a Christian who gives up the fight of faith and goes back to serving the enemy

Target = A Christian as a target for persecution (Hebrews 10:32-33, MSG), A Christian as the target of enemy attack (Ephesians 6:16), an indication of a coming enemy attack, the wicked as a target of God's judgment (Jeremiah 44:27, MSG), one who suffers abuse, the devil's kingdom as the target of warfare prayer by the saints **bulls-eye** – a very accurate prophetic word (Mark 7:6, MSG), a direct hit by the enemy, *My question: What are God-worshipers like? Your answer: Arrows aimed at God's bull's-eye.* (Psalm 25:12, MSG)

War = The spiritual battle between the Kingdom of God and the kingdom of darkness (Ephesians 6:11-13), the battle between one's spirit and the sinful nature or flesh (Galatians 5:16-17)

Weapons = Prayer, the Word of God (Ephesians 6:17), love and kindness: *Therefore if thine enemy hunger, feed him; if he thirst, give him drink: for in so doing thou shalt heap coals of fire on his head.* (Romans 12:19-21, KJV), praise and worship (2 Chronicles 20:20-22) ***weapons of the enemy*** – fear (Romans 8:15), bitterness (Hebrews 12:15), temptation (Matthew 6:13, NIV), lies (John 8:44)

SPORTS TERMS

At Bat = Fulfilling one's responsibility (stepping up to the plate)

Blocked Shot (Basketball) or Blocked Field Goal Attempt or Punt (Football) = The enemy hindering the efforts of God's people, God's people hindering the work of the enemy through prayer, obedience, unity, discernment, etc

Carrying the Ball (Football) = Taking on a responsibility

Curve Ball = An attempt by someone to deceive another person or to catch him/her off guard

Defeated = *satan is* defeated (Revelation 20:7, CEV), overcome by sin (1 Corinthians 10:3, MSG), an attitude of defeat

Flags (Auto Racing) = *green* – time to move forward *yellow* – Slow down, possible danger ahead *red* – Stop until new direction is given *white* – Your assignment or goal is almost complete, this season in your life is almost over *checkered flag* – Mission completed *black* – You will be delayed due to sin or compromise

Foul or Penalty = Sin (Job 8:4, NIV), offense

Full Court Press (Basketball) = Great pressure exerted by the enemy to hinder God's people from moving forward (1 Samuel 13:6, NIV), Great pressure exerted by the people of God through prayer to hinder the work of the enemy, an extremely stressful and exerting situation (1 Samuel 14:24, NLT, 2 Corinthians 4:8)

Fumble or Error = To make a mistake or shirk one's responsibility (drop the ball)

Handoff (Football) = To give up control of something to another person who has a better chance of moving it ahead,

Hardball = A very tough and difficult challenge, the kingdom of darkness standing in opposition to the Church (2 Thessalonians 2:3-5)

Home Run = A great achievement

Lay-up (Basketball) = An achievement that is easily attained

Opponent = Those who reject the Gospel who oppose the work of the Lord through persecution (Titus 2:8, Matthew 10:17, AMP), the rebellious (Numbers 16:3, NIV), *O Lord, oppose those who oppose me. Fight those who fight against me.* (Psalm 35:1, NLT), false teachers and prophets opposing the truth (Galatians 1:6, AMP), the sinful nature standing in opposition to the spirit (Galatians 5:16-17)

Overtime = A long running spiritual battle, a critical, high stress situation, it's your time to shine, weariness

Race = Running hastily to commit sin (Proverbs 6:18, NLT), striving with the wicked (Jeremiah 12:5), **one's Christian walk** – *However, I consider my life worth nothing to me, if only I may finish the race and complete the task the Lord Jesus has given me - the task of testifying to the gospel of God's grace.* (Acts 20:24, NIV), trying to earn God's favor through human effort (Romans 9:16, AMP) **marathon** – a long-term commitment that requires great effort and endurance **sprint** – a short term commitment, a short time span in which there is a great deal of activity **relay race** – teamwork

Rookie = A new believer, someone who is inexperienced in ministry or a particular job

Sacked (Football) = Temporarily knocked over by the enemy or by a difficult trial

Sacrifice Bunt (Baseball) = A call to give sacrificially to the poor and needy (Acts 10:4, AMP), *Dear friends, God is good. So I beg you to offer your bodies to him as a living sacrifice, pure and pleasing.* (Romans 12:1, CEV), **suicide squeeze** = Taking a major, all or nothing risk to achieve a goal

Scoreboard = Comparing yourself to other people, a person's fear that he or she doesn't measure up, competition, pride, rejection, *Don't ever say, "I'll get you for that!" Wait for God; he'll settle the score.* (Proverbs 20:22 MSG), keeping score of the sins of others (1 Corinthians 13:5, MSG)

Slam Dunk = A dramatic and forceful victory in a situation, a sure thing

Softball = A challenge that can be easily answered

Steal (Basketball) = *Make sure your treasure is safe in heaven, where thieves cannot steal it.* (Luke 12:33, CEV), the work of the devil: *to steal and kill and destroy* (John 10:10)

Strikeout = A failed attempt at something

Timeout = A need to step away and get direction from the Lord, a time of rest

Touchdown = Achieving a large goal

Victorious = The people of God overcoming satan and his kingdom (1 John 2:14), *Who is it that is victorious over (that conquers) the world but he who believes that Jesus is the Son of God* (1 John 5:5, AMP), those who live a life of obedience and are not overcome by sin and temptation (Revelation 2:25)

FISHING TERMS

Bait = Methods of outreach and evangelism which have as their goal the bringing of souls into the Kingdom of God (Matthew 4:17-19)

Fishing Pole = Outreach and evangelism (Matthew 4:17-19), rest and relaxation

Hook = *The adulteress stalks and snares (as with a hook) the precious life (of a man).* (Proverbs 6:26, AMP), sin, addiction, someone caught in wrongdoing and held accountable, a soul giving his/her life to Christ.

Lure = *And now I'm afraid that exactly as the Snake seduced Eve with his smooth patter, you are being lured away from the simple purity of your love for Christ.* (2 Corinthians 11:3, MSG), the work of the devil in using temptation to lure people into sin (1 Timothy 3:7, MSG), the enticement of worldly pleasures (Matthew 13:22, NLT).

Net = A hidden trap set by the enemy (Psalm 10:8-10), *Whoever flatters his neighbor is spreading a net for his feet.* (Proverbs 29:5, NIV), evil times or sudden tragedy (Ecclesiastes 9:12), outreach and evangelism (Matthew 4:17- 19)

Snag = The entanglement of sin (Hebrews 12:1), a hindrance

MATH TERMS

Addition = Souls being saved and added to the church (Acts 2:41), *For through me your days will be many, and years will be added to your life.* (Proverbs 9:11, NIV)

Division = *I appeal to you, brethren, to be on your guard concerning those who create dissensions and difficulties and cause* **divisions***, in opposition to the doctrine (the teaching) which you have been taught. (I warn you to turn aside from them, to) avoid them (Romans 16:17, AMP), For in the first place, when you assemble as a congregation, I hear that there are cliques (**divisions** and factions) among you; and I in part believe it* (1 Corinthians 11:18, AMP)

Multiplication = *But I will make Pharaoh's heart stubborn so I can multiply my miraculous signs and wonders in the land of Egypt.* (Exodus 7:3, NLT), *Before I could get my breath, my miseries would multiply.* (Job 9:18, CEV), *No one who has sacrificed home, spouse, brothers and sisters, parents, children—whatever—will lose out. It will all come back multiplied many times over in your lifetime.* (Luke 18:29-30, MSG), *And the message of God kept on spreading, and the number of disciples multiplied greatly in Jerusalem* (Acts 6:7, AMP), *And (God) Who provides seed for the sower and bread for eating will also provide and multiply your (resources for) sowing and increase the fruits of your righteousness* (2 Corinthians 9:10, AMP)

Subtraction = Loss

ACTIONS, ACTIVITIES AND STATES OF BEING

Abandonment = Rejection, divorce, a wrong idea a person might have that God left them in their time of need, *A hired hand will run when he sees a wolf coming. He will abandon the sheep because they don't belong to him and he isn't their shepherd. And so the wolf attacks them and scatters the flock.* (John 10:12, NLT), *No I will not abandon you as orphans—I will come to you. Soon the world will no longer see me, but you will see me. Since I live, you also will live.* (the words of Jesus to the disciples (John 14:17-19, NLT), *Since they thought it foolish to acknowledge God, he abandoned them to their foolish thinking and let them do things that should never be done.* (Romans 1:28, NLT)

Advertising = *So whenever you give to the poor and do acts of kindness, do not blow a trumpet before you [to advertise it,* (Matthew 6:2, AMP), self promotion, the promotion of an event

Adultery = Idolatry (Jeremiah 3:8), a lustful heart (Matthew 5:28), one who loves the things of this world more than the Lord (James 4:8, AMP), see also **Sexual Activity**

Analyzing = A person analyzing in a dream often shows that he or she is intellectually trying to figure out what to do in a situation in contrast to simple faith and trust in God, judging the signs of the times (Matthew 16:3)

Appointment = God's appointed time for an answer to prayer (Genesis 18:14, NKJV), having a set time in one's devotional life, God's appointed times and season (1 Thessalonians 5:1)

Baby Shower = A coming public acknowledgement of the dreamer's or dream subject's call to ministry by others, a sign that a new beginning is ahead, The Lord's reassurance that He will provide what is necessary to birth His purpose (church, ministry, business, etc) through the life of the dreamer or dream subject

Backflip = Undo effort to try and win approval or to get attention, a complete reversal of one's opinion or attitude

Bathing or Showering or Washing = Repentance, cleansing of sin by the Holy Spirit (1 John 1:9), or by the washing with water through the word (Ephesians 5:26, NIV) *hand washing* – absolving oneself from guilt by declaring innocence (Matthew 27:23-24, Deuteronomy 21:6-7), totally breaking off a relationship (Zechariah 11:6, MSG), religious ritual and the traditions of men (Matthew 15:1-3, Mark 7:4), the repentance of ungodly actions (James 4:8) *feet washing* – servanthood (John 13:12-17) *face washing* – humility (Matthew 6:16-18), getting a grip on one's emotions (Genesis 43:30-31)

Bending Down = In intense prayer (1 Kings 18:42, NIV), *I am praying to you because I know you will answer, O God. Bend down and listen as I pray. (Psalm 17:6, NLT)*, grieving and mourning (Psalm 38:6-7, AMP), submission and reverence (Isaiah 60:14), crippling disease (Luke 13:11), submission to the Lord's will or to the will of man *bending over backwards* – Trying hard to accommodate or please someone

Birth = Being born again by the Holy Spirit (John 3:5-7), a ministry or God's purposes birthed in a life or a group, Christ becoming fully developed in our lives (Galatians 4:18- 20, NLT), the law giving birth to bondage (Galatians 4:18-20, NKJV), evil desire giving birth to sin and sin giving birth to death (James 1:14-16, NIV), the godless: *They conceive trouble and give birth to evil; their womb fashions deceit.* (Job 15:34-35, NIV), something new coming into the life of a person or group of people *birth pangs (pains of childbirth)* – desperate prayer and intercession before the Lord (Isaiah 26:17), fear and terror (Jeremiah 48:41, NLT), the groaning of all creation for Jesus to return bringing restoration and breaking the curse placed on the Earth after Adam and Eve sinned (Romans 8:21-22, NLT), the sudden and inescapable destruction of the wicked at the end of the age (1 Thessalonians 5:1-3, NLT), famines, earthquakes, wars and other disasters as a sign of Jesus' return (Matthew 24:1-8), a sign that the birthing of God's purposes in one's life, ministry , church, etc is at hand.

Bleeding = Emotionally wounded, the sacrifice of Jesus

Blinking = *It will happen suddenly, quicker than the blink of an eye* (1 Corinthians 15:52, CEV), sudden surprise or shock.

Blowing = Impartation of the Holy Spirit (John 20:21-23), the Lord easily disposing of the enemy (Psalm 68:1-3)

Camping = A temporary season where one is stretched past his/her comfort zone, fellowship and bonding

Catapulting = Sudden promotion, the favor of God suddenly greatly advancing a person forward in life

Chasing or Being Chased = God's people pushing back the enemy (Joshua 10:19), the enemy actively coming after the people of God (Matthew 23:34, NLT), one's life pursuits whether good or bad (including: money, fame, fashion, holiness, wisdom, etc), Jesus' love pursuit of the bride of Christ, fear or a spirit of fear (Romans 8:15)

Chess = A situation that will require divine strategy and wisdom in order to gain victory *checkmate* – a difficult problem that it appears will be a certain defeat *pawn* – a person who is being selfishly used or manipulated by someone else, a nation that is being manipulated by a more powerful nation *chess board* – a person's life, the world

Chewing = Thinking a matter through, bible study or meditating on the Word of God (Psalm 1:2, MSG)

Choking = Therefore, they must eat the bitter fruit of living their own way, choking on their own schemes. (Proverbs 1:31, NLT), The seed falling among the thorns refers to someone who hears the word, but the worries of this life and the deceitfulness of wealth choke the word, making it unfruitful. (Matthew 13:22, NIV), truth that is hard for a person to 'swallow'

Circus = An organization that operates in a way that is frenetic, disorganized and disorderly, *And we must not turn our religion into a circus as they did—"First the people partied, then they threw a dance."* (1 Corinthians 10:7, MSG), crowd pleasing based, pride driven ministry (2 Corinthians 11:17, MSG)

Clapping = Worship (Psalm 47:1-3), God's destruction of the enemy (Ezekiel 21:13-15), joy (Psalm 98:7-8), the Lord's indignation over wickedness (Ezekiel 22:13, NLT)

Climbing Up = Coming into the Lord's presence (Exodus 24:15-17, MSG, Psalm 24:2-4), self promotion (Psalm 37:7, MSG), rebellion against God (Isaiah 14:14, NLT), attempting to get over an obstacle or hindrance, a thief trying to sneak in or symbolically a false Christian trying to sneak into a Church undetected (John 10:1)

Clinging = Holding fast to the Lord (Jeremiah 50:13, NLT, Joshua 23:8, NLT), holding tightly to lies and deceit (Jeremiah 8:5, NIV), a relationship in which one person is inappropriately dependant on the other

Cooking = Preparing Bible lessons, sermons, teachings, etc., "I'm not deceived. I know what you're up to, the plans you're cooking up to bring me down." (Job 21:27, MSG), They spend all their time cooking up gossip against those who mind their own business. (Psalm 35:19-21), plotting or planning

Competition = Ministry that is more focused on surpassing others than on pleasing God, You're blessed when you can show people how to cooperate instead of compete or fight. That's when you discover who you really are, and your place in God's family. (Matthew 5:9)

Crawling = The enemies crawling in surrender to the Lord (Psalm 18:45, MSG), things moving along at a very slow pace, a new Christian being trained in the basics of the faith (learning to crawl before you can walk)

Dancing = Celebration among the people of God because the prodigals children are coming back to the Father (Luke 15:25), praising God (Psalm 150:4), rejoicing after a season of darkness (Psalm 30:11), a dance ministry, sinful revelry and idolatry (Exodus 32:19), to avoid being straightforward about an issue, worldly revelry **waltz** – an easy accomplishment or victory

Death and Dying = Eternal suffering and separation from God for those who reject Christ; also called the *"second death"* (Revelation 20:`11-15), the mind controlled by the sinful nature (Romans 8:6), the sinful nature succumbing to the spirit so that the life of Jesus will be seen in us (Romans 8:12-14, 2 Corinthians 4:9-11 NLT), an end to harmful attitudes, habits, addictions, etc, the death of Jesus on the cross so that we can have eternal life (1 Thessalonians 5:9- 11), the demonic spirit of death (Jeremiah 9:21), the end of something, a warning that something will die if not attended to, a time or place of great spiritual darkness (Matthew 4:16, MSG)

Digesting = Meditating on and studying the Word of God in order to absorb it, thinking through and assimilating new information

Digging = Someone creating a trap (Psalm 7:15), looking into the past (Deuteronomy 32:7, MSG), *An ungodly man digs up evil and it is on his lips like a burning fire.* (Proverbs 16:27, NKJV), redigging the wells of past moves of God covered up by the enemy (Genesis 26:17-19), burying our gifts and resources rather than using them to grow God's Kingdom (Matthew 25:17) **digging up dirt** – Uncovering information to be used as gossip (Job 10:6, MSG, Proverbs 3:29, AMP)

Diving = *The Spirit, not content to flit around on the surface, dives into the depths of God, and brings out what God planned all along.* (1 Corinthians 2:10, MSG), plunging into the River of God (Revelation 22:1), going deep into the realm of the Spirit of God seeking to uncover the secrets of the Lord (Deuteronomy 29:29)

Divorce = A warning against falling away from the Lord (Jeremiah 3:8), a warning that marital problems need to be addressed, a fear of losing a spouse

Drama = A prophetic act (Acts 21:10-11, MSG), a metaphor for life or a specific situation (Matthew 3:11-12, MSG), very stressful interaction with one or more people

Drinking = See **FOOD AND DRINK**

Driving = Moving in ministry, see also **MODES OF TRANSPORTATION**

Eating = Studying and meditating on the Word of God (Hebrews 5:12-14), feasting with great joy before the Lord (Deuteronomy 27:7, NLT), worldly partying (Isaiah 22:12-13, MSG), fellowship with believers (1 Corinthians 11:33-34) or non-believers (Luke 15:2), receiving spiritual nourishment from the Lord (John 6:27)

Embracing or Hugging = Agreement, acceptance, belief in someone or something, mutual love or affection, *Turn your*

back on sin; do something good. Embrace peace—don't let it get away! (Psalm 34:14, MSG)

Escaping = Avoiding the flames of hell by becoming born-again (Corinthians 3:10-15), fleeing from sinful temptation (2 Peter 2:18, NIV), running into the arms of the Lord for shelter (Psalm 31:20, MSG), to get safely away from the traps set by the enemy (Psalm 124:6-8)

Eviction = Deliverance ministry where demons are dislodged and cast out (Matthew 8:31)

Exercising = Putting into action the basic elements of our Christian walk such as faith, self control, patience, etc (2 Peter 1:4-6, AMP), performing religious rituals or traditions (religious exercises)

Experimenting = I said to myself, "Let's go for it—experiment with pleasure, have a good time!" But there was nothing to it, nothing but smoke. (Ecclesiastes 2:1, MSG), trying out new approaches and strategies

Exploring = See **Explorer**

Fainting = Yearning with great longing for the presence of God (Psalm 84:1-2), one who is overwhelmed by troubling circumstances (Psalm 61:2, AMP), *to grow weary and lose heart* (Hebrews 12:3, NIV), a *lack of courage* (Leviticus 26:36, AMP)

Falling = Succumbing to sin or temptation (Jude 1:24), fear and confusion (Leviticus 26:35-37), a loss of strength (Job 4:4, NLT), shame and humiliation or disgrace and dishonor (Jeremiah 20:11), drunkenness (Jeremiah 48:26, MSG), divine judgment (Luke 10:18), worship (1 Corinthians 14:25), turning away from the Lord (2 Thessalonians 2:3), an emotional collapse, a loss of authority or position, total defeat (Jeremiah

46:12), taking a tumble from prominence to obscurity

Field Trip = An evangelistic or ministry outing

Fighting = Anger, hostility or covetousness (James 4:1-2), division (Genesis 13:8, 1 Corinthians 1:10-12), the Lord defending His people (Exodus 14:25, NLT), resisting God (Acts 5:38-40), spiritual warfare (Ephesians 6:12), the battle between the flesh and the spirit (Ephesians 6:12)

Fishing = See **Fisherman** and **Fish**

Flying = Escape (Psalm 55:5-7), soaring in the Spirit above our earthly cares and temptations (Isaiah 40:31), caught up in the Third Heaven (2 Corinthians 12:1-3) *unable to take off* – hindrance of the enemy, bogged down by the cares and distractions of the world

Funeral = A season of great mourning and sorrow (Amos 8:10, NLT), the death of the sinful nature, see also **Death and Dying**

Gambling = Taking a risk based on impulse, human reasoning or one's own will rather than being Spirit led, greed

Gasping = Hope that is quickly fading (Job 11:20, NIV), a desperate cry for help (Jeremiah 4:31, NIV), astonishment (Jeremiah 19:8, NLT), to be horrified or appalled (Jeremiah 50:13, NLT)

Hiding = Avoiding the Lord because of shame (Genesis 3:7- 8), the Lord withdrawing His favor (Deuteronomy 31:17), the enemy preparing for a surprise attack (Judges 16:1), cowering in fear (1 Samuel 14:11), secret sin (Job 31:33), the Lord as our place of refuge and safety (Psalm 32:6-7), keeping secrets, covering over the truth

Hiking = Moving forward with the Lord in spite of obstacles and difficulties

Homesick = The backslider having a desire to return to the Father's house, *My soul yearns, yes, even pines and is homesick for the courts of the Lord* (Psalm 84:2, AMP)

Horseback Riding = See **Horse** and **Jockey**

Housecleaning = The Lord bringing the Church to repentance and restoration (Acts 7:31-32, MSG), *The phrase "one last shaking" means a thorough housecleaning, getting rid of all the historical and religious junk so that the unshakable essentials stand clear and uncluttered.*(Hebrews 12:25-27,MSG)

Hypnotizing = A person using manipulation and/or demonic influence to control another person, manipulating a person of the opposite gender through mesmerizing charm

Igniting (Fire) = To enrage (2 Kings 23:26, MSG), Jesus baptizing us with the Holy Spirit and fire (Matthew 3:11, MSG), *And the tongue is a flame of fire. It is a whole world of wickedness, corrupting your entire body. It can set your whole life on fire, for it is set on fire by hell itself.* (James 3:6, NLT), to incite someone to sin, fiery preaching or exhortation that precipitates burning passion in the hearts of God people

Investing = *Invest in truth and wisdom, discipline and good sense, and don't part with them.* (Proverbs 23:23, CEV), *Be generous: Invest in acts of charity. Charity yields high returns.* (Ecclesiastes 11:1, MSG), the Lord pouring blessing and grace into His people with the expectation that they will bear fruit (Romans 11:1-2, MSG), to devote one's time, talents resources, etc. into the Kingdom of Heaven (Matthew 25:13- 29), sin and idolatry that leads to a bankrupt existence (Isaiah 42:17, MSG)

Itching = A restless desire or longing *itching ears* – *For the time will come when men will not put up with sound doctrine.*

Instead, to suit their own desires, they will gather around them a great number of teachers to say what their itching ears want to hear (2 Timothy 4:2-4, NIV), a deep desire to listen to gossip (Proverbs 17:4, MSG)

Journey = *Your life is a journey you must travel with a deep consciousness of God* (1 Peter 1:18, MSG)

Jumping or Leaping = Joy of the Lord (Psalm 28:6, MSG), praise and thanksgiving (Acts 3:8), jumping to conclusions (1 Samuel 1:12-14, MSG, 2 Kings 13:21, MSG), panic (1 Kings 1:49), resurrection from the dead (2 Kings 13:21), freedom (Malachi 4:2) **long jump** – a leap of faith, moving a long way quickly toward your goal

Kissing = Worshipping Jesus (Luke 7:38), an honest answer (Proverbs 24:26, NIV), intimacy with Jesus (Song of Solomon 1:2), false compliments (Proverbs 27:6), sign of affection (Genesis 31:55), imparting the anointing (1 Samuel 10:1), worship of false gods (1 Kings 19:18, Job 31:27), seduction and temptation (Proverbs 7:10-14), betrayal by a friend (Matthew 26:47-49), the merciful love of the Father (Luke 15:20), brotherly love between Christians (Romans 16:16)

Kneeling = Prayer (1 Kings 8:54), reverence and honor (1 Kings 1:31), worship (2 Chronicles 29:29)

Knitting = *So all the men of Israel were gathered against the city, knit together as one man.* (Judges 20:11, KJV), *the soul of Jonathan was knit with the soul of David, and Jonathan loved him as his own soul.* (1 Samuel 18:1b, KJV), the love that unites the body of Christ (Colossians 2:2),

Knocking (On the Door) = Persistently seeking the Lord in prayer (Matthew 7:7-8), Jesus knocking on the door of the hearts of His people to invite them into intimate fellowship with Him (Revelation 3:20)

Laughing = Joyful celebration (Esther 8:16-17), mocking and scoffing (2 Kings 19:21), to dismiss seeming disaster as trivial because God is with you (Job 5:22), the joy of the Lord (Job 8:21, Philippians 4:4), the Lord scoffing at the wicked nations of the Earth who defy Him (Psalm 2:1-4), a joyful expression of praise to the Lord (Psalm 100:1-3, MSG)

Limping = A person lacking strength or stability in his/her Christian walk

Lost (One's Way) = Backslidden (Luke 15:32), separated from God because of not receiving the Lord's free gift of salvation in Jesus Christ (Luke 13:3, AMP)

Lying Down = Soaking in the presence of the Lord (1 Samuel 3:3-4), the Lord's enemies bowing before Him (1 Samuel 3:3- 4, NLT), living in peace and safety (Zephaniah 3:13, NLT), sexual sin (Genesis 19:33, NLT), a surprise attack of the enemy (Numbers 35:20, NKJV), intimacy (Song of Solomon 1:1, NLT), humility, prayer and worship (Nehemiah 8:6), see also **Sleeping** and **Resting**

Marching = God's army of believers moving in unity (Joel 2:7), spiritual warfare **marching orders** – notice that it is time for action, specific direction from God

Maturing = We also pray for this, that you be made complete [fully restored, growing and maturing in godly character and spirit—pleasing your heavenly Father by the life you live] 2 Corinthians 13:9, AMP)., becoming more responsible, growing in faith, Acquire understanding [actively seek spiritual discernment, mature comprehension, and logical interpretation) – (Proverbs 4:5, AMP)

Measuring = *The more talk, the less truth; the wise measure their words.* (Proverbs 10:19, MSG), *For in the same way you*

judge others, you will be judged, and with the measure you use, it will be measured to you. (Matthew 7:2, NIV), *Give, and it will be given to you. A good measure, pressed down, shaken together and running over, will be poured into your lap. For with the measure you use, it will be measured to you.* (Luke 6:38, NIV), cautiously weighing options in place of acting in pure faith

Musical Notes = Worship, music ministry

Naked = Poverty (Job 24:7), shame (Isaiah 47:3, Micah 1:11), humiliation (Lamentations 1:8, NLT), defeat (Amos 2:16, NIV), weeping and mourning (Micah 1:8, NIV), a fear of being exposed (Revelation 16:15, NIV) idolatry, (Ezekiel 23:29), *Naked a man comes from his mother's womb, and as he comes, so he departs. He takes nothing from his labor that he can carry in his hand* (Ecclesiastes 5:15, NIV), sexual sin, drunkenness (Genesis 9:20-23), transparency and total openness, walking in sin and depravity (Revelation 3:15-18)

Packing (Up) = Preparing for transition, getting ready to move on

Panting = Great thirst for the presence of God (Psalm 42:1- 2), failing strength (Psalm 38:10, NKJV)

Parade = *In the Messiah, in Christ, God leads us from place to place in one perpetual victory parade.* (2 Corinthians 2:14, MSG), publicly displaying one's good works in order to be seen and receive praise from man (Luke 20:46, NLT, Isaiah 58:5, MSG), *The look on their faces testifies against them; they parade their sin like Sodom; they do not hide it* (Isaiah 3:9, NIV), worship that appears elaborate and extravagant but is done with a wrong heart, great celebration, an occasion to honor someone

Planting or Sowing = Evangelism (Matthew 13:18-19),

troublemakers "sowing mistrust and suspicion in the minds of the people" (Acts 14:2, MSG), financial giving to the work of the Lord (2 Corinthians 9:6), the enemy placing false Christians in the Church (Matthew 13:38-40), ministry to believers such as teaching (1 Corinthians 9:11), good works in the Lord (Galatians 6:7-9), works of evil and corruption (Galatians 6:7-9), peacemakers spreading seeds of peace (James 3:18)

Plowing = The sinful actions of the wicked (Proverbs 21:4), inner cleansing and repentance (Jeremiah 4:3-4, NLT), divine judgment against evil (Jeremiah 26:17-18)

Pouring Out = Unburdening ones soul to the Lord (1 Samuel 1:14-16, NIV), outpouring of the Holy Spirit (Isaiah 32:15), idolatry (Jeremiah 32:29), the Lord pouring out blessings on His people (Jeremiah 33:9, MSG), God's wrath poured out (Ezekiel 9:6-8, NIV), drunkenness – pouring out wine (Habakkuk 2:15), healing (Luke 10:34), God's children pouring out love one to another (Ephesians 4:1-3, MSG), the oil of joy poured out on God's people (Hebrews 1:9, NLT), God's people pouring out praise (Hebrews 13:13, MSG), a life sacrificially poured out in service to the Lord even unto death (2 Timothy 4:6), the end-time outpouring of God's wrath on the wicked (Revelation 14:19-20, MSG)

Poverty = *The poor in spirit (the humble, who rate themselves insignificant) for theirs is the kingdom of heaven!* (Matthew 5:3, AMP), the state of the lukewarm Christian in the eyes of God (Revelation 3:16-18)

Prosperity = *...life-joy and satisfaction in God's favor and salvation* (Matthew 5:3, AMP), great success

Pruning = The work of God the Father whereby He cuts away from the lives of His people everything that hinders them from bearing fruit in their lives (John 15:1-2), examining one's life and ridding oneself of sin and unproductive behavior

Rape = Violation (Jeremiah 13:22), abuse, violent oppression

Reaping or Harvesting = See **Harvesters** and **Harvest-Time**

Rejection = A demonic spirit of rejection, an expression of one's inner feelings of rejection, persecution

Repairing = The restoration of: a broken dream, a relationship, a ministry, damaged emotions, etc

Resting = The security of knowing that as a New Testament believer you are accepted by God and that you don't have to work to earn His love (Hebrews 4:8-11), giving your heavy burdens to Jesus while finding rest for your soul through faith and trust in Him (Matthew 11:28-29)

Rioting = Lawlessness, rebellion against authority, *Wine is a mocker, strong drink a riotous brawler; and whoever is intoxicated by it is not wise.* (Proverbs 20:1, AMP), mass persecution (Luke 23:23-25, MSG)

Resurrection = The born-again experience (John 5:24, John 11:25), a lost soul who returns and recommits him/herself to the Lord (Luke 15:24), the Jewish people finding Jesus their Messiah (Romans 11:7-15), things in one's life such as a prayer life or passion or dreams that had "died" but have been restored

Running = Escaping or fleeing danger (Genesis 31:20), sinful frenzy (Exodus 32:25), pursuit (2 Kings 5:21), one who moves eagerly toward sinful pleasures (Proverbs 6:18), repentant sinners hastening to the Lord (Isaiah 55:5, NLT), fleeing from God's purposes and direction (Jonah 1:3), living in obedience to the Lord (Galatians 5:7), the pursuit of a godly life (1 Timothy 6:11, NLT), freedom

Scrubbing = Hard scrubbing can signify trying to do spiritual cleansing or deliverance by human strength rather than by means of divine power and grace

Sexual Activity = Adultery or fornication (Leviticus 18:19- 21), idolatry (2 Kings 17:16-17, MSG, Ezekiel 16:22-24, MSG), marital intimacy (1 Corinthians 7:3, NLT), a lustful heart (Matthew 15:18-20), a demonic spirit of lust

(To Be) Shaken = To be rattled by afflictions and troubles (1 Thessalonians 3:3, NKJV), caused to be anxious or fearful (Isaiah 32:10, AMP), see also **Shivering or Trembling**

Shaking = The Lord bringing great turmoil to the Earth (Haggai 2:6), the Lord's judgment coming upon the Church for the purpose of bringing repentance and restoration (Hebrews 12:25-27, MSG)

Shaking Hands = Agreement, friendship, covenant

Shifting Gears (Car) = An abrupt change in strategy, attitude or behavior, *in gear* – things are running on a consistently smooth level *in high gear* – a high level of activity, activities done very efficiently *gearing down* – preparing to move at a lower rate of intensity

Shivering or Trembling = Fearful (Job 4:15, NLT), to be in awe of God (Job 4:15, Psalm 119:120, MSG), the fear of the Lord (Acts 7:31-32), great fear (Psalm 55:5, NKJV), grief (Isaiah 15:4, MSG), see also **Shaken**

Shooting = Releasing the power of God, hatred, spiritual warfare (Ephesians 6:12), gossip, slandering or cursing others, speaking truth (straight shooter)

Shouting or Screaming = Joyful Praise to the Lord (Psalm 47:1-3), panic (Judges 7:21), victory (Judges 15:14, NLT), a war cry (1 Samuel 17:20, NIV), the ranting of the enemy (1 Samuel 17:23), celebration (1 Kings 1:40-42, NLT), worship of false gods (1 Kings 18:26), praying for help (Psalm 88:13), a warning (Jeremiah 20:7-10), terror (Jeremiah 47:1-4) **unable to scream for help** – a hindrance to one's prayer life

Shrinking = Walking in fear (Job 6:21, MSG), humbling oneself or being humbled by the Lord (2 Kings 22:19, Psalm 110:1, NLT), living in shame and condemnation (1 John 2:28, NLT)

Singing = Worshipping God (Revelation 5:13, 2 Chronicles 23:18), Worshipping a false god or idol (Exodus 32:18), rejoicing (Genesis 31:27), an expression of being at peace and rest (Isaiah 14:7), the Lord's delight and love for His people (Zephaniah 3:17), giving thanks to the Lord (Psalm 28:6, MSG) warfare (2 Chronicles 20:20-22), see also **Musician**

Sinking or Drowning = Overwhelmed with sorrow and grief (Job 5:8-11, MSG), great financial loss (Deuteronomy 28:43, NIV, Ezekiel 27:27, NIV), great trouble (Psalm 69:14), the ultimate destruction of an unrepentant and wicked nation (Jeremiah 51:64, Amos 8:8, NIV), loss of honor or prestige (Job 14:21, NLT), shrinking back in fear (Job 23:13, MSG), death (Psalm 30:9), despair (Psalm 142:3, MSG), a great enemy attack (Ezekiel 26:19, NLT), a failing ministry

Sitting = Authority or rulership (1 Kings 1:46), inactivity or complacency (Jeremiah 8:14, James 2:19-20, MSG), fellowship (Matthew 26:20 NLT), repentance, negotiation, sitting in judgment (James 4:11, NIV), rest

Sleeping = Spiritually dull and not alert (Isaiah 56:10-11, MSG, Mark 13:36), prayerlessness (Jonah 1:4-6, Matthew 26:40-41), death for a Christian who will one day be resurrected (Matthew 7:52), rest **sleeplessness** – prayer and worship through the night (Ecclesiastes 5:2, MSG), wide awake with passion for Jesus (Song of Solomon 3:1), mourning (Psalm 102:7, AMP), lack of trust in the Lord, striving **overslept** – a warning that one may miss his/her appointed time or season for a breakthrough because of spiritual slumber or giving up (Galatians 6:9), a fear that one will miss his/her appointed time or season

Sowing (Seeds) = See **Sower**

Speaking = See **Lips**, **Mouth** and **Tongue**

Spitting = Mockery and disdain (Isaiah 50:6), physical healing (Mark 7:33, Mark 8:23)

Stabbing = Betrayal (1 Samuel 29:4, MSG), gossip and slander (Psalm 50:20, MSG), an attack that comes from someone in close relationship, destroying the works of the enemy with the sword of the Spirit which is the Word of God (Ephesians 6:17) **backstabbing** – Betrayal (1 Samuel 29:4, MSG)

Staggering = *They grope in the dark without a clue, lurching and staggering like drunks."* (Job 12:25 MSG), exhaustion (Psalm 107:4-9, MSG), wailing in defeat (Psalm 107:4-9)

Standing = Refusal to compromise, right relationship with God (Psalm 24:5, NLT), refusal to give up (Psalm 88:13-14, MSG)

Stealing = See **Thief**

Stirring (Up) = Always stirring up trouble, always at odds with his family.(Genesis 16:12, MSG), healing: For an angel went down at a certain time into the pool and stirred up the water; then whoever stepped in first, after the stirring of the water, was made well of whatever disease he had. (John 5:4, NKJV), attempting to cause something to happen, whether good or bad, see also **Cooking**

Strutting = *I told you but you wouldn't listen. You rebelled at the plain word of God. You threw out your chests and strutted into the hills.* (Deuteronomy 1:43, MSG), *We've all heard of Moab's pride, that legendary pride, the strutting, bullying, puffed-up pride, the insufferable arrogance.* (Jeremiah 48:29-33, MSG)

Stumbling = The staggering of the wicked through spiritual darkness (1 Samuel 2:9, MSG), one struggling through trouble (Job 12:5, MSG), suffer shame (Psalm 69:6, MSG), fall into sin (James 2:10, NIV), to stagger in exhaustion (Psalm 107:5, MSG), an ability to articulate one's thoughts, making mistakes (James 3:2, NLT)

Suffocating = *the cares of the world and the pleasure and delight and glamour and deceitfulness of riches choke and suffocate the Word, and it yields no fruit.* (Matthew 13:22, AMP), a lack of a devotional life, feeling totally suppressed, stifled and severely limited by others or by circumstances

Sunbathing = Soaking in the Lord, vanity

Swallowing = Believing a lie (Jeremiah 7:8, MSG), a bitter pill to swallow (Ruth 1:13, MSG), a consuming attack of the enemy (2 Samuel 17:16, KJV), the Lord's wrath annihilating the wicked (Psalm 21:9), swallowing one's pride (Proverbs 6:3, NLT), the Lord swallowing up death in victory (Isaiah 25:7-9, KJV), the wicked swallowed up by their own wine (Isaiah 28:7, NKJV)

Swatting (Flies) = Exposing and casting aside the lies of the enemy

Sweeping = See **Broom**

Swimming = Escape from danger (Acts 27:41-42), moving or ministering in the Holy Spirit (Ezekiel 47:3-5), enjoying God

treading water = activity that doesn't seem to lead to progress or advancement

Talent Contest = Ministry that has as its goal pleasing and impressing people rather than God, competition, pride vanity

Tasting = Spiritual discernment (Job 34:2-4, NIV), to experience bitterness of soul (Job 27:2 NIV), to experience wealth (Job 21:25, NLT), to experience happiness (Job 21:25, MSG), to venture into an experience with God in order to see that He really is good and kind, (Psalm 34:9), to experience the sweetness of God's Word (Psalm 119:103, Hebrews 6:5), to experience the ministry of the Holy Spirit (Hebrews 6:4), ***bad taste*** – a feeling that there is something wrong about a person or situation, see also **Bitter Tasting**, **Sour Tasting** and **Sweet Tasting**

Travelling or Journeying = Your life is a journey you must travel with a deep consciousness of God (1 Peter 1:18-21), life transition, repositioning yourself

Uncovering = *And the king of Assyria uncovered a conspiracy by Hoshea; for he had sent messengers to So, king of Egypt* (2 Kings 17:4, NKJV), *He will punish your iniquity, O daughter of Edom; He will uncover your sins!* (Lamentations 4:22, NKJV), *Nothing in all creation is hidden from God's sight. Everything is uncovered* (Hebrews 4:13, NIV)

Uprooting = The Father weeding false Christians out of the Church (Matthew 15:13), Moving away from one's home to live elsewhere

Vomiting = Purging, revulsion, overindulgence (Proverbs 25:16), derision (Jeremiah 48:26), *These things says the Amen, the Faithful and True Witness, the Beginning of the creation of God: "I know your works, that you are neither cold nor hot. I could wish you were cold or hot. So then, because you are* *lukewarm, and neither cold nor hot, I will vomit you out of My mouth.* (Revelation 3:16),

Waking Up = Resurrection (2 Kings 4:31-35, NIV), the arousal of love (Song of Solomon 2:7), the Lord moving into action to defend His people (Psalm 35:23), shaking off laziness and apathy (Proverbs 6:9, NLT), the Lord opening our ears to hear His voice (Isaiah 50:4-5, MSG), to heed a warning (Jeremiah 46:14, MSG), to become alert to the consequences of one's sin (Joel 1:4-6), to wake up to reality (Amos 6:1), to realize how much one is lacking in his/her spiritual state (Romans 13:11), to soberly examine one's behavior in the light of the Holy Spirit (1 Corinthians 6:5-6, MSG), Repent and obey! (Revelation 3: 2-3, NIV)

Walking = The way in which one conducts is/her life; whether following the ways of the Lord (Deuteronomy 8:5-7) or following one's own stubborn path of sin (Deuteronomy 29:19, NLT), following in the path of those who went before; whether good (2 Chronicles 11:17) or evil (1 Kings 15:33) **paralyzed** – a fear of helplessness, paralyzed with fear, a hindrance to moving ahead, see also **Feet** and **Shoes**

Wandering = Aimlessness or lack of purpose, *A man who wanders out of the way of understanding shall abide in the congregation of the spirits (of the dead).* (Proverbs 21:16, AMP)

Winking = *...signaling their deceit with a **wink** of the eye, a nudge of the foot, or the wiggle of fingers.* (Proverbs 6:13, NLT), flirtation or seduction (Isaiah 3:16, CEV), giving approval to wrongdoing by ignoring it (Leviticus 20:4, AMP)

Witchcraft = Rebellion (1 Samuel 15:23), a false prophet (Isaiah 44:25, AMP, Jeremiah 14:14, AMP), counterfeit miracles which are performed using satanic powers (2 Thessalonians 2:8-10), a seduction (Proverbs 7:21), legalistic teaching that leads God's people into a gospel of works rather than grace (Galatians 3:1-3), control and manipulation

Writing = Journaling dreams, testimonies, revelations etc. for remembrance, Then the Lord said to me, "Write my answer plainly on tablets so that a runner can carry the correct message to others. (Habakkuk 2:2, NLT), a calling to be an author, *handwriting on a wall* – God's judgment (Daniel 5:5), a foregone conclusion

Wounded = Having one's feelings hurt, the negative internal affect of an attack by the enemy such as loss of faith, depression or a broken heart

Yard Sale or Garage Sale = Ridding one's life of memories that bring hurt or bitterness, unburdening oneself of the old so that God can impart the new, a sign that a life season is coming to an end

U.S. STATE MOTTOS

*At times, a dream location might be a state with which the dreamer has no association or connection. I have felt to include a list of US state mottos which might offer a clue as to the state's symbolic significance in a dream. I am including also several state slogans and or nicknames that might be pertinent.

Alabama = We dare to defend our rights – Share The Wonder

Alaska = North to the future – Beyond Your Dreams, Within Your Reach – Last Frontier

Arizona = God enriches

Arkansas = The people rule

California = Eureka (which means "I have found it")

Colorado = Nothing without Providence or Nothing without the Deity – Enter a Higher State

Connecticut = He who transplanted sustains (It is believed that this motto is taken from Psalm 80:9-10: *You cleared the ground for us, and we took root and filled the land. Our shade covered the mountains; our branches covered the mighty cedars.*, NLT) – Full of Surprises

Delaware = Liberty and independence

Florida = In God we trust

Georgia = Wisdom, justice, and moderation

Hawaii = The life of the land is perpetuated in righteousness

Idaho = It is forever

Illinois = State sovereignty, national union

Indiana = The crossroads of America – Restart Your Engines

Iowa = Our liberties we prize and our rights we will maintain – Life Changing; Fields of Opportunity

Kansas = To the stars through difficulties

Kentucky = Let us give thanks to God (adopted 2002) – Unbridled Spirit

Louisiana = Union justice and confidence – Come as you are. Leave Different

Maine = "I direct" (symbolizes the state guiding the people)

Maryland = Manly deeds womanly words

Massachusetts = By the sword we seek peace but peace only under liberty

Michigan = I will be defended, If you seek a pleasant peninsula look around you

Minnesota = "I long to see what is beyond"

Mississippi = By valor and arms

Missouri = Let the good of the people be the supreme law – Where the Rivers Run

Montana = Gold and silver

Nebraska = Equality before the law

Nevada = All for our country – Wide Open

New Hampshire = Live free or die

New Jersey = Liberty and prosperity – Come See For Yourself

New Mexico = It grows as it goes

New York = Ever Upward!

North Carolina = To be rather than to seem

North Dakota = Liberty and union now and forever one and inseparable (from their Great Seal), Strength from the soil (from their Coat of Arms)

Ohio = With God all things are possible -- So Much to Discover

Oklahoma = Labor conquers all things

Oregon = She flies with her own wings – We Love Dreamers

Pennsylvania = Virtue liberty and independence -- State of Independence

Rhode Island = Hope

South Carolina = While I breathe I hope, Ready in soul and resource – Smiling Faces. Beautiful Places

South Dakota = Under God the people rule

Tennessee = Agriculture and commerce

Texas = Friendship

Utah = Industry – Life Elevated

Vermont = Freedom and Unity

Virginia = Thus always to tyrants (meaning the total defeat of tyranny)

Washington = Bye and bye (meaning into the future or "I will see you in the future")

West Virginia = Mountaineers are always free – Open for Business

Wisconsin = Forward – Stay Just a Little Bit Longer

Wyoming = Equal rights – Like No Place on Earth

EVERYTHING ELSE
INCLUDING THE KITCHEN SINK

Air Conditioner = Refreshing of the Holy Spirit, The need to 'cool off' after an argument or angry episode.

Air Purifier = The Holy Spirit cleansing the spiritual atmosphere, prayer, worship

Alarm = Crying out to God for protection from the enemy (Numbers 10:9-10), *I also sent prophets to warn you of danger, but when they sounded the alarm, you paid no attention.* (Jeremiah 6:17, CEV), the cry of the prophetic watchman that the enemy is at hand (Ezekiel 33:3, NLT), a call to repentance to avert judgment (Joel 2:1-17), warning, danger

Alarm Clock = A wake up call to shake off spiritual slumber, a new beginning

Altar = Sacrifice (Genesis 8:20), worship (Genesis 13:4)

Amnesia = A desire to block out the past rather than finding true inner healing, *Fear not; you will no longer live in shame. Don't be afraid; there is no more disgrace for you. You will no longer remember the shame of your youth and the sorrows of widowhood.* (Isaiah 54:4, NLT), *For I will be merciful to their unrighteousness, and their sins and their lawless deeds I will remember no more* (Hebrews 8:12, NKJV), a Christian who forgets his/her true identity in Christ

Amplifier = The Lord providing new opportunities for your message or music to be heard by many more people, a call to lift one's voice and not be silent, an increase of power

Amulet = Putting one's trust in something or someone other than the Lord for protection, the occult or superstition

Anchor = Hope in Christ (Hebrews 6:19), Jesus as our source of stability

Ankle Bracelet = An abusive or unhealthy relationship centered around control and constant scrutiny, shame or condemnation, the work of the religious spirit in inhibiting one's freedom

Anorexia = A Christian who spends little or no time reading the Scriptures, One who has attaining worldly standards of beauty as a goal in place of God's standard, self rejection due to a distorted self-image

Answering Machine = A message from the Lord or others

Antibiotic = The Holy Spirit exposing and destroying the hidden work of the enemy, see also **Medicine**

Antique = Something from the past such as a lesson learned or an ancient truth that continues to have value in our times. Something that is outdated or no longer relevant.

Appetite = Sinful and lustful desires (Proverbs 13:2, NLT, Romans 8:8, MSG), hunger for God (Matthew 5:6, MSG)

Apron = Servanthood (Luke 17:8, NLT), a calling to teach the Word of God, physical healing and deliverance (Acts 19: 11-12)

Arrow or Dart = Divine judgment (Deuteronomy 32:23), warning (1 Samuel 20:20-22), deliverance and victory over the enemy (2 Kings 13:17), words (Psalm 64:3), *Children born to a young man are like arrows in a warrior's hands* (Psalm 127:4, NLT), a prophet (Isaiah 49:2) lies (Proverbs 25:18), famine and great hunger (Ezekiel 5:16), demonic attack (Ephesians 6:16), spiritual warfare

Axe = *Even now the axe of God's judgment is poised, ready to sever the roots of the trees. Yes, every tree that does not produce good fruit will be chopped down and thrown into the fire.* (Matthew 3:10, NLT), anointing, resentment **sharp axe** – wisdom (Ecclesiastes 10:10b) **dull axe** – human strength (Ecclesiastes 10:10a)

ATM = prosperity, a wrong view of God as a money machine

Baby Bottle = The elementary teachings of the Christian faith (Hebrews 5:12), great immaturity, emotional dependence, (1 Corinthians 3:1-3, Hebrews 5:12-14), the mentorship of a new believer

Backpack = Carrying your past memories or experiences which have become a burden, carrying stress or great responsibility

Badge = Authority

Balloons = Christians who although fragile in themselves are indwelt with the Holy Spirit which causes them to soar, rapid increase (ballooning at a fast rate), freedom, a person puffed up with pride **lead balloon** – a flop, a suggestion that is strongly declined

Bankruptcy = The fruitless results of sin and corruption (Psalm 119:11, MSG), to be lacking moral character

Belt = The righteousness of Christ (Isaiah 11:5), authority (Isaiah 22:21, NKJV), The Lord binding His people to Him as a belt around His waist (Jeremiah 13:11, NIV), God's truth (Ephesians 6:14, NIV) **tightening one's belt** – the need or desire to budget and/or spend less money

Banner = Victory in the Lord (Psalm 20:5), the intimate love

Jesus has for His bride – the Church (Song of Solomon 2:4), Jesus as: *a banner of salvation to all the world.* (Isaiah 11:10b, NLT), a call to war (Jeremiah 51:27)

Banquet = Intimate and joyful fellowship with the Lord (Song of Solomon 2:4), the future Marriage Supper of the Lamb (Revelation 19:9), a great time of eating the Word of God and drinking of the Spirit (Matthew 23:4, MSG), worldly revelry and celebration (1 Samuel 25:35-37), an occasion to honor a person or group of people (Esther 1:3)

Barrel = A large quantity of something (Psalm 102:9, MSG), moving ahead recklessly (barreling forward)

Barrier = Hindrance, "Even now," says the *Lord*, "Turn and come to Me with all your heart [in genuine repentance], With fasting and weeping and mourning [until every **barrier** is removed and the broken fellowship is restored) (Joel 2:12, AMP), "And that's not all. You will have complete and free access to God's kingdom, keys to open any and every door: no more barriers between heaven and earth, earth and heaven." (Matthew 16:19, MSG), a hindrance in a relationship, a person who is unwilling to open his/her heart to others

Beacon = A warning signal, a Christian as a light in the darkness (Philippians 2:15, AMP), the Bible which gives illumination to a dark world

Bed = Intimacy with Jesus our Bridegroom (Song of Solomon 61:16), sickness (Psalm 41:3, NIV), laziness (Proverbs 6:6-11, MSG), sexual temptation and sin (Proverbs 7:11-18, MSG), marital intimacy (Hebrews 13:4)

Billboard = A message from the Lord, evangelism

Binoculars = Prophetic revelation, the seer anointing

Blanket = Spiritual covering, sleep, rest, protection

Bleach = Spiritual cleansing and repentance (Malachi 3:1-3, NLT)

Blueprint = God's revealed design, strategy or plan of action (1 Chronicles 28:12, MSG, Isaiah 14:24, MSG)

Boomerang = *What a bad person plots against the good, boomerangs; the plotter gets it in the end.* (Proverbs 21:18, MSG)

Bottle = *You keep track of all my sorrows. You have collected all my tears in your bottle. You have recorded each one in your book.* (Psalm 56:8, NLT), an unhealthy repressing of emotions and feelings

Bowl = God's end-time judgment poured out on the wicked (Revelation 16), prayers of the saints (Revelation 5:8)

Bracelet = Beauty, prosperity, a gift from God (Ezekiel 16:11)

Brick = Hard labor (Exodus 1:12-15, NIV) or bondage (NKJV), human rather than divine effort **brick wall** – a hard and seemingly immovable obstacle (Isaiah 1:5, MSG)

Briefcase = One's identity, business plans or strategy, a calling to business or a profession, prosperity

Broom = Repentance and cleansing of sin, inner healing, the Lord wiping out the enemy (Isaiah 14:22-23), a symbol of witchcraft, deliverance (Matthew 12:44)

Bruise = Hurt feelings

Bubble = An illusion, a comfortable environment in which there is no real challenge, something in life that lasts for a moment and then fades away *a burst bubble* – disillusionment

Buffet = Gluttony, a time of being faced with many choices, A Church or ministry that offers a wide variety of classes, seminars, conferences, etc where one can be fed spiritually

Cage = A fear of being trapped in a situation with no way out, a confining and overly restrictive situation from which it seems there is no escape (Job 6:1-3, MSG)

Candle = The light of God piercing the darkness (Psalm 18:28, KJV), a frail or vulnerable person (Matthew 12:19-21, NLT), religious ritual and tradition, the occult

Canteen = The Lord's provision during a dry desert season of one's life, a call to continually drink of the water of the Spirit in spite of feeling dried up and weary

Cartoon = an attitude of not taking life seriously enough, unrealistic expectation, immaturity, childlikeness, a larger than life person

Centerpiece = ...*take a good hard look at Jesus. He's the centerpiece of everything we believe* (Hebrews 3:1, MSG), the thing that is central in someone's life whether good or bad

Certificate = Achievement, authority, qualified to minister, qualified professionally, shows that official recognition is coming to a minister, ministry, business, etc.

Chain = Imprisonment (Ezekiel 7:22-24, AMP), bondage to sin or addiction, defeat (Nahum 3:10, AMP), unity (believers linked together as one)

Chair = Seat of authority (1 Samuel 1:9) *rocking chair* – laziness, old age, motherhood

Cigarette = Spirit of death (Jeremiah 9:21), addiction

Circle = Symbol of eternity, one's sphere of influence, endless unfruitful activity or conversation (going around in circles), a group of people who are closest to an authority figure (inner circle)

Cloak or Coat = A spiritual mantle of authority and anointing (2 Kings 2:14, NIV), shame and disgrace (Psalm 109:28-30, NIV), being cloaked in secrecy (Proverbs 21:14, NIV), the zeal of the Lord (Isaiah 59:16-18), the Lord's covering (Ezekiel 16:8), divine healing (Matthew 9:21, NIV), a cover-up for evil (1 Peter 2:16, NKJV) *cloaks spread out on the road* – worship of Jesus as King (Matthew 21:8, NIV)

Clock or Watch = God's timing, things working out perfectly or people working together with great precision (like clockwork)- Note the time on the clock and check the **Numbers** section. The time can also represent a Scripture verse or a calendar date. *stop watch* – feeling of being pressured to accomplish something in a limited time period, a time constraint, a competitive attitude

Clothes or Garments = Covering, clothes are indicative of one's inner state *dirty clothes* – Shame and disgrace (Psalm 109:29, MSG), sin (Zechariah 3:3) *torn clothes* – repentance and/or mourning (2 Samuel 13:31) *clean clothes* – righteousness (Zechariah 3:4-5), see also **Colors** *as the color of clothes are often essential in understanding symbolic meaning*

Clutter = Less important things that fill one's time so that there is little room for that which is truly worthwhile such as prayer or family time, thoughts of the cares and pleasures of this world which distract the mind from focusing on the Lord or other truly important matters

Cork = Self control or self restraint

Cross = The sacrificial death of Jesus bringing us forgiveness of sin and reconciling us with God (Ephesians 1:7-10, MSG, Colossians 1:19-21), *Those who belong to Christ Jesus have nailed the passions and desires of their sinful nature to His cross and crucified them there.* (Galatians 5:24, NLT) the power released through Jesus' death to break curses off of our lives (Galatians 3:13), persecution (Galatians 6:12), humility and obedience (Philippians 2:8-9), Jesus' total victory over the enemy (Colossians 2:15)

Crown = Authority (Esther 6:8), glory and honor (Psalm 8:5), *He redeems me from death and crowns me with love and tender mercies* (Psalm 103:4, NLT), *For the LORD takes delight in his people; he crowns the humble with salvation.* (Psalm 149:4 NIV), *A wife of noble character is her husband's crown* (Proverbs 12:4, NIV), *Grandchildren are the crowning glory of the aged* (Proverbs 17:6, NLT), everlasting joy (Isaiah 35:10, NIV), *To all who mourn in Israel, he will give a crown of beauty for ashes* (Isaiah 61:3, NLT), *And now the prize awaits me—the **crown** of righteousness, which the Lord, the righteous Judge, will give me on the day of his return. And the prize is not just for me but for all who eagerly look forward to his appearing.* (2 Timothy 4:8, NLT)

Cup = One's portion or lot in life or life season (Psalm 16:5, NIV) whether the abundant blessings of God (Psalm 23:5) or bitterness and sorrow (Lamentations 3:15, NLT), salvation (Psalm 116:12-14), the wrath of God (Isaiah 51:17), ruin and desolation, NLT), a person (Matthew 23:26), the cup of Communion representing the blood of Jesus (Matthew 26:27)

Curtain = The heavens (Psalm 104:2), secret sin, a secretive person ***pulling the curtains closed*** – the ending of something (Matthew 13:49, MSG), secrecy

Cymbal = Rejoicing (1 Samuel 18:6, NLT), bold praise and worship (Psalm 150:5), religious speech which is void of love (1 Corinthian 13:1)

Dam = Religious spirit (stopping up the free flowing movement of the Holy Spirit), the Lord as the one who holds back the floods of the enemy, the work of the enemy in attempting to hinder the flow of God's blessings to His people, repression of one's emotions

Deadline = An urgent need to complete a task, a sense of undue pressure, a sense of fear or worry about not measuring up

Debris = Residual damage from a bad situation such as hurt feelings or broken relationships

Deed or Title = *Now faith is the assurance (the confirmation, the **title deed**) of the things (we) hope for, being the proof of things (we) do not see and the conviction of their reality (faith perceiving as real fact what is not revealed to the senses.)* (Hebrews 11:1, AMP), a sign of future ownership of property, house, car, etc, a reminder that we God's people belong to Him (John 8:47), the ownership of the land of Israel by the Jewish people (Ezekiel 45:5-7)

Defibrillator = The work of the Holiday Spirit in healing and restoring a broken heart, The Holy spirit restoring a backslider, resurrection power

Desk = Bible study, academics, writing

Dominoes = Unleashing chariots and horses and an armada of ships, he'll blow away anything in his path. As he enters the beautiful land, people will fall before him like dominoes. (Daniel 11:40-41, MSG),

Drain = Sudden terror and disease draining away life (Leviticus

26:16, NIV), courage draining away for fear (Joshua 5:1, MSG), misery draining away strength (Psalm 31:10, NLT), shame draining away power (Isaiah 37:27, NIV), repentance draining away sin

Drugs (Illegal) = Spirit of death (Jeremiah 9:21), addiction, witchcraft: pharmakia which is the Greek word used for sorceries in Revelation 9:21 is the root word for drug – drugs (potions) have long been used in sorcery

Earring = *a wise man's rebuke to a listening ear* (Proverbs 25:12, NIV), beauty, having the ability to hear and discern God's voice

Empty = Things of this World that have no eternal value (1 Samuel 12:21, NKJV), *A lazy life is an empty life, but "early to rise" gets the job done.* (Proverbs 12:27, MSG), *A pretentious, showy life is an empty life* (Proverbs 13:7, MSG), *"Look at that man, bloated by self-importance— full of himself but soul-empty. But the person in right standing before God through loyal and steady believing is fully alive, really alive.* (Habakkuk 2:4, MSG), ideas, philosophies, teaching, etc that are void of truth and substance (Colossians 2:8), religion that is focused on tradition, ritual, and human effort rather than on the true love, grace, power and purity of the Spirit of God (1 Peter 1:18, NLT and MSG)

Eyeglasses = An increase in prophetic vision

Fabric = framework, structure, organization, infrastructure, *They show that God's law is not something alien, imposed on us from without, but woven into the very fabric of our creation.* (Romans 2:14-16 MSG)

Fairy Tale = An unrealistic expectation, an unrealistic expectation that comes true, a false report or lie

Famine = *Behold the days are coming, says the Lord, when I will send a famine through the land— not a famine of food or a thirst for water, but a famine of hearing the words of the Lord.* (Amos 8:11, NKJV)

Feces or Dung = Something worthless (Philippians 3:7-9), sin, spiritual filth

Fence = A barrier or obstacle to moving ahead (Job 19:8, NKJV), a boundary, a feeling of being fenced in **barbed-wire fence** – protection from the enemy, a person who doesn't allow others to become close **sitting on the fence** – *Elijah challenged the people: "How long are you going to sit on the **fence**? If God is the real God, follow him; if it's Baal, follow him. Make up your minds!"* (1 Kings 18:21, MSG)

Ferris Wheel = Religious ritual and tradition, a ministry that is going nowhere, an unfruitful strategy, fruitless cycles of behavior, fun and relaxation

Firecracker = Emotional outburst, celebration, an energetic person, an outspoken person

Fire Extinguisher = *In addition to all this, take up the shield of faith, with which you can extinguish all the flaming arrows of the evil one.* (Ephesians 6:16, NIV), a church leader who disallows prophecy (1 Thessalonians 5:18-20) a peacemaker, sin which quenches the fire of God

Fireworks = Self promotion, a display of great anger, spectacular activity with little substance

Flight Simulator = Training for ministry, leadership training

Found (A Person Who Had Lost His/Her Way) = A lost soul brought into the Kingdom of God through faith in Jesus Christ (Luke 15:4-7)

Fragrance (Sweet Smelling) = The sweet smelling fragrance of Jesus (Song of Solomon 1:3), the sweet smelling fragrance of the Church before the Lord (Song of Solomon 4:10), worship (John 12:3), *Now thanks be to God who always leads us in triumph in Christ, and through us diffuses the fragrance of His knowledge in every place.* (2 Corinthians 2:14, NKJV), the sacrifice of Jesus (Ephesians 5:2, AMP), sacrifice and offerings to the Lord (Numbers 28:27)

Freedom or Liberty = *But Jesus said to the woman, your faith has saved you; go (enter) into peace (in freedom from all the distresses that are experienced as the result of sin).* (Luke 7:50, AMP), living under the New Covenant of grace rather than under the Old Covenant based on keeping the law (Romans 6:14, NLT), freedom from eternal death for the believer (1 Corinthians 15:53, AMP), the enabling grace the Lord gives His people to no longer be bound by sin and addictions (2 Corinthians 3:17, AMP), fearlessness in one's Christian walk (Philippians 1:14, AMP), freedom for the believer to come boldly into God's presence (Hebrews 10:19, AMP)

Full = *I came that they may have and enjoy life, and have it in abundance [to the full, till it overflows].* (John 10:10, AMP), fullness of joy in Jesus (John 15:11), *Therefore, brethren, seek out from among you seven men of good reputation, full of the Holy Spirit and wisdom* (Acts 6:3, NKJV), *And Stephen, full of faith and power, did great wonders and signs among the people.* (Acts 6:8, NKJV), *Then he said, "You son of the devil, full of every sort of deceit and fraud, and enemy of all that is good! Will you never stop perverting the true ways of the Lord?* (Acts 13:10, NLT)

Gangrene = *moral or spiritual corruption and decadence that pervades an individual or group* – quoted from dictionary.com

Garbage = Gossip (Proverbs 18:8, NIV), sin (Isaiah 1:25, MSG), idols (Isaiah 30:22, MSG), things that have worldly value but no eternal value (Philippians 3:8, NLT), worthless or useless, see also **Junk Food**

Garden = The fruitful heart of a Christian in which the Lord takes delight (Song of Solomon 5:1), the Jewish people in the eyes of God (Isaiah 5:7), the Lord's provision (Ezekiel 34:29, MSG) *a garden locked up* – the place in the heart of a Christian that is preserved for intimacy with God alone (Song of Solomon 4:12, NIV)

Gate = *You can enter God's Kingdom only through the narrow gate. The highway to hell is broad, and its gate is wide for the many who choose that way.* (Matthew 7:13, NLT), Jesus as the only way to access the Kingdom of Heaven (John 10:7), rulership over a city or region (Genesis 23:18, Deuteronomy 21:19)

Gift = An offering unto the Lord (Genesis 4:3-4, NLT, Numbers 7:3, NIV), the birth of a child as a gift from God (Genesis 30:20), the blessings of the Lord (James 1:17, John 1:16), *As each of you has received a gift (a particular spiritual talent, a gracious divine endowment), employ it for one another as (befits) good trustees of God's many-sided grace* (1 Peter 4:10, AMP), *Peter replied, "Each of you must repent of your sins and turn to God, and be baptized in the name of Jesus Christ for the forgiveness of your sins. Then you will receive the gift of the Holy Spirit.* (Acts 2:38), *For the wages of sin is death, but the free gift of God is eternal life through Christ Jesus our Lord.* (Romans 6:23, NLT)

Glass = Transparency, fragility *stained glass* – Religious ritual and the traditions of men (Mark 7:8), see also **Window**

Globe = The nations

Glue = The Holy Spirit joining people together in true

relationship, a unifying person, a unifying truth or doctrine, a cause people will gather together to rally around, marriage

Gong = religious speech which is void of love (1 Corinthians 13:1)

Hammer = *Those who belong to Christ Jesus have nailed the passions and desires of their sinful nature to His cross and crucified them there.* (Galatians 5:24, NLT), *God wiped out the charges that were against us for disobeying the Law of Moses. He took them away and nailed them to the cross.* (Colossians 2:14, CEV) the Word of God (Jeremiah 23:29), a great and very powerful nation in war (Jeremiah 51:20, MSG), a call to build up the Kingdom of God on Earth

Handkerchief = Physical healing and deliverance (Acts 19: 11-12), weeping

Harp = Worship (Psalm 43:4), rejoicing and celebration (Genesis 31:27), deliverance (1 Samuel 16:23), prophesying (2 Kings 3:15-16)

Hat = Glory and beauty (Exodus 28:40, NKJV), a role, office or position (the type of hat may give more clarification, as for example a hard hat or a firefighter's hat)

Headline = Strong prophetic word or declaration, powerful word of knowledge

Hourglass = Time is running short, it's time for action

Hunger = *God—you're my God! I can't get enough of you! I've worked up such hunger and thirst for God, traveling across dry and weary deserts.* (Psalm 63:1, MSG), a great desire for the Word of God (Psalm 119:20, MSG), *fools are hungry for foolishness.* (Proverbs 15:14a, CEV), a longing for true love (Song of Solomon 2:5, CEV), a non-believer who feels empty inside along with an inner hunger for something more in life, *Blessed are they which do hunger and thirst after righteousness: for they shall be filled.* (Matthew 5:6, KJV), a lust for material wealth and possessions (2 Timothy 3:2, MSG)

Incense = Prayer (Revelation 8:4), *the heartfelt counsel of a friend is as sweet as perfume and incense* (Proverbs 27:9, NLT)

Inheritance = *For what has God above chosen for us? What is our inheritance from the Almighty on high? Isn't it calamity for the wicked and misfortune for those who do evil?* (Job 31:2-3, NLT), *The king proclaims the LORD's decree: "The LORD said to me, 'You are my son. Today I have become your Father. Only ask, and I will give you the nations as your inheritance, the whole earth as your possession.* (Psalm 2:7-8, NLT), *Lord, you alone are my inheritance, my cup of blessing. You guard all that is mine.* (Psalm 16:5, NLT), *What joy for the nation whose God is the Lord, whose people he has chosen as his inheritance.* (Psalm 33:12, NLT), *But the meek [in the end] shall inherit the earth and shall delight themselves in the abundance of peace.* (Psalm 37:11, AMP), the promises of God (Psalm 119:6, AMP), *The wise shall inherit glory (all honor and good)* (Proverbs 3:35, AMP), *Those who love me inherit wealth. I will fill their treasuries.* (Proverbs 8:21, AMP), *wisdom* (Ecclesiastes 7:11), eternal life as the inheritance of the children of God in Christ (Matthew 19:29), the passing down of spiritual gifts, mantles, callings, etc from those who have gone before (2 Kings 2:13-15)

Iron (Clothes) = The Word of God which removes the wrinkles of sin in our lives (Ephesians 5:25-27), continuous sin that sears the conscience of the wicked (1 Timothy 4:2, NIV)

Jar = The Lord's provision (Jeremiah 13:12, NLT, 2 Kings 4:5-7, NIV, Ruth 2:9, NIV), a Christian as a container of the Holy Spirit

Yarmulke or Kipa = Judaism, spiritual covering

Jewel = *Gold there is, and rubies in abundance, but lips that speak knowledge are a rare jewel.* (Proverbs 20:15, NIV), great beauty (Ezekiel 16:7), the outshining of the glory of God (Revelation 21:11), a child of God (Malachi 3:17, KJV), a very special person, wealth, see also **GEMSTONES**

Junk Mail = Distracting thoughts that come during one's prayer time

Key = Wisdom as the key to life (Proverbs 4:8-14, NLT), kingdom authority (Isaiah 22:22), the fear of the Lord as the key to: *a rich store of salvation and wisdom and knowledge* (Isaiah 33:6, NIV), *I am the Living One; I was dead, and behold I am alive for ever and ever! And I hold the keys of death and Hades.* (Revelation 1:18)

Knife = Sacrifice unto the Lord (Genesis 22:9-12), betrayal (Psalm 144:11, MSG), the Word of God (Ephesians 6:17), circumcision which is a type of the Lord cutting away sin from our hearts (Exodus 4:25), see also **Stabbing**

Knot = A complicated problem (Daniel 5:16, AMP), marriage, a very close relationship

Ladder = Jesus as the bridge between Heaven and Earth (Genesis 28:11-13), a vehicle for promotion and prosperity as signified by climbing up the ladder (Deuteronomy 28:43, MSG), a way of escape, **bottom rung** – at the lowest level of status, a beginning, **top rung** – highest status level

Lamp = The Word of God (Psalm 119:105), *The spirit of man [that factor in human personality which proceeds immediately from God] is the lamp of the Lord, searching all his innermost parts.* (Proverbs 20:27, AMP), *"Your eye is a lamp that provides light for your body. When your eye is good, your whole body is filled with light.* (Matthew 6:22, NLT), a Christian who shines forth the light of God from his/her life (Mark 4:21), the Church (Revelation 1:20)

Landmark = The barrier between right and wrong (Hosea 5:10, AMP), a significant event in the life of a person, an organization, a region, a nation, etc – an example of this would be a wedding as a landmark event in one's life

Lie Detector = The gift of discernment, the Holy Spirit as the Spirit of Truth (John 16:13)

Linen = Wealth (Luke 16:19, Revelation 18:16), *Let us rejoice and be glad and give him glory! For the wedding of the Lamb has come, and his bride has made herself ready. Fine linen, bright and clean, was given her to wear." (Fine linen stands for the righteous acts of the saints.)* (Revelation 19:7-8)

Lock = Emotional and spiritual bondage from which it seems there is no escape (Lamentations 3:5-6, MSG), a bad situation in which someone feels entrapped (Lamentations 3:7-9, MSG), the secrets of the Lord (Daniel 12:4, MSG), *But the Scripture declares that the whole world is a prisoner of sin, so that what was promised, being given through faith in Jesus Christ, might be given to those who believe. Before this faith came, we were held prisoners by the law,* **locked** *up until faith should be revealed*, a locked door which speaks of an opportunity or desired outcome that is or seems unattainable.

Lost (One's Way) = Living an unrepentant life of sin and rebellion (Genesis 6:12, AMP, Luke 13:3, AMP), a person who is or has become separated from God (Matthew 18:11)

Magic = Counterfeit miracles performed through satanic powers (2 Thessalonians 2:8-10), a false prophet (Genesis 41:23-25, Jeremiah 14:14, AMP), lies and illusions (Isaiah 30:9-11, AMP), see also **Magician**

Magnet = Someone or something that attracts such as a church that draws a lot of congregants or a charismatic person who draws people to him/herself

Magnifying Glass = Sharp prophetic insight, seeing yourself through the lens of self-importance and pride (Daniel 8:25, AMP), making a big issue out of a small one. Oh, magnify the Lord with me, And let us exalt His name together. (Psalm 34:3, NKJV)

Map = The Lord's direction or strategy, a sign of someone being without direction, *and if you stay on course, keeping your eye on the life-map and the God-signs as your father David did, I'll also give you a long life."* (1 Kings 3:14, MSG)

Masquerade Costume = A sign of covering up one's true inner thoughts and feelings while showing a facade, hypocrisy or hidden sin, ... *for Satan himself masquerades as an angel of light. It is not surprising, then, if his servants masquerade as servants of righteousness* (2 Corinthians 11:14-15, NIV), A call to the arts or drama ministry, performance in place of Spirit-led ministry

Mat = Sickness (Mark 6:55, Acts 5:14-16) ***doormat*** – an often abused person (Proverbs 29:21, MSG)

Maze = A difficult situation with many twists and turns (Psalm 88:8-9, MSG), the wicked who travel *paths that go nowhere, wandering in a maze of detours and dead ends.* (Proverbs 2:14-15, MSG)

Measuring Cup = Increasing levels of sin (Genesis 15:16, NIV, Matthew 23:32), God's judgment (Psalm 28:4, NLT), *For in the same way you judge others, you will be judged, and with the measure you use, it will be measured to you.* (Matthew 7:2, NIV), *"Give and you will receive. Your gift will return to you in full—pressed down, shaken together to make room for more,* *running over, and poured into your lap. The amount you give will determine the amount you get back"* (Luke 6:38, NLT), the measure of godly spiritual qualities in one's life such as kindness and love (2 Peter 1:6-8) **beyond measure** – great abundance of provision (Genesis 41:49), God's glory (2 Corinthians 4:17), the grace of God (1 Timothy 1:14), God's love, *for God gives the [gift of the] Spirit without measure [generously and boundlessly]!* (John 3:34, AMP)

Medicine = A cheerful heart (Proverbs 17:22), Brutal *Ephraim is himself brutalized— a taste of his own medicine!* (Hosea 5:11, MSG), correction or rebuke from a godly person (Psalm 141:5, NLT), healing prayer (James 5:15), the Word of God

Merry-Go-Round = Endless activity with little variety, religious tradition and ritual

Microphone = Public prominence in ministry, business or other endeavors, a prideful desire to be in the spotlight

Microwave = A method of making things happen quickly regardless of quality, an unrealistic expectation of instantaneous results

Mirror = The Word of God (James 1:22-24), Jesus as a reflection of the Father (Hebrews 1:3, MSG), vanity (1 Timothy 2:8-10, MSG), the Church which is to reflect the glory of the Lord (2 Corinthians 3:17-18)

Money = An offering to the Lord (2 Kings 12:16, NLT), greed (Proverbs 1:19, NLT), investing (Matthew 25:16, NLT), idolatry, corruption (Mark 11:15), counting the cost (Luke 14:28, NLT), deception (Jude 1:11, NLT)

Music = Worshipping the Lord (Judges 5:3), celebration (Luke 15:25), worship of false gods (Daniel 3:4-6), worldly revelry *harmony* – Unity (Psalm 133:1, NLT), one with the Lord (Psalm

7:9, AMP) **symphony** – *Wilderness and desert will sing joyously, the badlands will celebrate and flower— Like the crocus in spring, bursting into blossom, a* **symphony** *of song and color. Mountain glories of Lebanon—a gift. Awesome Carmel, stunning Sharon—gifts. God's resplendent glory, fully on display. God awesome, God majestic.* (Isaiah 35:1-2, MSG), agreement and unity (Matthew 18:19, AMP) **cacophony** – Loud conflict and disagreement

Necklace = Love and faithfulness (Proverbs 3:3, NIV), vanity (Isaiah 3:17-18), *Therefore pride serves as their necklace; Violence covers them like a garment.* (Psalm 73:6), A Christian who yields his or her will to the Lord (Song of Songs 4:9), inner or outer beauty (Ezekiel 16:10-12, NIV), prosperity

Newspaper Headline = The foretelling of a future event, an expression of fear that a frightening event will take place, an inner desire for fame, *Your marvelous doings are headline news; I could write a book full of the details of your greatness.* (Psalm 145:6, MSG), a desire for fame, a prophetic word or word of knowledge in the headline itself

Odor (Foul Smelling) or Stench = Wickedness and sin (Proverbs 10:7, MSG, Jude 1:22, MSG), a Christian as *the smell of death* to those who reject Christ (2 Corinthians 2:16, NIV), *Religious performance by the wicked stinks* (Proverbs 21:27a, MSG)

Oven or Stove = Murderous rage (Hosea 7:6-8), the consuming nature of God's wrath poured out on the wicked (Psalm 21:9, AMP), great suffering and tribulation (Lamentations 5:10, AMP), fresh baked bread symbolizing fresh revelation, *They're a bunch of overheated adulterers, like an oven that holds its heat* (Hosea 7:4, MSG) **backburner** – Something that for a time is given less focus or attention

Padlock = *An offended friend is harder to win back than a*

fortified city. Arguments separate friends like a gate locked with bars. (Proverbs 18:19, NLT), an instruction to keep a revelation or prophetic word to yourself (Daniel 12:4, MSG,) depression, a person who locks up his/her heart to avoid intimacy due to past hurts and abuse, fear (John 20:19, NLT), *Write this to Philadelphia, to the Angel of the church. The Holy, the True— David's key in his hand, opening doors no one can lock, locking doors no one can open* (Revelation 3:7, MSG), a call to keep the door locked to the enemy

Paint or **Paint Brush** = Creation or creativity, to describe someone or something in a particular way from a particular viewpoint (2 Corinthians 10:1-2, MSG), beauty, a calling to the prophetic or worship arts

Parachute = The Lord as the object of our faith

Patch = A strategy to mend a broken relationship, an attempt to cover over a problem without really dealing with it

Pen = The Spirit of God guiding the words of a true worshipper of Jesus (Psalm 45:1-3), writing or journaling (Jeremiah 36:18, MSG)

Pension = Work hard for sin your whole life and your pension is death. But God's gift is real life, eternal life, delivered by Jesus, our Master. (Romans 6:22, MSG), God's promise of perpetual provision

Perfume = Sexual temptation (Proverbs 7:16-18), *the heartfelt counsel of a friend is as sweet as perfume and incense* (Proverbs 27:9, NLT), the sweet smelling fragrance of Jesus (Song of Solomon 1:3), the sweet smelling fragrance of the Church before the Lord (Song of Solomon 4:10), a heart poured out in worship (Matthew 26:6), the knowledge of Christ (2 Corinthians 2:14, NLT), see also **BIBLICAL SPICES AND PERFUMES**

Pesticide = Deliverance ministry, the power of God, the Word of God, intercessory prayer

Phone = Prayer, communication whether spiritual or natural, a need to reach out to another person

Pillow = Rest, spiritual slumber

Photograph = Memories or images from the past

Photo Album = Ordering past memories in order to put them in proper prospective, an unhealthy focus on the past, a journal of past dreams and visions

Piggy Bank = Saving money, a little bit adding up to a lot, a grassroots funding campaign, small mindedness, greed

Plate or Dish = A person: the outside of the plate speaks of one's outward appearance and reputation while the inside represents the inner person (Luke 11:38-40), a person's schedule (full plate = full schedule), a teaching or Bible study tool or the vehicle through which the Word of God is presented

Pocketbook or Wallet = One's identity, personal finances (Proverbs 7:20, MSG)

Poison = Idolatry or false religion (Deuteronomy 29:18, NIV), evil words such as gossip or slander (James 3:8, Psalm 140:9, MSG), wine (Deuteronomy 32:32-34), trusting a fool (Proverbs 26:6, NLT), divine judgment (Jeremiah 8:14, NLT), false doctrine or teaching, the spirit of death (Jeremiah 9:21)

Pot = A person (Isaiah 29:16), a teaching ministry, *broken pot* – A broken hearted person, a teaching ministry in trouble, *I am forgotten as though I were dead; I have become like broken pottery.* (Psalm 31:12, NIV)

Potter's Wheel = Symbolic of God molding and shaping us into his image (Jeremiah 18:6)

Pressure Cooker = A very stressful and demanding situation (Psalm 32:4, MSG)

Prize = The eternal reward of the Christian (1 Corinthians 9:25) The Church in the eyes of Jesus (Hebrews 12:2, AMP), Jesus in the eyes of His people

Puppet = A false prophet (1 Kings 22:23, MSG), a person who is being controlled and/or manipulated by another

Puzzle = *The heart is hopelessly dark and deceitful, a puzzle that no one can figure out* (Jeremiah 17:9, MSG), a situation or statement that one's mind cannot make sense of (Matthew 19:25), a complicated matter, a challenge that will take a lot of detailed understanding to complete

Rags = Great poverty (1 Corinthians 4:11, NIV), drunkenness (Proverbs 23:19, NIV), *We are all infected and impure with sin. When we display our righteous deeds they are nothing but filthy rags.* (Isaiah 64:6, NLT)

Report Card = A works versus grace mentality (Ephesians 2:8-10), The Judgment Seat of Christ (2 Corinthians 5:10)

Recipe = A means of attaining a goal or desired state: *I've found the recipe for being happy whether full or hungry, hands full or hands empty. Whatever I have, wherever I am, I can make it through anything in the One who makes me who I am* (Philippians 4:12-13, MSG) behavior that will lead to an unwanted end such as taking drugs and smoking as a recipe for disaster

Reward = Long life and salvation for those who love the Lord

(Psalm 91:13-16, NLT), *Behold, children are a heritage and gift from the Lord, The fruit of the womb a reward.* (Psalm 127:3, AMP), honor (Proverbs 3:35, MSG*), The reward of humility [that is, having a realistic view of one's importance] and the [reverent, worshipful] fear of the Lord Is riches, honor, and life.* (Proverbs 22:4, AMP), finding joy in marriage (Ecclesiastes 9:9, AMP), *For the Son of Man will come in the glory of His Father with His angels, and then He will reward each according to his works.* (Matthew 16:27, NKJV)

Ring = Wealth (James 2:2, NIV), authority (Esther 8:8), eternity, marriage, vanity commitment, covenant

Robe = Covering **multi-colored (KJV)** *or* **richly ornamented (NIV) robe** – favor (Genesis 37:2-4), **purple robe** – royalty (Daniel 5:7), **white robe** – righteousness (Isaiah 61:10, Revelation 6:11), **blue robe** – priestly intercession and worship (Exodus 39:22)

Rod = Punishment and discipline (2 Samuel 7:13-15), correction or rebuke (Proverbs 29:15), rulership (Isaiah 14:5, NIV)

Rollercoaster = An unpredictable season of life with many twists and turns and ups and downs and sudden changes

Rotten = Sin and corruption (2 Kings 21:2, MSG), death and hell (Psalm 68:5, MSG), envy and jealousy (Proverbs 14:30), pride (Jeremiah 13:9, NLT), sinful motives (Galatians 4:17, MSG), the moral decay of society (2 Peter 1:4, AMP)

Sackcloth = Mourning (Genesis 37:34), repentance (Joel 1:13)

Saw = Division, broken relationship, the cutting away of areas of one's life that are harmful or unfruitful (John 15:2)

Scale = Justice (Job 31:6, NLT), honesty (Proverbs 11:1b,), dishonesty (Proverbs 11:1a), God's measure of a person's character (Daniel 5:27), famine (Revelation 6:5-6)

Scarecrow = Something harmless that seems scary or intimidating, an idol (Jeremiah 10:5, AMP),

Scotch Tape = A temporary solution to a bigger problem

Scrapbook = An unhealthy focus on reliving memories of the past, documenting testimonies of what the Lord has done, A church, ministry or denomination that focus on their past victories while having little interest in what God would have them do today

Screwdriver = A need for a person to make adjustments in or tighten up one's schedule, relationships, way of thinking, etc.

Scroll = The Word of God (Deuteronomy 17:18, NLT), a vision or prophetic message from the Lord (Isaiah 29:11, AMP, Jeremiah 36:4, NLT), the title deed of the Earth (Revelation 5:1-3)

Seal = Authority (Esther 8:8), *And he received the sign of circumcision, a **seal** of the righteousness of the faith* (Romans 4:11, KJV), the Holy Spirit (Ephesians 1:13), ownership, a Christian as a seal upon the heart of Jesus or vice versa according to one's interpretation of the Scripture (Song of Solomon 8:6), divine end-time judgment poured out on the Earth (Revelation 6:5), God's seal of protection upon His people: *Then locusts came from the smoke and descended on the earth, and they were given power to sting like scorpions. They were told not to harm the grass or plants or trees, but only the people who did not have the seal of God on their foreheads.* (Revelation 9:3-4, NLT)

Sewage = Sin and pride (Isaiah 25:11, MSG)

Sewer = A place of sin and corruption (Genesis 6:11, MSG)

Shackles = Sin, addiction, imprisonment (Psalm 149:8, AMP), demonic possession (Mark 5:4)

Shawl = God covering over a life, prayer

Shelf = A time of inactivity (Psalm 71:9,MSG), a period of waiting on the Lord before being released into one's ministry, something important that a person has ignored such as prayer or ministry (Revelation 22:6, MSG – heading)

Shoes = *And having shod your feet in preparation (to face the enemy with the firm-footed stability, the promptness, and the readiness produced by the good news) of the Gospel of peace.* (Ephesians 6:15, AMP), one's individual walk in life (Galatians 4:12, MSG), evangelism (Isaiah 52:7) *snow shoes* – standing and walking on the Word of God, see also **Feet**

Shovel = See **Digging**

Shower or Bathtub = Repentance and cleansing, inner healing

Sickle = Divine judgment of the wicked poured out in the end-times (Joel 3:12-14), soul winning evangelism (Mark 4:26-29)

Sign = red sky in the morning means foul weather all day.' You know how to interpret the weather signs in the sky, but you don't know how to interpret the signs of the times! (Matthew 16:3, NLT), [The Signs of the Times and the End of the Age] Now as He sat on the Mount of Olives, the disciples came to Him privately, saying, "Tell us, when will these things be? And what will be the sign of Your coming, and of the end of the age?" (Matthew 24:3, NLT), Miracles that confirm the truth of the Gospel and the lordship of Jesus (Mark 16:17), a miracle performed by a false prophet, teacher, etc. designed to lead people astray (Mark 13:22), speaking in tongues when witnessed by a non believer (1 Corinthians 14:22), what is written on a sign can be a prophetic message or word of knowledge

Silence = Wisdom (Job 13:5, AMP), a period of time where God seems quiet and inactive and not meeting our expectations (Job 21:4-16, Psalm 28:1, MSG), quiet reverence (Habakkuk 2:20), peace in the land (Judges 8:28, KJV), inner peace (Job 3:26, NLT)), quiet meditative prayer, a time of quietly reflecting on God's Word

Silk or Velvet = Luxury (Isaiah 3:18, MSG), smoothness or softness

Sink = Repentance and cleansing of sin

Sleeping Bag = Travel, finding peace and rest regardless of the situation, vacation or travel, laziness

Slide = Falling into sin (Ephesians 5:3, MSG), *But there were also lying prophets among the people then, just as there will be lying religious teachers among you. They've put themselves on a fast downhill slide to destruction* (2 Peter 2:1, 3, MSG), a sign that a difficult time is ahead

Slingshot = God's grace and power working through our weakness (1 Samuel 15:20), *Honoring a fool is as foolish as tying a stone to a slingshot.* (Proverbs 26:8, NLT)

Soot = Poverty and lack (Lamentations 4:8)

Splinter = *And to keep me from being puffed up and too much elated by the exceeding greatness (preeminence) of these revelations, there was given me a thorn* (a splinter) *in the flesh, a messenger of Satan, to rack and buffet and harass me, to keep me from being excessively exalted.* (2 Corinthians 12:7, AMP), harassment (Numbers 33:55, NLT)

Sponge = Someone who retains a great deal of knowledge, a Christian who soaks up the glory and presence of God, a person who takes advantage of the generosity of others

Spoon or Fork = A bible study tool such as a concordance or bible dictionary, a teacher or teaching ministry

Spotlight = A prideful person who likes to draw attention to him/herself (Proverbs 25:6, MSG, Matthew 23:4-6), self-promotion (Philippians 1:15, MSG), the Lord promoting a person or ministry into the forefront (John 8:54, MSG), one who likes to brag about his/her accomplishments to impress others

Staff or Cane = Rulership and authority (Genesis 49:10, NIV), signs and miracles (Exodus 4:17, NIV), old age (Zechariah 8:4, NKJV), favor (Zechariah 11:10, NIV), brotherhood (Zechariah 11:14, NIV), guidance, a need for support

Stage or Platform = God creating opportunities for a person to be seen and/or heard in a public way (Matthew 10:17-19, MSG), public ministry, worship done as performance without focus on God, *backstage* – work done behind the scenes, see also **Spotlight**

Stain = Sin (Jude 1:23, Jeremiah 2:22), *blood stain* – bloodguilt (Isaiah 59:3 NIV,1 Kings 2:5), the garments of the Lord stained with the blood of the wicked when he pours out His wrath in the end-time judgment (Isaiah 63:3)

Statue = Idolatry (Judges 17:3-4, MSG), earthly kingdoms (Daniel 2:34-35), worshipping man rather than God (Daniel 3:5)

Statue of Liberty = Symbolic of the United States, freedom, liberty

Straightjacket = Severe mental illness, the restrictions of religious tradition and ritual, a severe restriction or limitation, a controlling and restrictive relationship

Stretcher = A healing ministry (Matthew 9:1-3, MSG), a person in crisis, emotional collapse, a person who cannot make it on his/her own

Suitcase or Baggage = Travel, heavy burdens that one carries around

Table = The Lord's blessing and provision (Psalm 23:5), fellowship with the Lord (Psalm 22:26, MSG), fellowship with believers (Mark 16:14, NKJV), sitting and sharing the Gospel with non-believers (Luke 5:29), worldly abundance and luxury (Psalm 69:22, AMP), family life (Psalm 128:3), authority (Luke 22:27), *I tell you, many will come from east and west, and will sit at the table with Abraham, Isaac, and Jacob in the kingdom of heaven* (Matthew 8:11, AMP), the Lord's supper (1 Corinthians 10:16, NLT), fellowship with demons through idolatry, the occult and false religions (1 Corinthians 10:20), marriage supper of the Lamb (Revelation 19:9) **under the table** – a bribe (Proverbs 17:23, MSG), a deceitful plan, drunkenness **head table** – honor, authority, presumptuous pride (Luke 20:46, NLT) **overturned tables** – divine anger over corruption in the Church (John 2:15), *The Holy of Israel, says: "Just for you, I will march on Babylon. I'll turn the tables on the Babylonians. Instead of whooping it up, they'll be wailing.* (Isaiah 43:14-15, MSG), vengeance, justice

Tabloid = Gossip, an evil report (Genesis 37:2, KJV)

Tambourine = Celebration and joy (Genesis 31:27, NLT), praising the Lord (Psalm 150:4, AMP)

Tape Measure = Comparing oneself to others, judging other people see **Measuring Cup**

Tapestry = The beauty of the body of Christ who in its diversity are: *woven into a tapestry of love* (Colossians 2:2, MSG)

Tarot Cards, Ouija Board, Crystal Ball, Séance, Horoscope, etc = The occult (Leviticus 19:26), witchcraft, a false prophet

Tea = Relaxation, a social gathering

Teddy Bear = Childhood, childlikeness, someone who appears rough but is actually gentle, a bad situation that will turn out okay

Telescope = Prophetically seeing into the future (Revelation 4:1)

Television = One's thought life, prophetic vision, idolatry

Test = A difficult situation or trial which the Lord allows in a person's life in order to prove and try his/her faith, love, commitment, obedience, motives, etc (Genesis 22:1-3, AMP, Exodus 16:4, 1 Peter 1:7, AMP), " ... *and you shall be kept in prison, that your words may be tested to see whether there is any truth in you*" (Genesis 42:16, NKJV), asking God for a sign as a confirmation of His will on a matter (Judges 6:39- 40), the process of discerning whether a prophetic word is a true revelation from the Lord (1 Thessalonians 5:20-22), the process in which the leadership of a Church or ministry determines whether a potential leader has the necessary character and maturity (1 Timothy 3:9-10), the process of discerning whether a person is operating in the Holy Spirit or demonic power: *"Dear friends, do not believe every spirit, but test the spirits to see whether they are from God, because many false prophets have gone out into the world"*. (1 John 4:1-3), *Examine and test and evaluate your own selves to see whether you are holding to* *your faith and showing the proper fruits of it. Test and prove yourselves (not Christ). Do you not yourselves realize and know (thoroughly by an ever-increasing experience) that Jesus Christ is in you--unless you are (counterfeits) disapproved on trial and rejected?* (2 Corinthians 13:5, AMP)

Thirst = *What chance do humans have? We are so terribly evil that we thirst for sin.* (Job 15:16, CEV), *As a deer gets thirsty for streams of water, I truly am thirsty for you, my God.* (Psalm 42:1, CEV)

Throne = Rulership and authority (Luke 22:30), The Lord's rule over the universe (Revelation 5:13), the kingdom of darkness (Revelation 2:13)

Ticket (to an event or destination) = *I'm happy from the inside out, and from the outside in, I'm firmly formed. You canceled my ticket to hell— that's not my destination!* (Psalm 16:9-10, MSG), God's promises (2 Peter 1:4, MSG), favor, opportunity, God's invitation

Torch = Guidance to get through a dark situation (Psalm 78:14), salvation radiating through the people of God (Isaiah 62:1), angelic appearance (Ezekiel 1:13), *Seven torches, which are the seven spirits of God, were burning in front of the throne.* (Revelation 4:5b), undying love, faithfulness, destruction (Revelation 8:10-11)

Toilet = Inner healing, repentance, cleansing **backed up toilet** – Guilt, shame, condemnation

Towel = Servant-hood (John 13:3-5), surrender, cleansing

Treasure = Israel in the eyes of the Lord (Exodus 19:5), a person in the eyes of a close friend (1 Samuel 19:1, MSG), the Lord in the eyes of His people (Job 22:25, NLT), the Word of God (Job 23:12), wisdom (Proverbs 2:3-5), knowledge (Proverbs

10:14), worldly riches (Proverbs 15:15-16), a wife (Proverbs 18:22, NLT), the Church in the eyes of Jesus (Song of Solomon 4:9, NLT), *He will be the sure foundation for your times, a rich store of salvation and wisdom and knowledge; the fear of the LORD is the key to this treasure.* (Isaiah 33:6, NIV), one's children (Ezekiel 24:25, NLT), that which a person considers as the most valuable things in life; whether earthly riches or eternal blessings (Matthew 6:19-21), *A good man out of the good treasure of his heart brings forth good things, and an evil man out of the evil treasure brings forth evil things.* (NKJV), eternal rewards stored up in Heaven (Matthew 19:21), the power and glory of God placed inside of the children of God (2 Corinthians 4:6-7

Trophy = Competition, victory, achievement, success, a desire for human recognition

Trumpet or Shofar = A call for God's people to gather together (Isaiah 27:13), the heralding of the manifestation of the presence and glory of God (Hebrews 12:19), worship (2 Samuel 6:15), the battle cry (2 Chronicles 13:12), warning of danger (Ezekiel 33:3, Jeremiah 4:5-6), a call to repentance and fasting (Joel 2:15), pride and hypocrisy (Joel 2:15), the return of Jesus to gather His bride (Matthew 24:31), the resurrection of the dead (1 Corinthians 15:52), a call to prepare for a heavenly encounter (Revelation 4:1), the end- time outpouring of God's wrath on the wicked (Revelation 8:6-10:7), A child of God proclaiming the gospel or proclaiming the Word of the Lord (Isaiah 58:1)

Tuxedo = A special occasion, luxury, formality

Ugly = A distorted view of oneself, sin, evil

Umbrella = The Lord as our protection from life's storms, a denomination, apostolic network or other organization that acts as a spiritual covering and offers accountability

Vacation = Time of rest and refreshing

Video = Memories or images from the past

Wax = The enemy melting away in the presence of the Lord (Psalm 68:1-3), a person who is easily manipulated, a broken heart (Psalm 22:14)

Wheelchair = A person who has become emotionally crippled, a person who is emotionally dependant, a person who sees him/herself as unable to move forward

Whip = Bondage (Exodus 5:14, NLT), the wrath of God (Isaiah10:25-26, NLT), the healing available to us because of Jesus' suffering (Isaiah 53:5, NLT), the persecution of the righteous (Jeremiah 20:2, NLT, Matthew 10:17, NLT), punishment (1 Corinthians 4:21), someone lashing out with angry words

Wool = Purity (Isaiah 1:18), asking God to supernaturally confirm His Will on a matter (Judges 6:36-38, NIV)

Wrinkle = Sin or imperfection (Ephesians 5:27), a disagreement

X-Ray = *Test me, O Lord and try me, examine my heart and my mind* (Psalm 26:2, NIV), gift of discernment

Yo-Yo = Life's ups and downs, emotional turmoil

MOTTOS OF THE NATIONS

Afghanistan = There is no god but God; Muhammad is the messenger of God.

Algeria = By the People and for the People

Andorra = Virtue, Unity, Strength

Antigua and Barbuda = Each Endeavoring, All Achieving

Argentina = In Union and Liberty

Armenia = One Nation, One Culture

Aruba = Always progressing

Azerbaijan = The Land of Fire

Azores = Rather die as free men than be enslaved in peace

Bahamas = Forward, Upward, Onward Together

Barbados = Pride and Industry

Bavaria = Steadfast in loyalty

Belgium = Unity Gives Strength

Belize = Under the Shade I Flourish

Benin = Fellowship, Justice, Labor

Bermuda = Whither the fates carry us

Bolivia = Unity Is Strength

Brazil = Order and Progress

Brittany = Rather Death than Dishonor

Brunei = Always In Service with God's Guidance

Bulgaria = Union Makes Strength

Burkina Faso = Unity, Progress, Justice

Burundi = Unity, Work, Progress

Cambodia = Nation, Religion, King

Cameroon = Peace, Work, Fatherland

Canada = From Sea to Sea

Central African Republic = Unity, Dignity, Work

Chad = Unity, Work, Progress

Czech Republic = Truth prevails

Chile = By Reason or By Strength

Colombia = Freedom and Order

Comoros = Unity, Justice, Progress

Democratic Republic of the Congo = French, Justice, Peace, Work

Republic of the Congo = Unity, Work, Progress

Côte d'Ivoire = Unity, Discipline, Labor

Cuba = Homeland or Death

Czech Republic = Truth Prevails!

Denmark = God's Help, The Love of the People, Denmark's Strength (the royal motto of Denmark)

Djibouti = Unity, Equality, Peace

Dominica = After the Good Lord, We Love the Earth

Dominican Republic = God, Country, Liberty

East Timor = Honor, Homeland and People

Easter Island = May God let the clarity of this vital light be extended to all peoples

Ecuador = Liberty and Order

El Salvador = God, Union, Liberty

Equatorial Guinea = Unity, Peace, Justice

Estonia = Positively Surprising

European Union = United in Diversity

Falkland Islands = Desire the Right

Fiji = Fear God and Honor the Queen

France = Liberty, Equality, Fraternity

Gabon = Union, Work, Justice

Georgia, Strength Is In Unity

Ghana = Freedom and Justice

Gibraltar = Conquered By No Enemy

Greece = Liberty or Death

Grenada = Ever Conscious of God We Aspire, and Advance as One People

Guatemala = Grow Free and Fertile

Guinea = Work, Justice, Solidarity

Guinea-Bissau = Unity, Struggle, Progress

Guyana = One People, One Nation, One Destiny

Haiti = Freedom, equality, brotherhood

Honduras = Free, Sovereign and Independent

India = Truth Alone Triumphs

Indonesia = Unity in Diversity

Iran = Independence, Freedom, Islamic Republic

Isle of Man = Whithersoever you throw it, it will stand

Jamaica = Out Of Many, One People

Jordan = God, Country, Sovereign

Kenya = Let's Work Together

Kiribati = Health, Peace and Prosperity

North Korea = Prosperous and Great Country

South Korea = Benefit All Mankind

Kosovo = Honor, Duty, Homeland

Laos = Peace, Independence, Democracy, Unity and Prosperity

Latvia = for Fatherland and Freedom

Lesotho = Peace, Rain, Prosperity

Liberia = The Love of Liberty Brought Us Here

Liechtenstein = For God, Prince and Fatherland

Lithuania = The Strength of the Nation Lies In Unity

Luxembourg = We Wish to Remain What We are

Macedonia = Freedom or Death

Madagascar = Land, Liberty, Progress

Malawi = Unity and Freedom

Malaysia = Unity Is Strength

Mali = One People, One Goal, One Faith

Mauritania = Honor, Fraternity, Justice

Mexico = The Homeland is First

(Federated States of) Micronesia = Peace, Unity, Liberty

Monaco = With God's Help

Morocco = Allah, the Country, the King

Namibia = Unity, Liberty, Justice

Nauru = God's Will First

Nepal = Mother and Motherland are Greater Than Heaven

Netherlands = I Will Preserve

Nicaragua = In God We Trust

Niger = Fraternity, Work, Progress

Nigeria = Unity and Faith, Peace and Progress

Nuevo Leon = Always Ascending

Pakistan = Unity, Faith, Discipline

Panama = For The Benefit Of the World

Papua New Guinea = Unity in Diversity

Paraguay = Peace And Justice

Philippines = For God, People, Nature and Country

Portugal = This is my Beloved Happy Motherland

Rwanda = Unity, Work, Patriotism

Saint Helena = Loyal and Unshakeable

Saint Kitts and Nevis = Country Above Self

Saint Lucia = The Land, the People, the Light

Saint Vincent and the Grenadines = Peace and justice

San Marino = Liberty

Saudi Arabia = There is no God other than God and Muhammad is His Prophet

Scotland = No One Provokes Me with Impunity

Senegal = One People, One Goal, One Faith

Seychelles = The End Crowns the Work

Sierra Leone = Unity, Freedom, Justice

Sint Maarten = Always progressing

Solomon Islands = To Lead Is To Serve

South Africa = Unity in Diversity

South Georgia and the South Sandwich Islands = Let the lion protect his own land

Spain = Further Beyond

Sudan = Victory Is Ours

Suriname = Justice, Piety, Loyalty

Swaziland = We Are the Fortress

Switzerland = One for All, All for One

Tanzania = Freedom and Unity

Togo = Work, Liberty, Homeland

Trinidad and Tobago = Together We Aspire, Together We Achieve

Tunisia = Freedom, Order and Justice

Turkey = Peace at Home, Peace in the World (unofficial)

Uganda = For God and My Country

United Arab Emirates = God, Nation, President

United Kingdom = God and My Right (Royal Motto)

United States = In God We Trust

Uruguay = Liberty or Death

U.S. Virgin Islands = United In Pride and Hope

Uzbekistan = The Strength is in The Justice

Vanuatu = Let Us Stand Firm in God

Vietnam = Independence, Liberty and Happiness

Zimbabwe = Unity, Freedom, Work

BIBLIOGRAPHY

The American Heritage® Dictionary of the English Language, *Fourth Edition* from *dictionary.com* website

biblegateway.com biblemaster.com

Columbia Electronic Encyclopedia, from *reference.com* website:

Crystal Reference Encyclopedia. Crystal Reference Systems Limited. http://www.reference.com

Dictionary.com Unabridged *(v 1.1)* from *dictionary.com* website: http://dictionary.reference.com

Easton's 1897 Bible Dictionary, from *dictionary.com* website: http://dictionary.reference.com

genealogy.about.com godsgenerals.com

Hitchcock's Bible Names Dictionary, from *biblegateway.com* website

Holman Bible Dictionary from *studylight.org* website

ihsworshiparts.com

Interpreting the Symbols and Types by Kevin J. Conner, City Christian Publishing, Portland, Oregon (1999)

nationalgeographic.com

newfoundationspubl.org/types.htm

Roget's New Millennium™ Thesaurus, *First Edition* from *thesaurus.com* website

Smith's Bible Names Dictionary from *studylight.org* website

The International Standard Bible Encyclopedia from *studylight.org* website

studylight.org

Wikipedia, *the free encyclopedia* from *reference.com* website

A Dictionary of Bible Types by Walter Wilson, Hendrickson Pub., Peabody, Massachusetts (1999 – originally published 1957)

weather.com/glossary

WordNet® *2.1* from *dictionary.com* website: http://dictionary.reference.com

COMPREHENSIVE INDEX

Aaron (Bible), 189
Aaron (Name), 157
Abandon Ship, 95
Abandoned Vehicle, 91
Abandonment, 252
Abigail, 157
About Face, 239
Above, 105
Abraham (Bible), 189
Abraham (Name), 157
Absent without Leave, 239
Acacia Tree, 124
Accelerator, 91
Accountant, 167
Accuse, 219
Accuser, 167
Acid, 131
Acid Rain, 111
Acorn, 125
Acquit, 219
Acrobat, 167
Actions, 252
Activities, 252
Actor, 167, 237
Ada, 157
Addition, 251
Adelaide, 157
Adopted Child, 171
Adulterer, 167
Adultery, 252
Adventurer, 167
Adversary, 219
Advertising, 252
Advocate, 167, 219
Afghanistan, 310
Agate, 129
Aida, 157
Aidan, 157

Aimee Semple McPherson, 204
Air, 131
Air Conditioner, 277
Air Purifier, 277
Air Raid Siren, 239
Air Traffic Controller, 168
Airbag, 91
Airplane, 36, 91
Airport, 38, 50
Airport Terminal, 238
Aisha, 157
Akita, 81
Alabama, 273
Alarm, 277
Alarm (Car), 97
Alarm Clock, 277
Alaska, 273
Albatross, 78
Albert, 157
Alberta, 157
Alberto, 157
Alexander, 44, 157
Alexandra, 157
Alexis, 157
Algeria, 310
Alice, 157
Alicia, 157
Alien, 119, 208
All Thumbs, 225
Alley, 103
Alligator, 39, 69, 77
Alligator Tail, 77
Almond, 139
Almond Tree, 124
Aloe, 122, 217
Altar, 277
Alyssa, 157

Ambassador, 168
Amber, 151
Ambulance, 91
Ambush, 239
Amethyst, 129
Ammunition, 239
Amnesia, 277
Amplifier, 277
Amulet, 277
Amy, 157
Analyzing, 252
Ancestor, 168
Anchor, 278
Andorra, 310
Angel, 157, 189
Angela, 157
Angelina, 157
Animal Shelter, 230
Animals, 77
Ankle Bracelet, 278
Anna (Bible), 189
Anna (Name), 160
Anorexia, 278
Answering Machine, 278
Ant, 83
Antelope, 82
Antenna, 92
Anthony, 157
Anti-Aircraft Artillery, 239
Antibiotic, 278
Antigua and Barbuda, 310
Antique, 278
Ape, 77
Appetite, 278
Apple, 140
Apple Tree, 124
Appointment, 252
Apron, 278
Aquarium, 230
Archaeologist, 168
Archer, 168
Architect, 168
Argentina, 310

Ariel, 158
Arizona, 273
Ark, 91
Arkansas, 273
Armadillo, 77
Armenia, 310
Armor, 239
Arms, 222
Army, 240
Arrow, 278
Arrows, 32
Aruba, 310
Ashes, 131
Assassination, 240
Astronaut, 119
Astronomer, 119
At Bat, 247
Athlete, 168
ATM, 279
Atmosphere, 109
Attic, 50, 232
Attorney, 32
Audience, 169
Aunt, 169
Aurora, 158
Author, 169
Auto Mechanic, 42, 169
Autumn, 52, 145
Ava, 158
Avalanche, 109
Avenue, 103
Axe, 279
Azerbaijan, 310
Azores, 310
Baboon, 77
Baby, 169
Baby Bottle, 279
Baby Shower, 252
Baby's Breath (Flower), 121
Baca, 211
Back, 105, 222
Backbone, 228

Backburner, 296
Backdoor, 51
Backfiring, 97
Backflip, 253
Backpack, 279
Backstabbing, 268
Backstage, 304
Backwards, 105
Backyard, 51, 232
Badge, 279
Badger, 77
Baggage, 305
Bahamas, 310
Bait, 250
Balaam, 189
Bald Eagle, 78
Balloons, 279
Ballroom, 230
Balm of Gilead, 124, 217
Baloney, 139
Balsam Tree, 125
Bamboo, 122
Bandage, 230
Band-Aid, 230
Bank, 230
Bankruptcy, 279
Banner, 279
Banquet, 280
Barbados, 310
Barbara, 158
Barbed-Wire Fence, 287
Bare Feet, 224
Bark, 131
Barking Dog, 81
Barley, 141
Barn, 230
Barnabas, 189
Barrel, 280
Barren Land, 114
Barrens, 114
Barricade, 240
Barrier, 280
Basement, 50, 232

Bassett Hound, 81
Bat, 78
Bathing, 253
Bathroom, 50, 232
Bathtub, 302
Battery, 92
Battery Charger, 92
Battle, 240
Battle Fatigue, 240
Battleground, 240
Battleship, 37, 91
Bavaria, 310
Bayonet, 240
Beach, 71, 114
Beachhead, 245
Beacon, 280
Beagle, 81
Bear, 32, 39, 70, 77
Beating One's Breast, 222
Beatrice, 158
Beauty Parlor, 230
Beaver, 77
Becky, 163
Bed, 59, 71, 280
Bed of Roses, 122
Bedrock, 131
Bedroom, 50, 232
Bees, 32, 83
Beetle, 83
Being Chased, 254
Belgium, 310
Belinda, 158
Belize, 310
Belly, 222
Below, 105
Belt, 279
Bending Down, 253
Bending Over Backwards, 253
Benin, 310
Benny Hinn, 201
Bermuda, 310
Bernice, 158

Beryl, 129
Beth, 159
Bethany, 211
Bethel, 211
Bethlehem, 211
Bethsaida, 211
Betty, 159
Beyond Measure, 295
Biblical Figures, 189
Biblical Places, 211
Biblical Spices and
  Perfumes, 217
Bicycle, 37, 91
Big Apple, 140
Big Fish, 82
Bill Johnson, 202
Billboard, 280
Billy Graham, 200
Binoculars, 280
Bird(s), 77
Birth, 253
Bitter Tasting, 139
Bitterroot, 121
Bittersweet Tasting, 139
Black, 151
Black Cat, 80
Black Eye, 223
Black Hole, 119
Black Sheep, 87
Blacksmith, 169
Blanket, 281
Bleach, 281
Bleeding, 254
Blind Guide, 175
Blindness, 223
Blinking, 254
Blizzard, 109
Blocked Field Goal
  Attempt, 247
Blocked Shot (Basketball),
  247
Blood, 222
Blood of Jesus, 222

Blood Stain, 304
Bloodhound, 81
Blossom, 131
Blowing, 254
Blue, 33, 151
Blueprint, 281
Bob Jones, 202
Bobby Conners, 199
Body, 222
Bodyguard, 169
Bog, 114
Boiling Water, 137
Bolivia, 310
Boll Weevil, 83
Bomb, 240
Bombardment, 240
Bones, 222
Bonsai Tree, 124
Booby Traps, 240
Boogeyman, 208
Book, 71
Boomerang, 281
Borrowed Vehicle, 91
Bottle, 281
Bottom Feeder, 82
Bouquet, 121
Bow and Arrow, 168
Bowed Neck, 227
Bowl, 281
Boy Scout, 170
Boyfriend, 169, 173
Bracelet, 281
Brain, 222
Brakes, 92
Bramble, 123
Branch(es), 131
Brass, 127
Brazil, 311
Bread, 139
Breast, 222
Breastplate, 241
Brian, 158
Brianna, 158

Brick, 281
Brick Wall, 281
Bride, 32
Bridegroom, 32
Bridge, 103
Bridge Ices Before Road, 100
Bridge is Out, 100
Bridget, 158
Briefcase, 281
Brier, 122
Brimstone, 131
Brittany, 158, 311
Broken Arm, 222
Broken Down, 97
Broken Down Car, 37
Broken Home, 51
Broken Pot, 298
Bronze, 127, 151
Brook, 114
Broom, 269, 281
Broom Tree, 125
Brother, 42, 170
Brother-in-Law, 170
Brown, 151
Bruise, 281
Brunei, 311
Bubble, 281
Bubbling Brook, 114
Bud, 131
Buffalo, 80
Buffet, 282
Buffy, 158
Bugs Bunny, 208
Builder, 170
Building, 230
Bulgaria, 311
Bull, 80, 81
Bulldog, 81
Bulletproof Vest, 241
Bulls-Eye, 245
Bully, 170
Bump, 100

Bumper, 92
Bumper Sticker, 92
Burkina Faso, 311
Burning Bridge, 103
Burning Rubber, 97
Burning Stick, 136
Burning Sulfur, 131
Burundi, 311
Bus, 91
Bus Depot, 38
Bus Terminal, 50, 238
Busboy, 170
Butter, 139
Butterfly, 84
Bypass Rte, 103
C. Peter Wagner, 206
C.S. Lewis, 203
Cabin, 230
Cacophony, 296
Cactus Flower, 121
Cage, 282
Cain, 189
Cake, 139
Cal Pierce, 203
Calamus, 217
Caleb, 158
Calf, 80
California, 273
Calvary, 212
Cambodia, 311
Camel, 80
Cameroon, 311
Camouflage, 241
Camphire, 121
Camping, 254
Cana, 212
Canaan, 212
Canada, 311
Candle, 282
Cane, 304
Cannibal, 170
Canteen, 282
Capernaum, 212

Capital Offense, 219
Captain, 180
Car, 36, 49, 91
Car Overheating, 92
Car Seat, 92
Cargo Ship, 95
Carjacker, 170
Carla, 158
Carlene, 158
Carlos Anacondia, 196
Carpenter, 170
Carrie, 158
Carrot, 139
Carrying the Ball
  (Football), 247
Cartoon, 282
Cascade, 117
Cassandra, 158
Cassia, 217
Cat, 38, 80
Catapulting, 254
Cataract, 223
Caterpillar, 84
Catherine, 158
Caution, 100
Cave, 114
Cavern, 114
Cease Fire, 241
Cedar Tree, 125
Ceiling, 232
Celebrity, 170
Centerpiece, 282
Central African Republic,
  311
Cereal, 139
Certificate, 282
Cesspool, 232
Chad (Country), 311
Chaff, 124
Chain, 282
Chair, 282
Chameleon, 84
Champion, 171

Channel, 114
Chariot, 93
Charles, 158
Charles Finney, 200
Charles Stanley, 205
Charlotte, 158
Chasing, 254
Che Ahn, 196
Checkmate, 254
Cheeks, 223
Cheerleader, 171
Cheetah, 80
Cherry Blossom, 121
Chess, 254
Chess Board, 254
Chewing, 254
Chicken, 78
Child, 32, 171
Childhood Home, 51, 232
Chile, 311
Chinchilla, 85
Choking, 255
Christian, 158
Christian Walk, 248
Christine, 158
Christmas, 148
Christopher, 44, 159
Chrysolite, 129
Chuck Pierce, 204
Cigarette, 283
Cindy Jacobs, 202
Cinnamon, 217
Circle, 283
Circus, 255
Circus Performers, 188
City, 230
Civil War, 241
Clam, 80
Clapping, 255
Claude, 159
Claudia, 159
Clay, 131
Cleft of the Rock, 134

Climbing Bittersweet, 122
Climbing Up, 255
Clinging, 255
Cloak, 283
Clock, 283
Closet, 232
Clothes, 43, 283
Cloudy, 53, 109
Clover, 122
Clown, 188
Clutter, 283
Coach, 171
Coal, 132
Coat, 283
Cockroach, 84
Coffee, 139
College, 65
Collie, 82
Collision, 97
Colombia, 311
Colorado, 273
Colors, 32, 33, 151
Comet, 119
Commander in Chief, 171
Comoros, 311
Competition, 256
Condemned, 219
Conductor (Musical), 171
Conduit, 114
Connecticut, 273
Connie, 159
Connor, 159
Constance, 159
Contortionist, 188
Convertible, 93
Convicted, 219
Cook, 171
Cookie, 139
Cooking, 255
Copper, 127
Coqui, 82
Coriander, 217
Corinth, 212

Cork, 283
Corn, 141
Cornerstone, 232
Corridor, 232
Côte d'Ivoire, 311
Counselor, 171
Counterattack, 241
Courthouse, 231
Courtroom Terms, 219
Cow, 80
Cowboy, 172
Co-Worker, 172
Crab, 80
Craftsman, 172
Crashing, 97
Crater, 119
Crawling, 256
Cream, 140
Crescent Moon (and Star),
    119
Crimson, 33, 152
Critic, 172
Crocodile, 77
Crooked Road, 100
Crop, 132
Cross, 284
Crossroad, 100
Crossroads, 103
Crow, 78
Crown, 284
Crystal Ball, 306
Cuba, 312
Cup, 284, 294
Cupid, 208
Curtain, 284
Curve, 100
Curve Ball, 247
Cyclops, 208
Cymbal, 284
Cypress Tree, 125
Czech Republic, 311, 312
Daisy, 121
Dalmatian, 81

Dam, 285
Damaged House, 51, 232
Damascus, 212
Dancing, 256
Danger, 100
Daniel, 44
Daniel (Bible), 190
Daniel (Name), 159
Danielle, 159
Dark Cloud, 109
Darkness, 40, 53, 65, 109
Dart, 278
Date, 140
Daughter, 42, 184
David (Bible), 189
David (Name), 159
David Yonggi Cho, 198
Dawn, 145
Day of Atonement, 148
Day of Pentecost, 148
Daytime, 145
Dead Battery, 97
Dead End, 100
Dead Sea, 212
Dead Wood, 137
Deadline, 285
Deafness, 223
Death, 38, 256
Deborah (Bible), 190
Debris, 285
Decay, 132
Deed, 285
Deep Sea Diver, 172
Deep Waters, 116
Deer, 80
Defeated, 247
Defense, 241
Defibrillator, 285
Delaware, 273
Delivery-Person (Food), 172
Democratic Republic of the Congo, 311

Demon, 190
Denmark, 312
Derek Prince, 204
Desert, 114
Deserter, 239
Desk, 285
Detour, 100
devil, 194
Dew, 109
Diamond, 129
Dictator, 185
Diego, 160
Digesting, 256
Digging, 256
Dinosaur, 81
Directions, 105
Dirt, 39
Dirty Hands, 225
Dirty House, 51
Dirty Vehicle, 97
Dish, 298
Dismissal, 219
Dispatcher, 172
District Attorney, 42, 172, 220
Divide and Conquer, 241
Diving, 257
Division, 251
Divorce, 257
Djibouti, 312
Do Not Enter, 100
Doberman Pincher, 81
Dock, 38
Doctor, 32, 43, 172
Doctor's Office, 231
Dog, 81
Dolphin, 82
Dominica, 312
Dominican Republic, 312
Dominoes, 285
Donald, 159
Donkey, 81
Door, 39, 233

Door Mat, 233
Doormat, 294
Doorstep, 233
Dora, 159
Dorothy, 164
Double Agent, 184
Doug Addison, 196
Dove, 29, 78
Dove's Eyes, 78
Down, 105, 262
Dr Jekyll and Mr. Hyde, 208
Dr. Michael L. Brown, 198
Dragon, 32, 208
Drain, 285
Drama, 257
Dream Journal, 26
Dream Message, 59, 64, 66, 70, 71
Dream Messages, 24
Dream Setting, 58, 63, 65, 69, 71
Dream Settings, 49
Dream Source, 60, 65, 66, 70, 71
Dream Subject, 25, 59, 64, 66, 70, 71
Dream Symbols, 29, 58, 64, 69
Dried Up Spring, 116
Drifting (Boat), 97
Drinking, 257
Drive, 93
Driveway, 233
Driving, 257
Driving in Neutral, 93
Driving in Reverse, 93
Drought, 109
Drowning, 267
Drug Dealer, 173
Drugs (Illegal), 286
Dung, 287
Dusk, 145

Dust, 132
Dutch Sheets, 205
Dying, 256
Eagle, 78
Earring, 286
Ears, 223
Earthquake, 39, 110
Earwax, 223
East, 105
East Timor, 312
East Wind, 113
Easter, 148
Easter Bunny, 208
Easter Island, 312
Eating, 257
Eclipse, 110
Ecuador, 312
Edelweiss, 121
Eduardo, 159
Edward, 159
Edwin, 159
Egg, 140
Egypt, 212
Eight, 33, 153
Eighteen, 154
El Salvador, 312
Elbow, 223
Electricity, 39
Elephant, 82
Elevator, 234
Eleven, 154
Elias, 159
Elijah, 159
Elijah (Bible), 190
Elim, 212
Elisha, 190
Elizabeth, 159
Elliot, 159
Embracing, 257
Emerald, 129, 151
Emergency Room, 231
Emily, 159
Emma, 159

Emmaus, 213
Empty, 286
Encroachment, 241
Enemy, 173, 242
Energizer Bunny, 208
Engine, 92
Engine Failure, 97
Enoch, 190
Enrique, 160
Ephesus, 213
Ephraim, 159
Equatorial Guinea, 312
Error, 247
Escaping, 258
Esther (Bible), 190
Esther (Name), 159
Estonia, 312
Ethan, 159
European Union, 312
Eva, 159
Evelyn, 159
Evergreen Tree, 125
Eviction, 258
Evidence, 220
Evita, 159
Exercising, 258
Ex-Husband, 173
Experimenting, 258
Explorer, 173
Exploring, 258
Exterminator, 173
Eyeglasses, 286
Eyes, 223
Ezekiel, 190
Fabric, 286
Facade, 233
Face, 224
Face to Face, 224
Face Washing, 253
Facedown, 224
Factory, 231
Failed Crop, 132
Failing Brakes, 37

Fainting, 258
Fairy Tale, 286
Faith (Name), 160
Falkland Islands, 312
Fall (Autumn), 52, 145
Falling, 258
Falling Star, 119
False Teeth, 228
Family, 173
Family Member, 41
Famine, 287
Far, 105
Farm, 50, 231
Farmer, 42, 173
Fast Lane, 104
Fat, 224
Fat Cat, 80
Fat Cow, 80
Father, 41, 173
Father Figure, 32
Father-in-Law, 173
Feast of Esther, 149
Feast of Tabernacles, 148
Feast of Trumpets, 148
Feast of Weeks, 148
Feathers, 78
Feces, 287
Federated States of
    Micronesia, 314
Feet, 224
Feet Washing, 253
Felicia, 160
Felix, 160
Fence, 287
Ferris Wheel, 287
Fertile Soil, 135
Fertilizer, 132
Fetus, 181
Field, 114
Field Trip, 259
Fifteen, 154
Fifty, 155
Fifty-Two, 155

Fig, 140
Fig Leaf, 125
Fig Tree, 125
Fighter Plane, 37
Fighting, 259
Fiji, 312
Finger of God, 225
Fingerprint, 225
Fingers, 225
Fir Tree, 125
Fire, 29, 132
Fire Escape, 233
Fire Extinguisher, 287
Firebrand, 136
Firecracker, 287
Firefighters, 174
Fireplace, 234
Firestorm, 133
Fireworks, 287
First Born, 174
Fish, 32, 58, 82
Fisherman, 174
Fishing, 259
Fishing Pole, 250
Fishing Terms, 250
Fishing Vessel, 93
Five, 32, 153
Flash Flood, 110
Flat Tire, 38, 98
Flax, 123
Flea, 84
fleece, 87
Flies, 84
Flight Simulator, 287
Flint, 133
Flood, 110
Floodgate, 110
Florida, 273
Flower, 40
Flowers, 121
Flying, 259
Fog, 110
Food, 66

Food and Drink, 139
Footprints, 224
Footsteps, 224
Forehead, 224
Forest, 114
Forest Ranger, 174
Forget-Me-Not, 121
Fork, 304
Fork In The Road, 100
Fortress, 231
Fortuneteller, 174
Forty, 155
Forward, 105
Fossil, 133
Foul, 247
Found, 287
Foundation, 234
Four, 32, 153
Fourteen, 154
Fourth of July, 148
Fox, 32, 82
Fragrance (Sweet
  Smelling), 288
France, 312
Frankenstein Monster,
  208
Frankincense, 217
Franklin Graham, 200
Freedom, 288
Freeze Free Season, 148
Freight Train, 95
Friend, 174
Frog, 82
Front, 106
Front Door, 51
Front Yard, 51, 234
Frontal Assault, 242
Frost, 110
Frozen, 137
Fruit, 58, 133, 140
Fuel, 92
Full, 288
Full Court Press

(Basketball), 247
Fumble, 247
Funeral, 259
Furnace, 234
Gabon, 312
Gabriel, 160
Gabrielle, 160
Gail, 157
Galatia, 213
Galbanum, 217
Gall Bladder, 224
Gambling, 259
Gangrene, 288
Garage Sale, 272
Garbage, 288
Garbage Truck, 93
Garden, 289
Gardener, 32, 174
Garlic, 141
Garments, 283
Gas Mask, 242
Gas Station, 231
Gas Tank, 92
Gasping, 259
Gate, 289
Gazelle, 82
Gearing Down, 266
Generational Blessings, 45
Generational Curses, 45
Generational Sin Patterns,
  45
Genie, 208
Geographical Symbols,
  114
Georgia, 273
Georgia (Country), 312
Germ, 133
German Shepherd, 81
Gethsemane, 213
Ghana, 313
Giant, 174
Gibeon, 213
Gibraltar, 313

Gideon, 191
Gift, 289
Gilgal, 213
Giovanni, 161
Giraffe, 82
Girl Scout, 170
Giselle, 160
Glass, 289, 294
Globe, 289
Gloria, 44, 160
Glue, 289
Glutton, 175
Gnat, 84
Gnome, 210
Goat, 58, 82
Goblin, 208
Gold, 64, 127, 151
Gold Mine, 115
Golgotha, 212
Goliath, 191
Gong, 290
Goshen, 213
Graduate, 175
Grains, 141
Grandparent, 175
Grapes, 140
Grass, 123
Grasshopper, 84
Gravity, 133
Gray, 151
Gray Hair, 151
Greece, 313
Green, 33, 151
Gremlin, 208
Grenada, 313
Grenade, 242
Greyhound, 81
Grim Reaper, 208
Grinch, 209
Groundhog, 83
Groundswell, 110
Guatemala, 313
Guide, 175

Guillermo, 165
Guilty, 220
Guinea, 313
Guinea-Bissau, 313
Gun, 242
Gutter (Street), 103
Guyana, 313
Gym, 231
Gymnasium, 49
Hail, 53, 110
Hair, 224
Hairpin Curve, 100
Haiti, 313
Haley, 160
Halloween, 148
Haman, 191
Hammer, 32, 290
Hand of God, 225
Hand Washing, 253
Handkerchief, 290
Handoff (Football), 248
Hands, 225
Handwriting on a Wall,
  272
Hang Glider, 94
Hangar, 231
Hanna, 160
Hannah (Bible), 191
Hannah (Name), 160
Hanukkah, 148
Hard Soil, 135
Hardball, 248
Harmony, 295
Harp, 290
Harry Potter, 209
Harvesters, 175
Harvesting, 265
Harvest-Time, 145
Hat, 290
Hawaii, 273
Hawk, 78
Hazard Lights, 92
Haze, 110

Head, 225
Headlights, 92
Headline, 290
Heart, 226
Hebron, 214
Heidi, 160
Heidi Baker, 196
Heir, 175
Helicopter, 93
Helm, 95
Helmet, 242
Hemlock, 123
Hen, 78
Henna, 121
Henrietta, 160
Henry, 160
Hibiscus, 121
Hidden Face, 224
Hiding, 259
High, 106
High Ground, 242
High Horse, 83
High Tide, 112
Highway, 103
Hiking, 259
Hilda, 160
Hill, 115
Hillary, 44, 160
Hog, 83
Hollow, 117
Holy Spirit, 29
Home Run, 248
Homeless Person, 175
Homesick, 260
Honduras, 313
Honey, 32, 141
Hook, 250
Horn, 83
Horn (Car), 92
Hornet, 84
Horoscope, 306
Horse, 83
Horseback Rider, 176

Horseback Riding, 260
Horsepower, 92
Hosea, 191
Hospital, 49, 231
Hot Air Balloon, 93
Hotel, 50, 231
Hourglass, 290
House, 50, 232
House in Disrepair, 51, 232
Housecleaning, 260
Hugging, 257
Hundred, 155
Hunger, 290
Hurricane, 110
Husband, 32, 41, 176
Husky, 81
Hyena, 83
Hypnotizing, 260
Hyssop, 123
Ice, 133
Iceberg, 115
ICU, 231
Idaho, 274
Igniting (Fire), 260
Illinois, 274
Imaginary Creatures or Beings, 208
Imposter, 176
In Gear, 266
In High Gear, 266
Incense, 291
India, 313
Indiana, 274
Indonesia, 313
Inez, 160
Infection, 133
Infiltration, 242
Inheritance, 291
Insect, 83
Interloper, 176
Intruder, 176
Invasion, 242

Investing, 260
Investor, 176
Iowa, 274
Iran, 313
Irena, 160
Irene, 160
Iris, 121, 160
Iron, 127
Iron (Clothes), 291
Isabella, 159, 160
Isaiah (Bible), 191
Isaiah (Name), 160
Island, 115, 160
Isle of Man, 313
Itching, 260
Itching Ears, 260
Ivory, 82
Ivy, 123
Jacinth, 129
Jack Coe, 198
Jack Hayford, 201
Jackal, 85
Jackie, 160
Jacob (Bible), 191
Jacob (Name), 160
Jacqueline, 160
Jamaica, 313
James (Name), 160
James Dobson, 199
James Goll, 200
Jane, 161
Jar, 291
Jason, 161
Jason Upton, 205
Jasper, 130
Jaw, 226
Jay, 78
Jeep, 94
Jentzen Franklin, 200
Jerame Nelson, 203
Jeremiah (Bible), 191
Jeremiah (Name), 161
Jeremy, 161

Jericho, 214
Jerusalem, 214
Jesse, 161
Jessica, 44, 161
Jet, 94
Jewel, 292
Jezebel, 191
Jim Baker, 197
Joanna, 161
Joanne, 161
Job (Bible), 192
Jocelyn, 161
Jockey, 176
Joel Osteen, 203
John (Bible), 192
John (Name), 44, 161
John and Carol Arnott, 196
John and Paula Sanford, 204
John Eckhardt, 199
John G. Lake, 203
John Hagee, 201
John Kilpatrick, 202
John Mark, 192
John Paul Jackson, 202
John the Baptist, 192
John Wesley, 206
John Wimber, 206
Jonah, 192
Jonathan, 44, 161
Jonathan Cahn, 198
Jonathan Edwards, 199
Joppa, 214
Jordan, 161
Jordan (Country), 313
Jordan River, 116, 214
Jose, 161
Joseph, 44, 161
Joseph (OT Bible), 17, 192
Joshua (Bible), 192
Joshua (Name), 44, 161
Journey, 261

Journeying, 270
Joy, 161
Joyce, 161
Juan, 161
Juana, 161
Juanita Bynum, 198
Jubilee, 149
Judah, 161
Judas Iscariot, 192
Judge, 32, 42, 176, 220
Judgment, 220
Judith, 161
Juggler, 188
Juice, 141
Juliet, 161
Jumping, 261
Jungle, 115
Juniper Tree, 125
Junk Food, 141
Junk Mail, 292
Justin, 161
Justine, 161
Kangaroo, 85
Kansas, 274
Karen, 158
Karl, 158
Katherine, 44
Kathryn Kuhlman, 203
Katrina, 158
Kayla, 158
Kelly, 161
Kenneth, 44, 161
Kenneth Hagen, 201
Kentucky, 274
Kenya, 313
Kernel, 124
Key, 292
Kidney, 226
Kim Clement, 198
Kim Walker Smith, 205
King, 32, 176
Kipa, 291
Kiribati, 313

Kirsten, 158
Kissing, 261
Kitchen, 51, 234
Kneeling, 261
Knees, 226
Knife, 292
Knife Thrower, 188
Knight, 176
Knitting, 261
Knocking (On the Door), 261
Knot, 292
Kosovo, 314
Kris Valloton, 205
Kylie, 161
Ladder, 292
Lake, 115
Lakeisha, 162
Lamb, 32, 85
Lame Foot, 224
Lamp, 292
Lance Wallnau, 206
Land Mines, 240
Landlord, 177
Landmark, 293
Landslide, 110
Laodicea, 214
Laos, 314
Laticia, 162
Latvia, 314
Laughing, 262
Launching Pad, 119
Laundromat, 235
Laura, 162
Laverne, 162
Law, 220
Lawyer, 42, 177, 220
Lawyer's Office, 235
Laying on of Hands, 225
Lay-up, 248
Lazarus, 192
Lead, 127
Leah, 162

Leaping, 261
Leaven, 143
Leaves, 133
Leech, 84
Left, 106
Left Hand, 225
Legion of Superheroes, 209
Legs, 226
Lemon, 140
Lemur, 85
Leonard, 162
Leonardo, 162
Leopard, 85
Lesotho, 314
Levee (Natural), 115
Liam, 162
Liberia, 314
Liberty, 288
Library, 235
Lie Detector, 293
Liechtenstein, 314
Life Guard, 177
Lifeboat, 94
Light, 29
Lighthouse, 235
Lightning, 53, 110
Lightning Rod, 111
Ligure, 129
Lily(ies), 121
Limited Sight Distance, 101
Limited View, 101
Limping, 262
Linda, 162
Linen, 293
Lion, 32, 85
Lion Tamer, 188
Lips, 226
Liquor, 141
Lithuania, 314
Liver, 226
Living Room, 51, 234

Llama, 85
Lock, 293
Locker Room, 235
Locust, 84
Loins, 226
Long Jump, 261
Loon, 78
Lost (One's Way), 262, 293
Lot, 192
Lotus, 121
Lou Engle, 199
Louis, 162
Louisa, 162
Louisiana, 274
Low, 106
Low Clearance, 101
Low on Air, 98
Low Tide, 112
Luis, 162
Lukewarm, 137
Lure, 250
Luxembourg, 314
Lynn, 162
Macedonia, 314
Madagascar, 314
Madeline, 162
Magdalene, 162
Magic, 293
Magician, 177
Magnet, 294
Magnolia Blossom, 122
Magnolia Tree, 125
Mahesh Chavda, 198
Mahogany Tree, 125
Maine, 274
Making Headway, 95
Malawi, 314
Malaysia, 314
Mali, 314
Mandrake, 122
Mansion, 235
Manuel, 162
Map, 40, 294

Maple Leaf, 125
Maple Tree, 125
Marathon, 248
Marauder, 180
Marble, 130
Marching, 262
Margaret, 162
Margarita, 162
Margot, 162
Maria, 162
Maria Woodworth-Etter, 199
Marian, 162
Mark, 44, 162
Marsh, 117
Marshmallow, 141
Martha, 193
Martin, 162
Martina, 162
Mary, 44, 162
Mary (Mother of Jesus), 193
Mary (of Bethany), 193
Maryland, 274
Masquerade Costume, 294
Massachusetts, 274
Master, 177
Mat, 294
Mat (Sleeping), 71
Matchmaker, 177
Math Terms, 251
Matthew, 162
Maturing, 262
Matzo, 141
Mauritania, 314
Maze, 294
Meadow, 115
Measuring, 262
Meat, 32, 141
Medicine, 295
Medium, 174
Megan, 162
Menorah, 148

Merchant, 177
Mercy, 220
Mermaid, 209
Merry-Go-Round, 295
Messenger, 177
Metals, 127
Meteor, 119
Mexico, 314
Michael, 44, 162
Michal (David's Wife), 193
Michelle, 162
Michigan, 274
Mickey Mouse, 209
Microphone, 295
Microwave, 39, 295
Midnight, 145
Midwife, 177
Migdalia, 162
Miguel, 162
Mike Bickle, 197
Military Strategy, 243
Military Terms, 239
Milk, 32, 142
Milkman, 178
Mine Sweeper, 243
Minefield, 243
Mink, 85
Minnesota, 274
Mire, 114
Mirror, 32, 295
Mississippi, 274
Missouri, 274
Mist, 111
Mitchell, 162
Mite (Insect), 84
Mobile Home, 94
Mockingbird, 78
Mole, 85
Mole Hill, 85
Molly, 162, 163
Monaco, 315
Money, 295
Monica, 163

Monkey, 85
Monster, 209
Montana, 274
Moon, 40, 119
Mordechai, 193
Morning, 146
Morning Star, 120
Morocco, 315
Moses, 193
Moth, 84
Mother, 41, 178
Mother-in-Law, 178
Motorboat, 37, 94
Motorcycle, 94
Mottos of the Nations, 310
Mountain, 38, 115
Mountain Climber, 178
Mountain Pass, 115
Mouse, 85
Mouth, 226
Movies, 23
Moving Truck, 37, 94
Mt Mariah, 214
Mt. Sinai, 214
Mud, 133
Muddied Spring, 117
Mulberry Tree, 125
Mule, 86
Multi-Colored, 152
Multiple Scenes, 66
Multiplication, 251
Mummy, 209
Murder, 220
Murderer, 178
Museum, 235
Music, 23, 295
Musical Notes, 263
Musician, 178
Mustard Plant, 123
Mustard Seed, 123
Myrrh, 217
Myrtle Tree, 125
Naked, 263

Name, 43
Name Meanings, 157
Namibia, 315
Nancy, 163
Nanny, 179
Naomi, 163
Narcissus, 122
Narrow Bridge, 101
Natalie, 163
Natasha, 163
Nathaniel, 163
Nature, 109, 131
Nauru, 315
Nazareth, 214
Near, 106
Nebraska, 275
Neck, 227
Necklace, 296
Neil, 163
Nepal, 315
Nephew, 179
Net, 250
Netherlands, 315
Nevada, 275
New Hampshire, 275
New Home, 234
New House, 51
New Jersey, 275
New Mexico, 275
New Wine, 143
New Year's Eve, 149
New York, 275
Newspaper Headline, 296
Nicaragua, 315
Nicholas, 44, 163
Nicole, 163
Niece, 179
Niger, 315
Nigeria, 315
Nighttime, 146
Nine, 33, 153
No Outlet, 100
No Parking, 101

No Passing Zone, 101
No U Turn, 101
Noah, 163
Noah (Bible), 193
Nomad, 179
Noon, 146
North, 106
North Carolina, 275
North Dakota, 275
North Korea, 314
North Wind, 113
Nose, 227
Nuevo Leon, 315
Numbers, 32, 153
Nurse, 179
Nut, 142
Oak Tree, 125
Oasis, 236
Oats, 141
Ocean, 116
Octopus, 86
Odor (Foul Smelling), 296
Offense, 220
Office, 49, 236
Ogre, 209
Ohio, 275
Ohio Buckeye Tree, 125
Oil, 29, 134, 142
Oklahoma, 275
Old Wine, 143
Older Brother, 170
Olive Branch, 126
Olive Tree, 125
Oliver, 163
Olives, 140
Olivia, 163
One, 32, 64, 153
One Hundred Ninety-
    Three, 155
One Hundred Ninety-Two,
    155
One Hundred Thousand,
    155

One Thousand, 155
One Way, 101
Onion, 142
Onyx, 130
Operating Table, 184
Opponent, 248
Oral Roberts, 204
Orange, 33, 59, 152
Orange Blossom, 122
Orbit, 119
Orchestra, 179
Orchid, 122
Orphan, 179
Orphanage, 236
Osprey, 78
Ostrich, 78
Ouija Board, 306
Out of Control, 98
Out of Fuel, 98
Outer Space, 119
Outstretched Hands, 225
Oven, 296
Overheated, 98
Overslept, 268
Overtime, 248
Owl, 79
Ox, 86
Oyster, 80
Pablo, 163
Packing (Up), 263
Padlock, 296
Paige, 163
Paint, 297
Paint Brush, 297
Pakistan, 315
Palace, 236
Palm, 227
Palm Tree, 126
Panama, 315
Panda, 86
Pansy, 122
Panting, 263
Paparazzi, 179

Papua New Guinea, 315
Parachute, 297
Parade, 263
Paraguay, 315
Paralyzed, 271
Paramedic, 179
Parasite, 134
Pardon, 221
Parking Lot, 38, 50, 238
Parrot, 79
Partner, 179
Partridge, 79
Parts of the Body, 222
Passenger, 179
Passover, 149
Pastor, 180
Pastureland, 115
Patch, 297
Path, 104
Patricia, 163
Patricia King, 202
Patrick, 163
Paul, 163
Paul (Bible), 193
Paula, 163
Pavement Ends, 101
Pawn, 254
Peace, 243
Peach, 140
Peacock, 79
Peak, 116
Pearl, 130
Peggy, 162
Pelican, 79
Pen, 297
Penalty, 247
Penguin, 79
Pennsylvania, 275
Pension, 297
People, 167
People In Dreams, 41
Perfume, 297
Pergamum, 215

Perry Stone, 205
Pesticide, 298
Peter (Bible), 194
Peter Pan, 209
Peter Wagner, 206
Phantom, 209
Pharaoh, 193
Pharmacy, 236
Philadelphia, 215
Philippi, 215
Philippines, 315
Philistia, 215
Phone, 298
Photo Album, 298
Photograph, 39, 298
Photographer, 180
Pier, 38
Pig, 86
Pigeon, 79
Piggy Bank, 298
Pillar, 234
Pillow, 298
Pilot, 180
Pine Tree, 125
Pinnacle, 116
Pinocchio, 209
Pioneer, 180
Pirate, 180
Places, 230
Plague, 134
Planet, 120
Plant, 236
Planter, 180
Planting, 263
Plants, 122
Plate, 298
Plateau, 116
Platform, 304
Platinum, 127
Plowing, 264
Plum, 140
Plumber, 180
Pocketbook, 298

Pointing Finger, 225
Poison, 298
Poison Ivy, 123
Police, 180
Politician, 180
Pomegranate, 141
Poodle, 81
Pool, 116
Popcorn, 142
Porch, 234
Portugal, 315
Possum, 86
Postman, 181
Pot, 298
Pothole, 101
Potter, 181
Potter's Wheel, 299
Pouring Out, 264
Poverty, 264
Prayer Plant, 123
Precious Stones, 129
Pregnant Woman, 181
Pressure Cooker, 299
Prince, 181
Princess, 181
Principal, 181
Prison, 39, 50, 236
Prison Guard, 181
Prisoner, 181
Prize, 299
Prophetic Character, 25
Prosperity, 264
Prostitute, 182
Pruning, 264
Psychic, 174
Psychologist, 182
Psychologist's Office, 236
Pulling Out Own Hair, 225
Pumpkin, 142
Punt (Football), 247
Puppet, 299
Puppeteer, 182
Purim, 149

Purple, 33, 152
Purpose of Dreams, 21
Puzzle, 299
Python, 86
Quagmire, 114
Quail, 79
Quarterback, 182
Queen, 182
Queen of Heaven, 182
Quicksand, 134
R.W. Schambach, 204
Rabbit, 86
Raccoon, 86
Race, 248
Racecar, 94
Radar, 243
Radiator, 92
Raft, 94
Rags, 299
Raid, 243
Rain, 52, 111
Rainbow, 111, 160
Ram, 86
Randy Clark, 198
Rape, 265
Raphael, 163
Rash, 228
Rat, 32, 86
Raven, 79
Raymond, 44, 163
Reapers, 175
Reaping, 265
Rear View Mirror, 38, 92
Rebecca, 163
Rebel, 182
Recipe, 299
Reconnaissance, 243
Record Keeper, 182
Recurring Dreams, 67
Red, 33, 152
Reed, 123
Referee, 182
Refiner of Metals, 182

Registrar, 182
Reinhard Bonnke, 197
Rejection, 265
Relay Race, 248
Rental Car, 94
Repairing, 265
Report Card, 299
Republic of the Congo, 311
Rescuer, 183
Restaurant, 50, 236
Resting, 265
Resurrection, 265
Retreat, 244
Reward, 299
Rhode Island, 275
Ricardo, 163
Rice, 141, 142
Rich Young Ruler, 194
Richard, 44, 163
Rick Joyner, 202
Rick Warren, 206
Right, 106
Right Hand, 225
Ring, 300
Rioting, 265
River, 116
Riverbank, 116
Road, 104
Road Closed, 101
Road Narrows, 101
Road Runner (Cartoon), 209
Road Signs, 100
Roadways, 103
Robe, 300
Robert, 163
Roberta, 163
Roberto, 163
Rocco, 163
Rock, 134
Rocket Ship, 94, 120
Rocking Chair, 282

Rod, 300
Rodney Howard-Browne, 202
Roll Bar, 92
Rollercoaster, 300
Roof, 51, 234
Rookie, 248
Rooster, 79
Root, 134
Rosa, 164
Rosalie, 164
Rose, 122, 164
Rosh Hashanah, 148
Rotten, 300
Rotten Food, 142
Rottweiler, 82
Rough Road Ahead, 101
Rowboat, 37, 94
Rubble, 244
Ruby, 130
Rudder, 95
Run Ashore or Aground (Boat), 98
Running, 265
Ruth, 44, 164
Ruth Ward Heflin, 201
Rwanda, 315
Ryan, 164
Sabbath, 149
Sackcloth, 300
Sacked (Football), 249
Sacrifice Bunt (Baseball), 249
Sailboat, 94
Saint Bernard, 82
Saint Helena, 315
Saint Kitts and Nevis, 315
Saint Lucia, 316
Saint Vincent and the Grenadines, 316
Sally, 164
Saloon, 236
Salt, 142

Salt Spreader, 94
Salvador, 164
Samantha, 164
Samaria, 215
Sample Dreams, 57, 63, 65, 69, 70
Samson, 194
Samuel (Bible), 194
Samuel (Name), 164
San Marino, 316
Sand, 71
Sand Dune, 116
Sandman, 209
Sands, 116
Santa Claus, 210
Sapphire, 130
Sarah, 164
Sarah (Bible), 194
Sardis, 215
Sardius, 130
satan, 194
Satellite, 120
Saudi Arabia, 316
Saul, 164, 194
Savior, 183, 231
Saw, 300
Scab, 134
Scale, 300
Scalpel, 184
Scar, 227
Scarecrow, 301
Scarlet, 33, 152
School, 50, 237
School Bus, 37, 95
School Bus Driver, 183
Scoreboard, 249
Scorpion, 86
Scotch Tape, 301
Scotland, 316
Scrapbook, 301
Screaming, 266
Screwdriver, 301
Scroll, 301

Scrooge, 210
Scrubbing, 266
Sea, 116
Sea Nymph, 209
Seal, 301
Sean, 164
Séance, 306
Season, 146
Seat Belt, 92
Seaweed, 123
Security Guard, 183
Seed, 134
Senegal, 316
Senna, 123
Serena, 164
Serpent, 32, 86
Servant, 183
Servants of the Lord, 196
Seth, 164
Seven, 33, 64, 153
Seventy, 155
Sewage, 301
Sewer, 302
Sexual Activity, 266
Seychelles, 316
Shackles, 302
Shade, 135
Shadow, 135
Shadrach, Meshach, and
  Abednego, 195
Shaken, 266
Shaking, 266
Shaking Hands, 266
Shaquille, 164
Shark, 87
Shauna, 164
Shavuot, 148
Shawl, 302
Shawn, 164
Shawn Bolz, 197
Sheep, 32, 87
Sheepdog, 82
Shelf, 302
Shell Shocked, 244
Shepherd, 42, 183
Shield, 244
Shifting Gears (Car), 266
Ship, 37, 95
Shirt, 64
Shittah Tree, 124
Shivering, 266
Shock Absorber, 92
Shoemaker, 183
Shoes, 302
Shofar, 308
Shooting, 266
Shoulder, 227
Shouting, 266
Shovel, 302
Shower, 302
Showering, 253
Shrine, 237
Shrinking, 267
Sickle, 302
Sid Roth, 204
Siege, 244
Sierra Leone, 316
Sign, 302
Silence, 303
Silk, 303
Silver, 127, 152
Simmering Water, 137
Singing, 267
Sink, 303
Sinking, 98, 267
Sint Maarten, 316
Siren, 209
Sister, 42, 183
Sister-in-Law, 170
Sitting, 267
Sitting on the Fence, 287
Six, 33, 153
Six Hundred Sixty-Six,
  155
Sixteen, 154
Sixty-Six, 155

Skateboard, 95
Skeleton, 227
Skin, 227
Skinny, Scrawny Cow, 80
Skunk, 59, 87
Skyscraper, 237
Slam Dunk, 249
Slate, 135
Slaughterhouse, 237
Slave, 183
Sled, 95
Sleeping, 267
Sleeping Bag, 71, 303
Sleeplessness, 267
Slide, 303
Slingshot, 303
Slippery When Wet, 101
Sloth, 87
Slow, 102
Smoke, 135
Smoke Screen, 244
Smyrna, 216
Snag, 250
Snail, 87
Snake, 70, 86
Snow, 53, 111
Snow Shoes, 302
Soapy Water, 64
Sodom, 216
Sofia, 164
Softball, 249
Soil, 135
Solar Flare, 120
Soldier, 42, 183, 244
Solomon, 195
Solomon Islands, 316
Son, 42, 184
Soot, 303
Soothsayer, 174
Sour Tasting, 142
Source of Dreams, 22
South, 106
South Africa, 316

South Carolina, 275
South Dakota, 275
South Georgia and the
    South Sandwich Islands,
    316
South Korea, 314
South Wind, 113
Sower, 180
Sowing, 263
Sowing (Seeds), 268
Spa, 237
Spain, 316
Spark Plug, 92
Sparrow, 79
Speaking, 268
Speeding (Illegally), 98
Speeding Vehicle
    (Illegally), 95
Spice, 142
Spider, 84
Spider Web, 39
Spider's Web, 136
Spikenard, 217
Spine, 228
Spinning, 98
Spinning Wheels (Without
    Forward Movement), 98
Spiritist, 174
Spiritual Inheritances, 45
Spitting, 268
Splinter, 303
Sponge, 304
Spoon, 304
Spotlight, 304
Spring, 52, 146
Spring (of water), 116
Spring Rain, 111
Sprint, 248
Spy, 184
Squall, 111

Squatter, 184
Squirrel, 87
St. Valentine's Day, 149
Stabbing, 268
Stacie, 164
Stadium, 237
Staff, 304
Stage, 304
Staggering, 268
Stain, 39, 304
Stained Glass, 289
Stairs, 234
Stale Food, 142
Stalker, 184
Standing, 268
Star(s), 120
States of Being, 252
Statue, 304
Statue of Liberty, 304
Steal (Basketball), 249
Stealing, 268
Steam, 136
Steel, 127
Steering Wheel, 93
Stench, 296
Stephanie, 164
Stephen, 164
Stephen (Bible), 195
Steve Hill, 201
Steven, 164
Stew, 143
Sticks, 136
Stiff-Necked, 227
Sting Ray, 87
Stirring (Up), 268
Stomach, 222
Stone, 136
Stop, 102
Stop Watch, 283
Stopping for Gas, 38
Storehouse, 238
Stork, 79
Storm, 32, 53, 111

Stove, 296
Straightjacket, 305
Strait, 117
Stream, 117
Stretcher, 305
Strikeout, 249
Stronghold, 245
Strongman, 188
Strutting, 269
Student, 184
Stumbling, 269
Subtraction, 251
Subway, 95
Succoth, 148
Sudan, 316
Suffocating, 269
Suicide Squeeze, 249
Suitcase, 305
Summer, 52, 146
Sun, 40, 120
Sunbathing, 269
Sunburst, 111
Sunflower, 122
Sunset, 146
Sunshine, 53, 112
Super Villain, 210
Superhero, 210
Supermarket, 237
Surgeon, 184
Suriname, 316
Surrender, 245
Susan, 164
Suspension, 93
Suzanne, 164
Swallow, 79
Swallowing, 269
Swamp, 117
Swan, 79
Swatting (Flies), 269
Swaziland, 316
Sweeping, 269
Sweet Tasting, 143
Swimmer, 184

Swimming, 269
Swimming Pool, 50
Swine, 86
Switzerland, 316
Sword, 32, 244
Sword Swallower, 188
Sycamore Tree, 125
Symphony, 296
Table, 305
Tabloid, 305
Taffy, 143
Tail, 87
Talent Contest, 270
Tamara, 164
Tambourine, 305
Tammy, 164
Tank, 37
Tanzania, 317
Tape Measure, 305
Tapestry, 306
Tares, 123
Target, 245
Tarot Cards, 306
Tasting, 270
TD Jakes, 202
Tea, 306
Teacher, 32, 184
Teddy Bear, 306
Teeth, 39, 228
Telescope, 306
Television, 23, 306
Temperature, 112
Temperature Gauge, 93
Ten, 33, 153
Ten Horns, 83
Tennessee, 275
Tent, 237
Teri, 164
Termite, 84
Terrorist, 184
Test, 306
Testimony, 221
Texas, 275

Thanksgiving, 149
Theater, 237
Theodore, 164
Theresa, 164
Thessalonica, 216
Thick Skinned, 227
Thicket, 117
Thief, 185
Thigh, 228
Thin Skinned, 227
Thirst, 307
Thirteen, 154
Thirty, 154
Thistle, 123
Thomas (Bible), 195
Thorn, 123
Thorn Bush, 123
Three, 32, 153
Three Hundred, 155
Throne, 307
Thunder, 53, 112
Thyatira, 216
Ticket, 307
Tidal Wave, 112
Tide, 112
Tiffany, 44, 165
Tiger, 87
Tightrope Walker, 188
Time of Day, 52
Timeout, 249
Times and Seasons, 52,
  145
Timothy, 165
Tin, 128
Tires, 38, 93
Titanium, 128
Title, 285
Todd, 165
Todd Bentley, 197
Todd White, 206
Togo, 317
Toilet, 64, 307
Tommy Tenney, 205

Tongue, 228
Topaz, 130
Torch, 307
Tornado, 53, 112
Torrent, 112
Touchdown, 249
Tow Truck, 95
Tow-away Zone, 102
Towel, 307
Tower, 237
Tractor, 95
Tractor Trailer, 37, 95
Tracy, 164
Traffic (Stuck in), 98
Traffic Cop, 180
Train, 36, 49, 95
Train Station, 38, 50, 238
Train Tracks, 95
Transmission, 93
Transportation, 36, 49, 91
Travelling, 270
Treading Water, 270
Treasure, 307
Tree, 39
Tree Frog, 82
Tree Planted by the
  Water, 124
Tree Stump, 124
Trees, 124
Trembling, 266
Trinidad and Tobago, 317
Trip (Journey), 66
Tripping, 98
Trojan Horse, 83
Troll, 210
Trophy, 308
Trumpet, 308
Tsunami, 112
Tugboat, 96
Tulip, 122
Tunisia, 317
Tunnel, 104
Turkey, 79

Turkey (Country), 317
Turn Signal, 93
Turning, 98
Turning Tide, 112
Turquoise, 130, 152
Turtle, 88
Tutor, 185
Tuxedo, 308
Twelve, 154
Twenty, 154
Twenty-Four, 154
Twenty-Six, 154
Twilight, 145
Twins, 185
Two, 32, 153
Tyrant, 185
U.S. State Mottos, 273
U.S. Virgin Islands, 317
Uganda, 317
Ugly, 308
Umbilical Cord, 229
Umbrella, 308
Umpire, 182
Unable to Get Started
  (Vehicle), 99
Unable to Scream for
  Help, 267
Unable to Take Off, 99,
  259
Uncle, 185
Uncovering, 270
United Arab Emirates, 317
United Kingdom, 317
United States, 317
University, 237
Unknown Man, 185
Unknown Woman, 185
Unleavened Bread, 141
Unnamed People, 71
Unseen Man, 185
Unseen Woman, 185
Up, 107
Uplifted Hands, 225

Uprooting, 270
Uranium, 128
Uruguay, 317
Utah, 276
Uzbekistan, 317
Vacation, 38, 309
Vagabond, 185
Valley, 117
Vampire, 210
Vanuatu, 317
Vapor, 111
Velvet, 303
Venom, 87
Ventriloquist, 186
Venus Flytrap, 123
Vermont, 276
Veronica, 165
Victor, 165
Victoria, 165
Victorious, 249
Video, 309
Vietnam, 317
Vine, 136
Vinegar, 143
Violet, 122
Viper, 88
Virgin, 186
Virginia, 276
Virus, 137
Visionary, 186
Volcano, 112
Vomiting, 270
Vulture, 79
Waiter, 42, 186
Waiting Room, 50, 238
Waking Up, 271
Walking, 271
Wall, 234
Wallet, 298
Wandering, 271
Wandering Star, 120
War, 246
Warehouse, 238

Washing, 253
Washington, 276
Wasteland, 117
Watch, 283
Watchdog, 81
Watchman, 186
Water, 29, 30, 32, 71, 137, 143
Waterfall, 117
Watershed, 117
Waves, 113
Wax, 309
Weapons, 246
Weasel, 88
Weather, 52, 109
Weather Forecaster, 186
Weeds, 123
Weightlessness, 120
Weightlifter, 186
Well, 118
Wellspring, 117
Werewolf, 210
West, 107
West Virginia, 276
West Wind, 113
Whale, 88
Wheat, 32, 123
Wheel, 93
Wheelchair, 309
Whip, 309
Whistle Blower, 186
White, 33, 152
White Cloud, 109
White Stone, 136
Wife, 41, 187
Wilderness, 114
Wiley Coyote, 210
William, 165
William Branham, 197
William Seymour, 205
Willow Tree, 126
Wind, 29, 113
Winding Road, 102

Window, 51, 235
Windshield, 93
Windshield Fogging Up, 99
Wine, 143
Wings, 77
Winking, 271
Winter, 52, 146
Wisconsin, 276
Witch, 187
Witchcraft, 271
Wolf, 32, 88
Woman, 160
Womb, 229
Wood, 64, 137
Wool, 309
Worm, 88
Wormwood, 124
Wounded, 272
Wrecked Car, 37
Wrinkle, 309
Writing, 272
Wrong Way, 102

Wyoming, 276
X-Ray, 309
X-Ray Technician, 187
Yacht, 96
Yard Sale, 272
Yarmulke, 291
Yeast, 143
Yellow, 59
Yellow, 33
Yellow, 152
Yellow Rose, 122
Yield, 102
Yo-Yo, 309
Zachary, 165
Zebra, 88
Zig Zagging, 99
Ziklag, 216
Zimbabwe, 317
Zinc, 128
Zombie, 210
Zookeeper, 70

Also by Gary Fishman:

Distorted Images of God's Heart:
Phariseeism in the modern-day Church
by Gary Fishman

The Pharisees stood as a constant wall between Jesus and the people of God, fighting tooth and nail to uphold their rigid, suffocating traditions in opposition to the liberty offered by the Son of God. Although the Pharisees are long gone, the religious spirit, which dominated their philosophies, is still alive and kicking in much of modern-day Christianity.

However, *"Christ has set us free to live a free life. So take your stand. Never again let anyone put a harness of slavery on you."* (Galatians 5:1-3, NLT) Distorted Images of God's Heart is a challenge to the people of God to do just that.

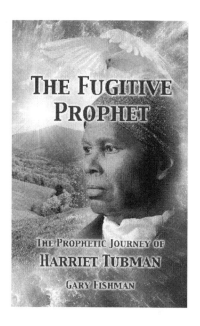

The Fugitive Prophet:
The Prophetic Journey of Harriet Tubman
by Gary Fishman

"Harriet Tubman had a destiny as a forerunner who would break out of unthinkable circumstances and open the door for others to follow. Harriet carried out her operations through the mechanism of what became known as the Underground Railroad. No matter what things looked like in the natural, she kept the dream alive in her heart until it came to pass. Many of God's children receive powerful dreams and visions of future victories and breakthroughs, but only a few dare to keep believing when the path seems dark and stormy. Harriet had a faith that couldn't be broken by beatings, hunger, cruelty, injustice, or racism. It is that aspect of her life that I hope I can adequately relate to readers of this book."

— From Introduction

This book was edited by:

Making a way for companies, organizations, and individuals through website services and more.

www.WaymakerMedia.com

Custom Web Design & Development

WordPress Websites

Content Management Systems

Search Engine Optimization

Website Promotion Services

Logo Design

Copy Editing

Gary Fishman may be reached at:

dreams@sanctuaryfellowship.org